Praise for *We Had a Little Re*

A Best Book of 2021 by *Esquire* a

"[Nesteroff] has carved out a niche as the premier popular historian of comedy because of his knack for unearthing such forgotten stories . . . [*We Had a Little Real Estate Problem*] provides context for an argument about the importance of representation."

—*The New York Times*

"[A]n illuminating and stereotype-busting history of Native Americans and comedy."

—*The Washington Post*

"[A] thoughtful, passionate, and extremely well-researched look at the rarely examined history of Indigenous American comedy . . . Nesteroff provides a history of one part of American life that also tells the story of something much more vast."

—*New York* magazine
("The Best Comedy Books of 2021 (So Far)")

"Stuck with living out contradictions between what America says and what it does, Native people transformed a hard world of irony into one of wry and satirical humor. Kliph Nesteroff takes readers on a journey through this uncharted Indian comic world—its pasts and presents, legendary heroes and rising stars, insider jokes and desperate performances. The result is a fascinating and rich picture of the life-affirming, revolutionary practices of Native comedy."

—Philip J. Deloria, Harvard University

"My uncle used to tell this one joke, it went—no, no, just read this instead. It's got the jokes and the jokesters, five hundred–plus years and counting."

—Stephen Graham Jones, bestselling author
of *The Only Good Indians*

"A remarkable book that takes the history of Native American comedy and turns it into a page-turner. It seems like there's a revelation in every one of its tight chapters. Applause for the book and the exciting artists who populate it."

—Steve Martin

"Kliph Nesteroff explores an overlooked side of comedy in *We Had a Little Real Estate Problem*. From its account of Native American marginalization to the Cherokee roots of Will Rogers, from the inspiring story of Charlie Hill to the new wave of young, hilarious, Indigenous comedians, this book is a game changer."

—Judd Apatow

"No one knows the inside story of comedy, and the trials and tribulations of the people who can't stop themselves from making it, like Kliph Nesteroff. It is so cool to observe how comedy lets people tell the truth—and Native Peoples certainly have a lot to release through making fun. If you love the story of comedy, this is an untold side (till now)."

—Bob Odenkirk

"Nesteroff has written a gem. *We Had a Little Real Estate Problem* tells the untold story of Native American comedy through contemporary interviews and historical analysis. He chips away at the myths of the stoic or long-suffering fate of 'the Indian.' In its place, he creates a vibrant counternarrative that exposes the hilarious, irreverent, ambitious heart of modern Native America."

—David Treuer, author of *Rez Life* and *The Heartbeat of Wounded Knee: Native America from 1890 to the Present*

"[A] fascinating picture of how an artistic tradition evolves . . . you couldn't have a better guide than Nesteroff."

—*National Post*

"A welcome introduction to an aspect of Native American life that merits broader exposure."

—*Kirkus Reviews*

"Richly researched and told through the vibrant voices of the comics themselves . . . Kliph Nesteroff's extraordinary *We Had a Little Real Estate Problem* chronicles a legacy deserving of inclusion in the history of comedy in the US."

—*BookPage* (starred review)

"[A] disturbing yet beautiful history."

—*Publishers Weekly* (starred review)

We Had
a Little
Real Estate
Problem

The Unheralded Story
of Native Americans in Comedy

Kliph Nesteroff

Simon & Schuster Paperbacks

New York   London   Toronto   Sydney   New Delhi

Simon & Schuster Paperbacks
An Imprint of Simon & Schuster, Inc.
1230 Avenue of the Americas
New York, NY 10020

First Simon & Schuster trade paperback edition February 2022

SIMON & SCHUSTER and colophon are registered trademarks of Simon &
Schuster, Inc.

For information about special discounts for bulk purchases, please contact Simon &
Schuster Special Sales at 1-866-506-1949 or business@simonandschuster.com.

The Simon & Schuster Speakers Bureau can bring authors to your live event. For
more information or to book an event, contact the Simon & Schuster Speakers
Bureau at 1-866-248-3049 or visit our website at www.simonspeakers.com.

Interior design by Carly Loman

10 9 8 7 6 5 4 3 2

The Library of Congress has cataloged the hardcover edition as follows:

Names: Nesteroff, Kliph, author.
Title: We had a little real estate problem / by Kliph Nesteroff.
Description: First Simon & Schuster hardcover edition. | New York :
    Simon & Schuster, 2021. | Includes index. | Summary: "From renowned
    comedy journalist and historian Kliph Nesteroff comes the underappreciated
    story of Native Americans and comedy"—Provided by publisher.
Identifiers: LCCN 2020020301 (print) | LCCN 2020020302 (ebook) |
    ISBN 9781982103033 (hardcover) | ISBN 9781982103057 (paperback) |
    ISBN 9781982103064 (ebook)
Subjects: LCSH: Indian comedians—United States—History. | Indian
    Comedians—Canada—History. | Indians of North America—Social conditions.
Classification: LCC E98.C67 N47 2021 (print) | LCC E98.C67 (ebook) |
    DDC 970.004/97—dc23
LC record available at https://lccn.loc.gov/2020020301
LC ebook record available at https://lccn.loc.gov/2020020302

ISBN 978-1-9821-0303-3
ISBN 978-1-9821-0305-7 (pbk)
ISBN 978-1-9821-0306-4 (ebook)

Table of Contents

TABLE OF CONTENTS

TABLE OF CONTENTS

TABLE OF CONTENTS

Author's Note

There was a stand-up special ten or fifteen years ago called *Welcome to Turtle Island*. It used to rerun on Canadian television all the time. It was a modest show with a low budget and no big names, but it had the unique distinction of an all-Indigenous lineup. It was the first of its kind.

At least three different Native comedians have told me that they were inspired to enter the stand-up racket after seeing that special. That seems like a pretty strong argument for proportional representation in media—and the effect that such representation can have.

I grew up in western Canada where First Nations issues were frequently in the news. The news was usually about land. The province of British Columbia was not the result of some ancient land deal brokered between the king of England and the Indigenous peoples who were already there. To the contrary, in a move now seen as a violation of international law, colonial powers moved in; laid claim to the land; established extensive logging, mining, and petroleum operations; subjugated the population; and established a British colony. British Columbia was established as a land heist. No treaty was proposed nor considered nor signed. The land was never ceded. It might be the longest-running squat in history.

As a kid I frequently saw George Manuel, the president of the Union of BC Indian Chiefs, discussing this discrepancy on television. He would accuse the government of violating the law and would inform viewers about something called the Doctrine of Discovery. He responded with wry bemusement as non-Native journalists baited him, trying to play devil's advocate. They knew little of land title, less of residential boarding schools, and nothing about inter-generational trauma, but they acted in a smug and condescending manner. They refused to believe Manuel when he told them that mining companies had poisoned the drinking water in Native com-munities all across the country and that the government had covered it up. And when he underscored that the provincial government of British Columbia had no title to the land, they laughed in his face. But it was obvious George Manuel knew what he was talking about: he who holds the land holds the wealth.

Decades later, I was working in a Vancouver neighborhood known colloquially as the Downtown Eastside, employed as a men-tal health worker and advocate for the "hard to house." Most of the people I encountered on a day-to-day basis had gone through some stage of Canada's brutal "residential school" system. In the darkest chapter of Canadian history, Native children were abducted by the federal government en masse, removed from their homes by white police, and transferred to industrial schools. The children were for-bidden to speak their own languages and denied visits from family members. Parents were given no choice in the matter. Those who resisted were arrested, imprisoned, or killed. The children were rou-tinely beaten and tortured. Where other schools had playgrounds, residential schools had cemeteries. It continued for a good hundred years until the final school was shut down in the 1990s. Survivors were left with severe trauma, the ramifications of which I could wit-ness every single day in the Downtown Eastside. Heavy, heavy stuff. The fact that many survivors could still find a way to laugh or joke was nothing short of remarkable.

Ten years ago I left British Columbia for California. I moved from a place with a fair amount of Native representation on television to a place where it is essentially absent. Even in Hollywood, where "diversity" is a mantra, Native Americans are seldom included. Even to me, a non-Native, this seemed preposterous.

We Had a Little Real Estate Problem does not include every Native comedian working today, but a cross section of comics representing a diverse range of styles and backgrounds. More than fifty people took part in this project, and I am grateful for their participation and trust.

Obviously First Nations and Native American peoples should be in charge of their own stories without the interference of non-Native interpretation. For this reason an effort has been made to quote each comedian at length and let them speak for themselves. I've worked with Jessica H. L. Elm, MSW, PhD, of John Hopkins University, to lend an Indigenous perspective to the manuscript. A citizen of the Oneida Nation and a descendent of the Stockbridge-Munsee Band of the Mohicans, Elm is also a huge fan of the late Charlie Hill, the revered Oneida comedian.

To this day Charlie Hill is the only Native American stand-up to have appeared on *The Tonight Show*, but as the scene profiled in this book makes clear, it's only a matter of time until that changes. Hill performed on *The Tonight Show Starring Johnny Carson*, *Late Night with David Letterman*, *The Richard Pryor Show*, and *The Arsenio Hall Show*. Telling jokes from a Native point of view, he inspired a whole wave of young Indigenous kids to enter the stand-up realm. The extent of Charlie Hill's influence is only now becoming clear. The many comedians in this book mention his name frequently. Charlie Hill is the perfect example of the enduring effect representation can have. It is for this reason we have chosen the title *We Had a Little Real Estate Problem*. It is the punch line to Charlie Hill's most famous joke.

My people are from Wisconsin. We used to be from New York.
We had a little real estate problem.

—CHARLIE HILL

Jonny Roberts Drives Five Hours to Every Gig and Five Hours Back

For an Ojibwe social worker and part-time stand-up in the Red Lake Nation, getting to the closest open-mic night requires an arduous five-hour drive. Jonny Roberts says good-bye to his wife, two children, and eight young foster kids before departing on this exhausting routine. Roberts is driving to Minneapolis to do a show for an audience that might not even show up. It's a long drive there and a long drive back—a total of ten hours—but it's the only way for this reservation comic to get himself some stage time.

After having logged several hundred thousand miles driving vast distances from gig to gig, his 2004 Chevy Silverado has stopped working. Roberts thinks the transmission is probably dead. He borrows his wife's black Dodge Nitro this afternoon and heads in the direction of Highway 89. "It's pretty much farmland all the way until Saint Cloud, Minnesota," says Roberts. "There are a few malls and gas stations, but mostly it's a lot of nothing." As he drives past the water tower with the Red Lake Nation insignia, he stops at the Red Lake Trading Post to fill up the tank. It'll cost $120 to get him to the gig and back—a gig that pays zero dollars, and will last seven minutes.

Red Lake encompasses eight hundred thousand acres of mostly flat landscape. Roberts grew up here, obsessively recording stand-up comedians off of television, hoarding VHS tapes of the 1980s comedy boom. Commuting is his only option. He has few neighbors who share his passion. "They've tried comedy shows at the casino here, but it's hard to get people to come out. There's not much interest for comedy shows in this area and not much opportunity for stage time. So I take the two-hundred-sixty-mile trip for the experience."

There is resilience in Red Lake, yet the reservation reels from intergenerational trauma in the form of addiction and suicide. A survey by the Minnesota Department of Health and Education determined that 48 percent of high school girls have attempted to end their life, and 81 percent have considered it. In a community with fewer than two thousand people, friends, neighbors, and family members are affected. In his capacity as a social worker, Roberts is only too familiar with the issues. As he heads toward the highway, he drives past a series of homemade billboards created by local schoolkids as part of a class project: UP WITH HOPE—DOWN WITH DOPE and IT'S LIFE—OR METH.

Thirty miles into the commute he enters Bemidji, Minnesota, and stops for a bathroom break. Down the street is a statue that stands eighteen feet tall. Made of concrete and plaster, the roadside attraction known as Paul Bunyan and Babe the Blue Ox has adorned thousands of postcards since 1937. Now armed with a bag of packaged popcorn, Roberts takes U.S. Route 2 out of the city and fumbles with a phone cord. He cues up a playlist of podcasts—*WTF with Marc Maron*, *Urban Indianz* hosted by Gabriel Night Shield, *Red Man Laughing* hosted by Ryan McMahon, and the *Monday Morning Podcast* with Bill Burr. He has four more hours to go.

Arriving in Minneapolis just as the sun is setting, he walks into the Spring Street Tavern, where fifteen young comedians are milling about. There are nine people in the crowd. Roberts sits in a corner, reviewing a notepad, scratching out some topics and adding others. Tonight is his first bout of stage time in forty-seven days.

Ninety minutes later, he's onstage telling jokes. "I think it's great that Bruce Jenner transitioned to Caitlyn Jenner," he tells the sparse crowd. "But I don't think she should have picked a young woman's name. I mean—she's seventy years old. Are you kidding me? Her name should be Gladys."

After the show, the other open-mic comedians are hanging out, smoking joints, talking about their next gig, but Roberts is already gone. He has to take his houseful of kids to day care in the morning. It's 11 p.m. and there's a five-hour drive ahead of him.

"I've been doing stand-up for eight years," says Roberts. "Sometimes I think I should just quit." Compared to his contemporaries in Los Angeles and New York, the amount of stage experience Roberts has is minimal. In New York, a comedian with eight years of experience can get onstage every single night. Someone who's really hustling can do as many as six shows in a single evening. Roberts is lucky if he gets onstage once a month. That makes it hard to move forward. Most open-mic hopefuls are between the ages of eighteen and twenty-three. Roberts is in his early forties. "It's an advanced age for sure," he says. "Although they said Rodney Dangerfield went back to comedy at forty-four. So that's always in the back of my mind."

Some of his ambition is motivated by a desire to get away from his job, and some of the things he has seen as a social worker have left him shaken. "I just want to walk away from the things I read about in the files. I just want to walk away from what I see on a daily basis. . . . I don't know how much longer I can deal with this. . . . I have no outlet." Roberts hopes stand-up is the answer.

"Degrading, Demoralizing, and Degenerating"

Go onstage or go to jail. That was the option presented to Native American prisoners of war during the final three decades of the nineteenth century when freedom of mobility was curtailed and free will suppressed.

P. T. Barnum and William "Buffalo Bill" Cody were the two most famous names of 1800s showmanship. One was a famous circus impresario, and the other staged Wild West re-creations. And they both subjugated Native peoples for the entertainment of white patrons.

In the 1840s Barnum presented Native Americans as sideshow attractions under the auspices of pseudo-anthropological nonsense. At P. T. Barnum's American Museum in New York City, Native Americans were showcased for their "authenticity." But the great showman wanted Native peoples to present *his* idea of "authentic." If they did something that was actually authentic, he flew into a rage. "These wild Indians seemed to consider their dances as realities," complained Barnum. "Damn Indians anyhow—they are a lazy, shiftless set of brutes—though they will draw [an audience]."

Sideshows were gaining traction at the time. So-called dime-museum freaks like the alligator man and the bearded lady were popular. Into the mix came Native captives who were paraded around with racist backstories. Typical freak show promotions included Yan-a-Wah-Wah, advertised as "an Indian Princess and Child rescued from one of the South Seas Islands by a Sailor." In reality they were a mother and child kidnapped from the plains of Iowa.

Natives were not participating of their own free will and could not have done so even if they wanted. Government policy kept them imprisoned on reservations where they were held at gunpoint. "If the reservation system is to be maintained, discontented and restless or mischievous Indians cannot be permitted to leave their reservation at will and go where they please," wrote E. A. Hayt, the commissioner of Indian affairs in 1878. "If this were permitted, the most necessary discipline of the reservations would soon be entirely broken up, all authority over the Indians would cease. . . ." Every movement was tightly controlled by the government and its military. Any Native who strayed from the reservation on which he or she had been forcibly placed was punished, beaten, or killed.

In a landmark court case, the Ponca leader Standing Bear challenged the laws restricting Native American freedom of movement in 1879. A federal judge ruled in favor of the "peaceful Indian to come and go as he wishes with the same freedom to a white man." However, that freedom was often overruled by the same authorities who determined who was or was not a "peaceful Indian."

It was at this time that rules concerning "blood quantum" were developed. The system imposed on Native Americans, blood quantum, was a way to diminish the number of Natives to whom the government owed something in exchange for land. Vine Deloria Jr., author of the influential book *Custer Died for Your Sins*, wrote of the laws "passed during and after the Civil War [that] systematically excluded Indian people. For a long time an Indian was not presumed capable of initiating an action in a court of law, of owning property, or of giving testimony against whites in court. Nor could an Indian vote or leave his reservation. Indians were America's captive people without any defined rights whatsoever."

There was nothing scientific about blood quantum. The "percentage of blood" assigned to Native Americans was arbitrary. Natives forced onto reservations were deemed "full-blood" or "half-blood" by a white government agent depending on their appearance. One man might be deemed "100 percent" while his sibling was labeled "50 percent." These capricious decisions cheated descendants out of land and annuities. The legacy of this practice endures to this day.

The erasure of Native religions and languages became government policy during the final thirty years of the nineteenth century. Native children were forcibly separated from their families and sent to boarding schools to indoctrinate them. In both Canada and the United States, violent subjugation was policy. Canada's first prime minister, Sir John A. Macdonald, made child separation a hallmark of his administration. Macdonald said, "When the school is on the reserve, the child lives with its parents, who are savages, and though he may learn to read and write, his habits and training mode of thought are Indian. He is simply a savage. . . . Indian children should be withdrawn as much as possible from the parental influence, and the only way to do that would be to put them in central training industrial schools where they will acquire the habits and modes of thought of white men."

Funded by the federal government and contracted to religious missionaries, the purpose of a residential school was to reprogram Native children—by force if necessary—eliminating their tribal beliefs, modes of dress, music, language, and thought. If they resisted, they were brutally abused. Known as residential schools because students were required to reside on campus, the institutions were notorious for their cruelty. When students spoke in their Native languages, they were punished by having their tongues punctured with sewing needles. At the St. Anne's residential school, run by the Oblate order in Fort Albany, Ontario, a makeshift electric chair was built to punish students with electric shocks. Those who vomited

6

in the wake of such abuse were forced to kneel and eat what they coughed up. Sexual abuse was especially rampant, and most schools had cemeteries on-site. Funerals were often presided over by the very priests who had abused the deceased.

An article in Canada's *Saturday Night* magazine published in 1909 stated "Indian boys and girls are dying like flies. . . . Even war seldom shows as large a percentage of fatalities as does the education system we have imposed on our Indian wards."

As First Nations peoples rose in objection, Prime Minister Macdonald said they were "forgetting all the kindness that had been bestowed upon them, forgetting all the gifts that had been given to them, forgetting all that the Government, the white people, and the Parliament of Canada had been doing for them, in trying to rescue them from barbarity. . . ."

With these policies in place, it is little wonder Natives were absent from show business while Jewish immigrants and African Americans flourished on the stage.

In 1883, Buffalo Bill Cody presented what would become his infamous re-creations of American history for the first time. Before entering show business, he participated in the forcible relocation of Kiowa and Comanche peoples with the Union army. Buffalo Bill scholar Deanne Stillman said Cody bragged about his exploits: "So, too, by his own account, did he kill an Indian in his youth—and others later—while he was employed as a wagon train hand."

His life was fictionalized in a series of bestselling pulp novels and magazines, many of which established the stereotypes that later emerged in western movies. One historian described Buffalo Bill's Wild West as "the most important commercial vehicle for the transmission of the Myth of the Frontier." The shows were filled with horse-riding stunts and patriotic fanfare. Native performers enacted scenes that ended with their very own subjugation. Buffalo Bill's slogan was "Everything Genuine," but his desire for realism appalled his cast when he insisted on using the actual scalps of murdered Natives as props.

Hundreds of Native American performers toured in Wild West shows at the turn of the century. Most considered it a respite from the oppressive reservation system, a lesser of two evils. Neither inexperienced nor naïve, some volunteered to join with P.T. Barnum and Buffalo Bill simply to escape the oppressive reservation system and attain an income on the side. It was reported that some split payments with Barnum and Cody to help recruit others. Those hired as interpreters secured favorable conditions and good pay. Harvard scholar Philip Deloria said that joining a Wild West show served "as a form of escape from agency surveillance." Nearly one hundred Natives were recruited from the Pine Ridge Reservation in South Dakota every year. "Indeed, the most significant regular flow of money onto that reservation between 1883 and 1913 may have come from Lakota performers traveling nationally and internationally," wrote Deloria. "The late 1880s and early 1890s in particular were starving times for many Indian communities, and performing represented, not simply escape, but also food and wages for Indian actors from a number of reservations."

The Office of Indian Affairs, later the Bureau of Indian Affairs, objected to both the Standing Bear decision and Buffalo Bill's recruitment process. They believed providing Natives with a taste of freedom would make their imprisonment unmanageable. Insisting that no Natives leave without the permission of the OIA, they fined Buffalo Bill several hundred dollars for doing something that the courts had already determined was perfectly legal.

Thomas J. Morgan, the new OIA commissioner, came up with a blackmail plan. He announced that anyone wishing to join a Wild West show was free to do so, but if they did, they would be stripped of their allotments and the annuities spelled out by treaty. He wrote in his annual report, "Indians must conform to white man's ways, peaceably if they will, forcibly if they must."

8

Suddenly it became much harder for Buffalo Bill to secure performers. Few were willing to risk losing their tribal status or the paltry annuities granted them in exchange for land. As a workaround, Buffalo Bill secured permission from federal authorities to offer potential Native American performers a plea deal: join the show or go to jail.

The famed Hunkpapa Lakota leader Sitting Bull fled to Canada after the Battle of Little Big Horn and the death of General Custer in 1876. After months in hiding, he was extradited back to the United States, where he was given the option of prison time or performing with Buffalo Bill. Reduced to a mere sideshow attraction, comedian Rich Hall observed in his 2012 television special *Inventing the Indian,* "It was as if a Guantánamo detainee suddenly had to appear on *X Factor*."

"About thirty Native Americans captured at Wounded Knee were forced by the army to tour with Buffalo Bill in lieu of prison sentences," explained historian Laura Browder.

Wild West shows were an escape from reservation life, but the conditions were far from ideal. The *New York Herald* quoted a performer in 1890: "All the Indians in Buffalo Bill's show are discontented, ill-treated, and anxious to come home." There were accusations of negligence, inadequate medical care, and poor living quarters. An investigation was opened after five Native performers died during an overseas tour, and Buffalo Bill was ultimately fined for the "mistreatment of seventy-five Indians."

A new policy was implemented in response. Any showman recruiting Native Americans for Wild West shows was now required to provide a cash deposit to the OIA. Depending on the number of performers requested, security bonds were as high as $10,000, to be refunded after they returned.

Some of the first students to graduate from government boarding schools used what they were taught to fight back against their captors, the very people who had forced them to learn English in the first place. One of the most notable was Chauncey Yellow Robe, who advocated for the end of the Wild West shows.

Born on the Rosebud Reservation in South Dakota, the future Lakota activist was shipped to the new Carlisle Indian School in Pennsylvania, where his long braids were cut off, his clothing replaced with a military suit, and his first language forbidden.

The Carlisle Indian School was founded by Captain Richard Henry Pratt, who got the idea while marching seventy-two Native Americans to Fort Marion, Florida. "After the captives were shackled for a period in a dungeon, Pratt took their clothes away, had their hair cut, dressed them in army uniforms, and drilled them like soldiers," wrote Roxanne Dunbar-Ortiz in *An Indigenous Peoples' History of the United States*. "This 'successful' experiment led Pratt to establish the Carlisle Indian Industrial School in Pennsylvania in 1879."

Chauncey Yellow Robe graduated from the Carlisle school in 1889. Equipped with fluent English skills, he was hired as an interpreter at the OIA. His first assignment was to translate the testimony regarding the mistreatment of Native men in Buffalo Bill's Wild West show. Yellow Robe was greatly disturbed by what he heard, and it led to the organization of a group devoted to Native rights—the Society of American Indians. At a mass gathering in Albany, New York, he asked the crowd, "What benefit has the Indian derived from Wild West shows? None but what are degrading, demoralizing, and degenerating."

It took several years, but Yellow Robe's agitation helped eliminate the genre. At the same time, the new medium of motion pictures was luring patrons away from Wild West theatrics. Buffalo Bill sensed the impending demise of his creation and decided to enter the new world of silent cinema. He planned a movie called *The Indian Wars*, which would re-create the Wounded Knee Massacre of 1890 on the very spot where the bodies were buried. The Society of American Indians expressed outrage. According to Philip Deloria, the showman "insisted that the filming take place on the actual battlefield itself, which included the site of the mass grave of Indian dead. Several Lakota performers refused to participate, threatening to shut down the production." A rumor made the rounds that the actors intended to replace the blanks in their prop guns with live ammunition. "Cody got wind of the murmurs in the Lakota camp," explained silent-film historian Kevin Brownlow. "[Buffalo Bill] spent the night before the battle riding between the Lakotas and the army, assuring each of the peaceful designs and blank cartridges of the other. But you can bet that he was worried as he galloped across the plains that day."

WILD WEST SHOWS are often confused with medicine shows. They emerged at the same time and operated concurrently, but a Wild West show was serious; medicine shows bordered on burlesque. It was the difference between a major motion picture and its *Mad* magazine parody. The purpose of a medicine show was to make money; the entertainment was merely a vehicle to hook gullible buyers into buying a bottle of bullshit. Just as the Wild West show laid the foundation for western movie clichés, medicine show hucksterism laid the foundation for commercial broadcasting, where entertainment was merely a catalyst to sell corporate products.

Parking a mobile stage in a town of yokels, the medicine show impresario would go into an obnoxious pitch like a modern-day street performer. Holding a bottle high overhead, the host would shout, "It is the only remedy the Indians ever use—and has been known to them for ages!" With few exceptions, the bottled product was marketed as an "ancient Indian cure," playing on the ignorance of local whites. Medicine show hustlers labeled their elixirs with phony tribal affiliations—Nez Perce Snuff, Pawnee Indian Remedy, and a product from the Kiowa Medicine Company that promised to cure "ulcers, scalds, burns, old sores, itch, piles, wounds, and all skin diseases."

Medicine shows employed Native American performers and crew. The OIA had contracts providing performers from different Native nations to several companies. Native participants presented ethnic caricatures and broad stereotypes and, in a push to assimilate them into European practices, were required to perform "Irish and blackface comedy."

In the late 1800s, humor writers wrote in character. They used pseudonyms as a smoke screen for incendiary comment, and many wrote in dialect. Samuel Clemens wrote as Mark Twain, Finley Peter Dunne as Mr. Dooley, Charles Farrar Browne as Artemus Ward, Henry Wheeler Shaw as Josh Billings, S. W. Small as Old Si, David Ross Locke as Petroleum V. Nasby, and Alexander Posey—a Muscogee Creek satirist—as Fus Fixico.

Alexander Posey created his character Fus Fixico in response to the General Allotment Act of 1887, which discouraged communal land ownership—the general default of most Native societies. Native lands were carved up into parcels not exceeding 160 acres, with the remaining land sold off to oil and railway interests.

"The allotment policy sought to divide Indian land held in common and to force Native people to occupy individual homesteads," explained Philip Deloria. "Allotment sought to forcibly impose a change in social evolutionary status. . . . From there, Indians would have, in theory, only a few short steps up the ladder to modern industrial capitalism." This infuriated Alexander Posey.

Born in 1873, Posey was a member of the Creek Nation. He grew up on the land that later became Oklahoma. He was surrounded by survivors of the Trail of Tears, the infamous forced migration ordered by President Jackson that resulted in scores of Indigenous deaths. Posey's literary themes were influenced by the people he saw around him. Elders told him stories about those who had perished due to government policy, and he witnessed a parade of white oil tycoons and railroad barons surveying the land. And he observed the infighting within his own tribe. Some resisted industry while others jumped at hollow promises of escaping poverty. All of it informed his work as a humorist. Posey's stories featured characters constantly "amazed, amused, and puzzled by the greed, materialism, political ambition, dishonesty, and hypocrisy in whites."

Posey ran the *Eufaula Indian Journal* and was the first Native American newspaper editor of the twentieth century. He used the platform to publish mock letters to the editor under the pseudonym Fus Fixico, tackling Native issues in a Muscogee Creek dialect. Between 1902 and 1906, he wrote seventy-two Fus Fixico letters, addressing controversies like the Allotment Act, the anglicizing of Indigenous names, and boarding schools:

> Well, so Big Man at Washington was made another rule like that one about making the Injin cut his hair off short like a prize fighter or saloon keeper. Big Man he was say this time the Injin was had to change his name just like if the marshal was had a writ for him. So, if the Injin's name is Wolf Warrior, he was had to call himself John Smith, or maybe so Bill Jones, so nobody else could get his mail out of the post office. Big Man say Injin name like Sitting Bull or Tecumseh was too hard to remember and don't sound civilized like General Cussed Her.

The accent was a hat tip to the locals, letting readers know that this character was one of their own. "The dialect was immediately understood by readers of the paper," wrote Posey biographer Daniel Littlefield. "It was obvious that the character of Fus Fixico was a Creek."

At the turn of the century, J. Ojijatekha Brant-Sera, a Mohawk theater impresario from the Six Nations reserve in Upper Canada, asked Posey to develop an act. A report said the producer "wanted him [Posey] to take his humor on the stage by joining a program of lectures that Brant-Sera was arranging for Indians from various

The 1491s in Their Underwear

"I wrote these commentaries when I was working in the communications department of the Seminole Nation, and they were sort of like Alexander Posey with his Fus Fixico letters," explains Sterlin Harjo. "Lumhee is my Native name, which means 'eagle,' and I called it 'News from the Woods by Lumhee Harjo.' They were letters to the editor, in which I would just talk shit and mess with people I knew in the community."

Sterlin Harjo grew up in Holdenville, Oklahoma. A prolific indie filmmaker, today he is editing a cinema verité documentary about contemporary Native artists and preparing to shoot a new television series for FX titled *Reservation Dogs*. Harjo has multiple projects to his name, but none has brought him as much joy as his five-man sketch comedy troupe, the 1491s.

The 1491s have a loyal following, and fans will travel hundreds of miles to catch one of their live shows. "We resonated and struck a nerve because we made fun of ourselves," says Harjo. "White people are easy to make fun of, and if you make fun of white people in front of Indians, you're sort of yelling into a vacuum. But we made fun of our weaknesses as Native people and held a mirror up to ourselves."

In addition to Harjo, the 1491s consist of Thomas Ryan Red-Corn, an Osage graphic designer; Migizi Pensoneau, a Ponca-Ojibwe screenwriter; Dallas Goldtooth, a Diné-Mdewakanton environmental activist; and Bobby Wilson, a Sisseton Wahpeton Dakota visual artist. Collectively they are the most respected Native comedians working today.

"My dad and my grandpa were both singer-songwriters," says RedCorn. "My grandpa wrote songs on piano and was in a barbershop quartet. But my teenage rebellion led me down the path of death metal. I was in an emo hard-core band as the front man. It was me, my brother, another Native guy who was Arapaho, and a couple of white guys who were tagging along. We were the most unserious death metal band you could imagine. In that [genre] you're surrounded by sadness and darkness, so my inclination was to do the opposite. It was comedy-centric, and a lot of our show just dealt with our demeanor. I left that band when my mom passed away and I was kicked out of school. I went through the yellow pages looking for a place that would give me an internship. I found this place called Trans-Digital in downtown Kansas City. One of the first jobs they gave me was editing a *How to Make Balloon Animals* video. It was just an hour of [balloon squeaking] *eek, eek, eep, eep*. We had these huge speakers for editing, and I was just listening to the sound of balloons squeaking for a full week, eight to ten hours a day. If I so much as look at one of those balloons today, every single crease makes that sound in my head. I can't be anywhere near them."

Suffering from balloon-animal PTSD, RedCorn became an accomplished editor and started collaborating with Sterlin Harjo. "I was friends with his cousin," says RedCorn. "I saw one of his films and it totally transformed the way I wanted to spend my energy and the kind of art I wanted to create. The 1491s were born out of these conversations with Sterlin: 'Man, I am so fucking *sick* of all these sad Indian movies.' Even among our own people that's what gets the funding and that's what was getting made. It was a lot of really heavy content—and I'm not saying that stuff shouldn't exist, but there's *gotta* be something else on the menu."

Together they made a short film called *Smiling Indians*, which sought to smash stoic stereotypes. Since the late 1800s, thanks to the famous black-and-white portraits by photographer Edward S. Curtis, the stereotypical image of the super serious Native American has endured, leaving whites with the impression that Native Americans never laughed, never joked, never smiled. RedCorn explained, "Laughter and joy is very much a part of Native culture.... A film like this is our way of trying to counterbalance the images that kids are exposed to in the classroom." The film's strength was its simplicity, a five-minute collage of contemporary Natives smiling, laughing, and being themselves.

Dallas Goldtooth and Migizi Pensoneau grew up obsessed with the same movies in the same Minnesota household. They could recite films like *Mad Max Beyond Thunderdome* by heart, and were completely smitten with Zucker brothers comedies like *Airplane!*, *The Naked Gun*, and *Hot Shots!* "Dallas and I, ever since we were little kids, we imitated the movies we liked," says Pensoneau. "Zucker brothers. Mel Brooks. Monty Python. Even up to high school we would do skits from MTV's *The State*." Their father, Tom Goldtooth, a celebrated environmental activist, led the family in ceremonies. Dallas Goldtooth explains, "My family is 'traditional,' meaning that we still practice a lot of our original ceremonies and traditional songs, and we used to do a lot of traditional gatherings. Through that upbringing, every time there was more than four people in the room, [we were] always joking . . . always laughing, always celebrating in some way, even in the darkest times."

Dallas and Migizi got their hands on a cheap Panasonic camera and started improvising short films in the early 2000s. Their first video was filmed in the woods behind their home. It was a takeoff on the Aboriginal Peoples Television Network, a Canadian cable channel known for its dry, didactic, and low-budget programming. "We had just watched one of those bad APTN shows, and it was clear the guys didn't know what they were doing," Pensoneau says with a laugh. "It was too funny. At that time there was some personal stuff going on at home, and I was bummed out. Dallas had this little white flip cam and he said, 'Let's just go out in the woods and record something to make ourselves laugh. Do that little rez accent that you do and we'll pretend like we're making one of those bad APTN shows.' We shot all day and then edited it down. It wasn't professional in any way. Later my mom told me she was worried because we had been quiet for so long. But then all of a sudden she heard us laughing—and laughing—for days." They posted the video for friends and family, but it somehow found its way to Thomas Ryan RedCorn, who felt like he was watching a pair of kindred spirits. Pensoneau says, "Ryan and Sterlin had been doing videos down in Oklahoma. Dallas and I were doing these videos in Minnesota. Sterlin contacted me: 'Dude, I'm going to be in Minnesota in a couple months—we should get together and do some stuff.'" Harjo and RedCorn came to Minneapolis to screen *Barking Water*, Harjo's latest film, at a local film festival. Sterlin, Thomas Ryan, Migizi, and Dallas came together for the first time, and Dallas dragged along his friend Bobby Wilson.

Raised in South Minneapolis along Franklin Avenue, Wilson had a tumultuous upbringing that saw him bouncing from one shelter to another. His parents had a volatile marriage, and his mother fled with the children. They ended up living in a shelter, and it was there that Wilson developed an ability to charm strangers and make them laugh. "When you grow up in these shelters and county facilities, you're locked up with *everybody*. Black people, Asian people, Hispanic people, you are all in this situation, and you can either be assholes to each other or you can figure out what we have in common. . . . It's a survival tactic, really. I guess that's why I kind of fell into this [comedy] and just started swimming."

At fourteen, Wilson learned the truth about his parents. "My dad was trying to get custody of us after we left and he was demanding blood tests, maternity tests, and that's when she told me she wasn't my biological mom." Wilson felt betrayed. "I ran away to Worcester, Massachusetts, on a Greyhound and stayed there for a couple months with this lady [who] had been a legal advocate at a battered women's shelter where we happened to be staying." Wilson slept in shelters by night and spent his days creating illicit art on the street. "Graffiti was a huge part of what defined me as a teenager. I was sixteen when I was arrested for graffiti, and they didn't know what to do with me because I didn't have any parents." He was sentenced to two years in a group home and a $50,000 fine. All the while, he continued to paint. His visual flourish showcased an obvious gift. Upon release, he focused on art and ended up at the Santa Fe Indian Market, selling his wares at the famed arts festival in New Mexico. "That's where I first met Ryan RedCorn and Sterlin Harjo," he says. "Ryan is a really social dude, so we just kind of started talking to each other and geeking out about art we were into. We had a lot of the same knowledge. . . . We were walking around, saying hi to folks, doing everything together until probably about two or three in the morning. He was like, 'Hey, man, you can come and stay at mine and Sterlin's hotel.' I had five dollars in my pocket, a bottle of water, and trail mix. I ended up staying with Ryan and Sterlin that night." Back in Minnesota, Wilson was hired at a youth shelter in Saint Paul, where he bonded with a fellow employee—Dallas Goldtooth. The two lived near each other, played video games on the regular, and became fast friends.

When Harjo and RedCorn arrived in town to screen *Barking Water*, the other movie theaters in town were showing *The Twilight Saga: New Moon*. The box office hit featured the "Wolf Pack," five chiseled Native Americans who transform into wolves. Sterlin, Thomas Ryan, Dallas, Migizi, and Bobby decided it was in need of mockery. It inspired their first sketch—"Wolf Pack Auditions"—in which they played a group of posturing incompetents auditioning for the role.

"Basically the idea of the video is about these Native actors ex-

KLIPH NESTEROFF

ploiting their Nativeness to get ahead," says Harjo. "That's something we had seen for a long time, and it was sort of based on real life. My dad and I had gone to this open audition for *Last of the Mohicans* or something. We were like, 'Yeah, we're Native. Let's go to this.' We sat down in the lobby and immediately felt weird about it. I had short hair and a Hawaiian shirt, which was definitely *not* what they were looking for. There were all these long-haired, chiseled Natives, and one guy had a choker on and was rubbing himself with baby oil to make himself shine. I had this feeling of, 'Man, are we real Natives?' What I realize now is that *we* were the real Natives in that scenario. So I thought it would be good to make fun of these people exploiting their culture to get a role and putting up a false front of who they are as Native people to please the white director or white producer."

"Dallas told me the idea," recalls Wilson. "I was like, 'Dude, that sounds fucking funny. I hate those [*Twilight* films].' I was doing a two-year mural [at] the Little Earth of United Tribes housing projects [and] they gave me an office key. I said, 'I've got a spot where we could film.'" A shirtless Dallas Goldtooth flaunted a loincloth, a shirtless Bobby Wilson wore red underwear, Migizi Pensoneau sported an incongruous fur coat, and Thomas Ryan RedCorn was nearly nude with only a plastic turtle to shield his groin. Wilson said, "What I *didn't* know was that there was a Sunday school that rented the place on the weekends. We pulled up there, and Ryan already had no shirt and a turtle over his dick. They were like, 'Uh, can we help you?' I was like, 'I *work* here!'"

Harjo says the shoot was an improvised delight. "We couldn't quit laughing. It felt like we tapped into this thing that was waiting to be tapped into. . . . It was a video by Indians for Indians. The idea of a Native American in a contemporary role—nobody's looking for that, but when we put it on YouTube, we got rid of that middle step and nobody said, 'We don't want to see Indians on the screen.' People *did* want to see it." It had ten thousand views in a matter of

20

hours. Wilson had no idea anyone had watched it until a bunch of schoolchildren recognized him. "I was teaching a weeklong poetry workshop in South Dakota at the Saint Francis Indian School," he says. "I got there on Monday. That video dropped on Wednesday. And on Thursday all the fuckin' kids in that school had already broke through their little firewalls to watch it—the whole school. Even the teachers were like, 'Shit, man, I fuckin' saw that video!'"

Simply by creating contemporary comedy, the 1491s smashed stereotypes. Pensoneau says, "This propaganda of a savage Indian or an overly peaceful and passive Indian—the work that we do seeks to reverse that completely."

Vaudeville Was Fraud-ville

Stereotype propaganda absolutely dominated vaudeville theater in the early 1900s. A quick glance at vaudeville listings from the turn of the century makes it seem like there were Native American acts touring all over, but the advertisements are deceptive. Vaudeville theaters presented Chief Poolaw, Chief Caupolican, Chief Wongo Newah, Chief Roaring Thunder, Princess Chinquilla, Princess Deer Horn, Princess Floating Cloud, Princess White Deer, Princess Red Wing, Princess Palanki, Princess Watahwaso, and Princess Wantura. Nearly all of them were white impostors wearing headdresses.

The actual Native Americans of vaudeville were generally there as part of their compulsory boarding-school curriculum. Students from the Carlisle Indian School toured vaudeville as "civilization success stories," and the purpose was to show how Native Americans had been successfully converted from "savagery" to "European refinement."

The most popular Native act in vaudeville was the Carlisle Indian Band, who served as de facto ambassadors for the school. The government saw to it that plenty of photos appeared in newspapers showing Carlisle students in their military haircuts and uniforms, looking very European as they held violins, cellos, and trombones. It was the government's way of assuring a settler population that the "Indian problem" had been solved. From now on, rather than be resentful of the white settlers on their land, Native Americans would be content to play the music of John Philip Sousa. It was never mentioned that the Carlisle school had a graveyard on campus where more than two hundred students had been buried.

In public it was pomp and circumstance, but in private correspondence, bureaucrats confessed that the whole process of indoctrinating Native children by force was a morbid disaster. Oliver La Farge of the Bureau of Indian Affairs privately described the schools as "penal institutions where little children [are] sentenced to hard labor for a term of years for the crime of being born to their mothers." William McConnell, an inspector for the BIA, wrote in 1899, "The word 'murder' is a terrible word, but we are little less than murderers if we follow the course . . . after the attention of those in charge has been called to its fatal results. Hundreds of boys and girls are sent home to die so that . . . institutions where brass bands [are] the principal advertisements may be maintained."

The school also presented European-style comedy in the form of comic operas. The *Philadelphia Inquirer* used an infamous racial slur in their February 1909 report:

Redskin Comedians is Carlisle's Latest. Advent of Aboriginal mirth-makers—A feature of great interest at this year's commencement of the Carlisle Indian School will be the production of a comic opera. . . . The cast, chorus, stage hands and orchestra will all be Indians. . . . In connection with this production will be the advent of Indian comedians, a novelty which fairly paralyzes those who know the Redskin, and are yet unfamiliar with his remarkable development at Carlisle. The school paper praised those Native students who "gave a particularly clever impersonation of negro comedians."

The success of the Carlisle Indian Band spawned several imitators, including the United States Indian Band. It followed the same basic formula, but with an added attraction: Pete Red Jacket, Oneida comedian.

Red Jacket was a four-year-old who did physical comedy while the band played behind him. He became such a popular draw that he turned solo in 1907. The child star toured with his father, who acted as the straight man in a "schoolroom act," the popular vaudeville genre where a teacher played straight to schoolkids delivering joke responses. Pete Red Jacket sat at a desk while the teacher looked approvingly at his model student. When the teacher turned his back, Red Jacket burst into a soft-shoe dance and made grotesque faces. When the teacher turned back around, Red Jacket would freeze in place with a metaphoric halo above his head. It was a bona fide crowd pleaser.

Red Jacket unveiled his new partner at a vaudeville house in Scranton, Pennsylvania, in 1911. The act was called "Pete Red Jacket and His Comedy Donkey" and featured a burro doing tricks in time to comic dialogue. Red Jacket had plenty of competition in this long-forgotten vaudeville field, among them Cotton's Comedy Donkeys, Bieler's Comedy Donkey, Pat West and His Comedy Donkey, and Honey Pot: World's Greatest Comedy Donkey. Red Jacket's popularity endured until the cute little boy grew into an awkward, lanky teenager. The writing on the wall was as plain as the acne on his face, and the comic whom the white press dubbed the "droll little redface comedian" left the business to start the Pete Red Jacket Coal Corporation.

The vacancy was filled by another Native American child, the offspring of an interracial vaudeville team. Sometimes billed as the Broadway Girl and the Indian, the team of Clifford and Wayne featured a Lakota husband and his Caucasian wife. Originally from South Dakota, the Lakota half of the duo was praised by the *Salt Lake Tribune* for his "impersonations of Joe Welch, the famous Hebrew comedian, and of Englishmen and Irishmen." They had marginal success, but with the birth of their son the act became a smash. Their first engagement as a family unit was in the autumn of 1916 in Wausau, Wisconsin. The poster in front of the venue said: "Bijou

Theatre—TONIGHT—Refined Vaudeville—See Baby Clifford—The Only Indian Baby in Vaudeville—Novelty Comedy."

Clifford and Wayne gave their son an exotic stage name—Master Karlh Wayne—and renamed the act the Clifford Wayne Trio. The diminutive child learned rapid dance steps, backflips, and celebrity impressions. Long before Sammy Davis Jr. became a child star in the Will Mastin Trio, Master Karlh was essentially doing the same shtick. He was considered a "positive riot over the entire Hippodrome circuit," and the *New York World* called him "the pocket edition of Fred Stone," referencing a famous vaudevillian who could do everything. His celebrity status gained him entry into the Boy Scouts of America, which up to that point had barred nonwhite children from membership.

Under the watchful eye of child protection organizations, children were barred from playing vaudeville in New York. The Clifford Wayne Trio, however, was able to bypass the regulations thanks to their status as Indigenous performers. *Variety* claimed that civil authorities had no jurisdiction over Natives who were "under the general supervision of the government Interior Department." The Lakota team was praised for avoiding stereotypes. "Indeed, he is a sort of a wonder child performer," wrote the *Dayton Daily News*. "There is not a war-whoop, a tomahawk or a wild and savage dance in the whole act." *Variety* agreed: "The Clifford Wayne Trio . . . have gotten away from the stereotyped regulation Indian act and only in the man's announcement is reference made to their race." Master Karlh succeeded as a "youthful versatile entertaining comedian" for ten years until the breaking of his voice destroyed his ability to do impressions. After one last tour through the vaudeville houses of Seattle, Portland, San Francisco, Denver, and Albuquerque, Master Karlh was doomed by puberty and retired from show business at the age of thirteen.

Adrianne Chalepah Pays the Price for Correcting Her History Teacher

Eight years in, Adrianne Chalepah has done stand-up in hundreds of tribal communities. Reservation to reservation, her performance conditions vary wildly. The casinos often have the ideal setup—professional lighting, good promotion, proper amplification—but beyond them, the gigs are unpredictable. "Worst-case scenario is you're booked for a show in a place that has never had comedy," she says. "No lights, no stage, no microphone—you just gotta roll with it. I was scheduled for an outdoor show at a rez in Utah at seven p.m. They didn't take into account that the sun would be down. It was dark. They had no lights. One of the other comedians drove her car up and shined her headlights on me. . . .

"I've done Albuquerque, Phoenix, Los Angeles, and Seattle, but most of my shows are outside the cities on the reservations. Native comedy is always disconnected from the other comedy scenes. I've done stuff in New York City where I'm the only Native in the entire room. But it's not on purpose that most of my work has been Native-related. It's an isolation thing. The comedy hubs are obviously New York and Los Angeles. Any comedian not in those places—you must plug into that industry. I'm just too far away, and I'm a mother of four. So I'm kind of in a weird spot. I get to do four shows a month, and each requires two or three days of travel. That's the biggest issue for Native people in comedy—isolation."

Cortez, Colorado, is 190 miles northwest of Albuquerque. Adrianne Chalepah is at home, preparing for a brief stand-up tour that will take her from the Four Corners area to the northeastern United States. She's trying to pack clothes into a pink, metallic roller bag as one of her four children is coughing and sneezing, struggling with a cold.

"I'm enrolled Kiowa and Plains Apache, and I grew up in several different towns," she explains. "To be a member of a tribal nation you have to be 'enrolled,' and each tribe has the right to set their own criteria for enrollment. You have some legitimate Natives who are not enrolled because their tribe's enrollment process is too strict. So they're not considered Native, but they really *are* Native. Some tribes enroll based on descendancy only. If you have an ancestor, then you're part of a tribal nation. Then there are other tribes with blood quantum where you have to have at least one 'full-blood' grandparent. And then there are tribes between those two scenarios, not based solely on enrollment or blood quantum but, whether or not you live on the reservation or have a parent who does. If a non-Native tells you their ethnicity, you wouldn't question it, but with Natives it's, like, x and y and z: 'Are you full-blood?' Do other human beings have the same type of criteria? No, there's no one else. Just horses, dogs, and us."

Growing up, she moved from town to town, school to school. "We were always moving because of the dysfunction in our family. By the age of six I had lived in Flagstaff, Gallup, Winslow—all of what we call border towns—the white towns next to the Southwest tribal reservations, although my tribes are from Oklahoma. I grew up mostly in Anadarko, Lawton, Cache, and Carnegie. Most of my childhood was spent on or near the Kiowa-Comanche-Apache Reservation in Oklahoma. By the tenth grade I had attended twelve different schools. My story is the cliché of the Native American family with the really tough upbringing, but at a young age my dad showed me Monty Python. And every Saturday night we watched *Saturday Night Live*. It was the *one thing* that was consistent. Sometimes things were really heavy. There were times when family members were homeless, family members were struggling with depression, family members were struggling with substance abuse, family members were in jail. Yet we could turn on the TV and watch comedy and laugh. It was such a fun time for *SNL*. It was the "Wayne's World" era. We would start mimicking the sketches and mimicking the characters, and pretty soon you've got inside jokes within your own family. And then my dad kind of caught me up and made sure that I knew about the original cast. My love for comedy just grew from there. My brothers and I, we became collectors of comedy. It shaped my worldview."

Her early obsessions included Mel Brooks and Cheech and Chong. "My dad had the Cheech and Chong cassette tapes, and I put them in my Walkman. When my dad realized that I had a love for comedy, he started showing me more stuff and gave me a little Comedy 101. He showed me Charlie Chaplin to give me a sense of the silent comedy era. And then when I was in middle school, he introduced me to Monty Python and Mel Brooks. I loved it. At one point I was watching *Blazing Saddles* every single day. To this day I can repeat it line for line. My dad was in and out of my life, but comedy kept me grounded. It was the one escape."

She hated school—a common trait of future stand-ups—even though her grades were pristine. During history class, she confronted a teacher for giving a whitewashed version of colonization. "My stepdad was Comanche and a real activist type, and he had schooled me on the relationship between the government and Natives. I got kicked out of public school for heckling my teacher. I was sent to Riverside Indian Boarding School [in Oklahoma], and I got in trouble right away. I always got straight As, so that wasn't the problem. It was my behavior. They put me in 'transition dorm,' which is like a boot camp. My boarding school had a bad reputation. It was established in 1871, but obviously it's different today than it was then—or even thirty years ago. Today it is run by the community and has a ninety-five percent Native staff. A lot of the staff had gone to school there, as had their parents and grandparents, and they knew the history of abuse. It used to be a place where you'd get a bad education and a violent education. But when I was there, the school was all about embracing our culture and uplifting the students. I can tell you, I didn't feel much pride in my culture until I went to that school. I was surrounded by the diversity of different tribes and realized we're still going strong. It was a really good thing for me. There were also some bad things about the school. It was very institutionalized and they searched us all the time, random searches of our belongings and bodies—looking for contraband. I knew my constitutional rights, and the searches were one of the things that I had a big problem with. Mostly because I was hiding contraband."

Today, her young boys—ages one, five, seven, and eleven—take up much of her time. Family obligations have limited her ability to be near a stand-up scene—so she carved one out where she lived. "I started doing comedy on the reservations out here in the Southwest," she says. "It was really different than if I had started at comedy clubs or at an open-mic night. Native American comedians started getting together on the reservation and hosting comedy shows by their own accord. They grew their own thing. Sometimes there's a language barrier. I don't speak the languages of the southwestern tribes, and sometimes you'll have half a crowd that doesn't speak English. And it's very rural where I live, so I have to travel to get to any show."

CHALEPAH IS DOING the ninety-minute drive from Cortez to the airport in Durango, Colorado. She's flying to San Bernardino, California, to participate in a taping of Native American stand-up comics. It's being produced for FNX, a digital subchannel devoted to Native content, distributed by PBS. Most people don't have it in

Will Rogers's Grandpa Is Murdered in a Vengeance Killing

"Durango is out of the way, and glad of it," said the Cherokee comedian who owed his notoriety to the newspapers. The Cherokee Nation established a newspaper of its own in Georgia in 1828. It was a new phenomenon. As with most Native American cultures, Cherokee storytelling was an oral tradition. Sequoyah, a famous Cherokee leader, created a syllabary that translated Cherokee to the page, and by 1809 political fact sheets focusing on Cherokee issues were being published. By the 1820s the Cherokee Nation established a written constitution and republican form of government as a means of defending themselves against Washington, D.C.

The Georgia legislature was alarmed by their progressive culture. In response they passed legislation declaring all Natives "incompetent" and forbade them from serving as "witness or party to any suit in which the defendant was a white man." Using the power of their newspapers, Cherokee leaders vehemently spoke out against it. In retaliation, the state of Georgia declared all Cherokee media illegal.

Andrew Jackson campaigned for president with a promise to remove Native peoples from Georgia and North Carolina with the purpose of securing their land for white settlement, and expand slavery. When he was elected in 1828, Jackson's supporters were emboldened. Thousands of white settlers illegally swarmed the area. Previously, federal troops had been stationed to protect Native peoples from white settlers who breached treaty conditions; after Jackson took office, he withdrew the troops and allowed the settlers to take over. The state of Georgia then sent in its own troops to protect the illegal settlements and passed a law preventing non-whites from extracting resources from Cherokee land. It led to a series of complex events ultimately resulting in the Indian Removal Act.

The Indian Removal Act was passed by Congress in 1830. Sixteen thousand people were forcibly removed by the U.S. cavalry with bayonets pointed at their backs. The Cherokee were forced to march through the winter on foot, seven hundred miles from Georgia to what the government dubbed Indian Territory. Over the course of six months many contracted dysentery, measles, whooping cough, and hypothermia. If someone was moving in a manner considered too slow for the cavalry, they were shot and left behind. By the time they reached the future Oklahoma, 25 percent were dead. It became known as the Trail of Tears.

In 1830, Robert Rogers, the grandfather of Will Rogers, was a resident of Tallapoosa, Georgia. He was among the minority of Cherokee citizens who cut a deal with the Jackson administration in 1830. In essence, the government told them, "Give up your land willingly—and we will give you agreeable terms in Indian Territory. You can go voluntarily or be relocated by force—either way, you're going." Approximately seventeen thousand Cherokee refused to go, while about two thousand agreed. Those who agreed received large plots of land and a $5 million payment to divide among themselves. They were nicknamed the Old Settlers. The Cherokee majority who refused to cede their land never forgave them.

Those who survived the Trail of Tears found themselves living among the Old Settlers, whom they resented. It created an immediate class distinction. Among the hated was Robert Rogers. The government gave him a substantial plot of land, and he became a prosperous rancher as a result. He welcomed a son, Clem, into the world in 1839. Three years later Cherokee vigilantes delivered retribution. Clem was just a toddler when his father was brutally murdered in a vengeance killing.

On his birthday, Clem Rogers received a cowboy starter kit from his family: a bull, four horses, twenty-five cows, and two Black enslaved people. The pressure on Native Americans to assimilate sometimes meant conforming with American slavery.

Clem became a full-time rancher, driving five hundred steers from Indian Territory to the stockyards of St. Louis, Missouri, for auction each year. A Cherokee woman named Mary Schrimsher was impressed with his rustic machismo, and they married in 1858.

With the Civil War approaching, the Cherokee were pushed to take a side. As his father had done in 1830, Clem Rogers hedged his bets. He joined the Confederacy and told the two people he kept enslaved, "You two can do as you wish, join whichever side you wish. If my side wins, I will come back after the war is over and you will be my slaves again. If the North wins, you will be free men and I will have no control over you." The enslaved person known as Rabb fought for the North. The enslaved person known as Huse fought for the South. After the war, Rabb had a child and named him after Clem Rogers.

A new treaty was signed with the federal government outlawing slavery in the Cherokee Nation. It also canceled the provision shielding Indian Territory from white settlement. Once again the Cherokee watched as squatters, railway interests, and oil speculators moved in. Rather than fight the coming of the railway, Clem Rogers developed a new ranch beside it. He used the emerging rail yard to ship cattle directly from his ranch to the stockyards of St. Louis, cutting down on labor and time. With this increase in profits, the Rogers family was quite wealthy by the time Will Rogers was born on November 4, 1879.

While just a young child, Rogers learned how to do dazzling

tricks with a lariat. He was taught the ways of the rope by Dan Walker, an African American cowboy who married the daughter of one of the people enslaved by the Rogers family. He spent hours with young Will, and the boy was enamored with this meditative diversion.

The Cherokee Nation allowed white settlers to lease their land without being paid up front. As it turned out, they would never be paid at all. Clem Rogers was livid, shouting, "Are we powerless to enforce our laws? Are we to submit to such great wrongs by white men not citizens[?] . . . There is not a single law in this country enforced. . . . We are fast, fast drifting into the hands of the white men."

His situation worsened when Henry L. Dawes, the Republican senator from Massachusetts, introduced the General Allotment Act of 1887, which would end tribal autonomy and outlaw communal land ownership in Indian Territory. As Alexander Posey had written about in the guise of Fus Fixico, Native Americans were restricted to a maximum of 160 acres of land. Clem Rogers lost 4,840 acres, and his ranching empire was destroyed. The federal government took the land and turned it over to white oil barons and railroad tycoons. The White House framed the move as a benevolent gesture, meant to protect Native Americans from armed settlers, but in their private correspondence they were more candid. In an internal memo, the House Committee on Indian Affairs wrote, "The real aim of this bill is to get at the Indian lands and open them up for settlement. The provisions for the apparent benefit of the Indian are but a pretext to get his lands and occupy them."

Will Rogers was listed on the Cherokee Authenticated Roll of 1880. Relatives listed on the roll included his mother, Mary A. Rogers, his grandmother Elizabeth Schrimsher, his aunt Sarah Catherine Schrimsher, his great-aunt Polly Smith, and his cousin Watt Smith. He referred to himself as "the boy from Indian Territory."

He was eleven years old when the U.S. Cavalry massacred three hundred Native men, women, and children at Wounded Knee in 1890. The U.S. government was pushing an aggressive assimilation strategy that punished Native Americans who defied the child-separation policies that forced their children into boarding schools. Prosperous one day, broken the next, Will Rogers gained a sense of political injustice. It would inform his worldview in the years to come as the world's most famous Native American comedian.

Jonny Roberts Is Nervous in San Berdoo

Today a towering mural of Will Rogers looks down benevolently upon the downtown core of San Bernardino, California. Affectionately nicknamed San Berdoo, the city is the last major stop before the vast mountain range gives way to a barren desert landscape. It is the traditional territory of the Cahuilla Nation, the Yuhaviatam of the Serrano–San Manuel Nation, and the Payómkawichum of the Luiseño Nation. Bisected by Route 66, Berdoo was once famous for its flagship Hells Angels clubhouse and an annual citrus festival where celebrity grand marshals like Bob Hope judged the annual Miss Citrus Pageant. The city used to host a Keep America Beautiful Day. It was named for the famous television commercial in which a generic Native American character stood silently, looking at a polluted landscape, as he shed a single tear. Known colloquially as "the crying Indian," the man in the commercial was a Sicilian American actor who worked under the phony name Iron Eyes Cody. He was one of the original Native poseurs.

"But he shed not a single tear Sunday when he rode an Appaloosa horse here to make a poster publicizing Keep America Beautiful Day," reported the *San Bernardino Sun* in 1979. "With a single eagle feather in his hair and carrying a shovel like a badge of office, Iron Eyes was followed by about twenty youngsters and a bevy of photographers as he rode the black-spotted white gelding, Pinto Pete, around San Bernardino City Hall."

In popular culture, San Bernardino was presented as an idyllic destination, famous for orange juice mascots and the happy-go-lucky song "Five Little Miles from San Berdoo." But today the city is neither happy nor lucky. The art deco towers downtown are boarded up, cordoned off with chain-link fences. There are miles of vacant lots, overgrown fields, and foreclosed houses in every direction.

Some of the roadside motels along Foothill Boulevard still flicker a bright neon at dusk. But when the bygone songwriter suggested people get their kicks on Route 66, he wasn't referring to the carousel of prostitution below the neon glow of Berdoo's sordid motels. Whatever kicks Route 66 had to offer here are long gone. The famed stretch of highway is in ruins. Near the industrial area, boxcars chug past the Astro Motel. With its space-age design and Googie-style architecture, it is an incongruous structure for low-income housing. Farther down the street is the abandoned drive-thru restaurant Queen's, "Home of the Grinder," with its rotting metal sign in the shape of a female carhop. A parking lot of mud-encrusted tractor-trailers sits beside the Wigwam Motel, a roadside landmark designed by architect Frank Redford in 1949. Its hotel rooms are freestanding concrete structures built in the shape of nineteen tipis, during the height of midcentury racial stereotyping. There is nothing resembling a wigwam on the premises.

A few blocks south of Route 66 is San Bernardino Valley College, a decent school with an affordable reputation. This month the school is hosting a series of television tapings showcasing twenty-five mostly new Native American comedians. There's no question the comics would receive a superior showcase in Los Angeles, but just as the education is affordable at Valley College, so too is the use of the auditorium. The venue was built in the 1930s, one of the many construction projects instigated by the Works Progress Administration under President Franklin Roosevelt's New Deal. The venue hosted a special broadcast of Bob Hope's radio program in 1947, and people lined up for blocks to get in. Tonight there is no line outside, no large crowd clamoring for seats. The Lyft drivers who come and go are mystified why anybody wants to be dropped off here in the dark—but for the comedians backstage, like Jonny Roberts and Adrianne Chalepah, it's exciting.

San Bernardino is an hour's drive from Los Angeles when the roads are clear and twice that during rush hour. It's just remote enough to go undetected by Hollywood. The studios used it as a secret testing ground for new movies back in the 1930s for this reason. If the film bombed, nobody would hear about it back in Tinseltown, and the studios could send it back for editing before it was released to the general public.

Such anecdotes don't bode well for the comedians here tonight, who are anticipating a full house in a theater that seats 570 people. Showtime is twenty minutes away and the auditorium is completely empty. Jonny Roberts is sitting at a table backstage, once again scribbling words and crossing out lines on his small notepad. He can barely focus on what he's writing. Sipping from a Diet Coke, he's overwhelmed with nerves. He has flown in all the way from the Red Lake Nation on his own dime, and even if he bombs tonight, the experience is essential. For an ambitious comic, there's nothing quite like doing television for the very first time. Roberts is trying to keep his cool, but his anxiety is obvious. "I don't think I've ever been so nervous in my life," he says. "They get this channel in the Red Lake Nation. My people are going to see this. That's all I'm thinking about. But even if I bomb, I guess it's better they see me doing this than getting busted for something on *Crimestoppers*."

San Berdoo may not be Hollywood, but it's the closest thing to it in his career so far. "It's pretty slow for me even in a busy year. I do maybe four or five shows a year. It'd be more if I was doing the open mics, but I can't get away. I can't get out there because I'm so busy with the kids." With ten children in his home, the fact that he does this at all is nothing short of amazing. "I respect the comedy game, but I've got mouths to feed and life insurance to pay for. I realize how much work it is to be a full-time comedian, and I act like a professional—even though I don't do that many gigs. I'm fortunate to get the gigs that I do, and I don't take them for granted. A lot of the Native comedians know the powwow scene and they know the traditions. I don't know any of that. That's just not my thing. I'm not very traditional, I'm not very religious, and I'm not very spiritual. I can't fake it. I just go by what I can see in front of me."

Roberts stares at his notes while a fellow Ojibwe comedian named Jim Ruel engages in backstage banter. Ruel belongs to the Bay Mills band of Ojibwe and is one of the few people here who has been on television in the past. He was in an NBC diversity program at the turn of the millennium, but it didn't amount to much. "I feel like this is a great opportunity for all the comics," says Ruel. "Native comedians—none of us have really broken through yet . . . so we need to support each other, push each other to get there . . . to try mainstream comedy clubs and the college circuit, not just performing for Native communities. What you get is what you put into it, and across the board all of us need to get funnier, which means getting better. . . . To me, the show we're doing tonight is all about us moving together into the mainstream. Because it hasn't happened ever." He pauses, and a grin crosses his face. "We're like the Columbus of Native comedians."

Chizz Bah, a middle-aged mother and amateur comic from Farmington, New Mexico, interrupts Ruel to ask, "Do you think this crowd understands Navajo? How many Navajo speakers do you think will be here tonight?" Doing half her act in English and half in Navajo is a big hit back home, but it's unlikely to go over among the five hundred–plus empty seats. There are now thirty people in the audience, and the taping is delayed while the camera crew devises a way to shoot around the sparse optics. Backstage the spread of salted snacks, licorice, and deli trays is looking the worse for wear. Vegetable selections under plastic Costco lids remain untouched, and an executive from FNX is double-fisting tiny sandwiches into

Will Rogers Learns Rope Tricks from an Enslaved Person

Will Rogers credited his sense of humor to his mother. She died of dysentery in 1890 when he was just eleven years old. Compounded with the loss of the family ranch, it left him in shock for the next several months. He never spoke of his mother's death again, the feelings of pain too raw and too deep. He could hardly believe it when his father married a new woman a short while later. It caused a rift in the family, and Rogers started acting out. He was bounced from multiple schools, fighting white students who heckled him with racist taunts. When a classmate compared Native Americans to a breed of horse, Rogers lunged at him and had to be restrained. His first romance was with a white girl, until her parents objected to the "dirty Indian." Angered as he may have been, it didn't compare to the sheer rage of his father. It was rumored that Clem Rogers hired vigilantes to police his daughter's love life. One night while she was lying in bed beside her fiancé, a gunman pointed a rifle through a window and shot him dead. Six months later, while May Rogers was walking home with a new boyfriend, a stranger materialized from the bushes and riddled him with bullets.

Death haunted the family. A murdered grandfather, the death of a mother, the assassination of two boyfriends—and then Clem's new wife dropped dead of a sudden illness. A few months later, Will was walking to get a haircut in Oologah, Oklahoma, when he was stopped by a panhandler. As he fumbled through his pockets for change, the building Rogers was headed toward collapsed, immediately killing a cashier, two customers, and his barber.

Will needed to escape. Equipped with the roping dexterity he'd learned as a child, he joined a traveling rodeo and toured through Des Moines, Memphis, San Antonio, and St. Louis. His twirling accuracy was impressive. He could halt a galloping horse by catching all four of its legs simultaneously with four different ropes. Rodeo patrons were impressed with the artistry, and he won several roping contests. While on the road he wrote love letters to Betty Blake, a white post office worker in Oologah whom he met shortly before leaving town. They took a liking to each other, but their interracial affection was cause for trepidation. "I know it would be a slam on your society career to have it known that you ever knew an ignorant Indian cowboy," wrote Rogers. "Now, Bettie [sic], please burn this up for my sake. Hoping you will consider what I have told you in my undignified way, and, if not, please never say anything about it and burn this up. I am yours with love."

Rogers learned to work a crowd amid the dust and dirt of the rodeo circuit. After five years he repurposed the act for vaudeville. He went to New York City and climbed the narrow stairwells above Broadway that led to the vaudeville booking agents. While vying for a contract, he spent his evenings doing rope tricks in a run-down Brooklyn burlesque house operated by the family of Bud Abbott, of Abbott and Costello fame. Rogers got lucky and landed with the most powerful of all vaudeville companies—the Keith Circuit. A gig with the Keith company meant a yearlong tour through ornate theaters around North America. Visiting nearly every major city, Rogers became hip to the sounds of contemporary popular music in the pre-radio era. Songs that were all the rage in Chicago and New York were completely unknown along the rural route. Whenever he returned to Indian Territory, a crowd of onlookers gathered as he demonstrated the latest Tin Pan Alley tunes on a banjo.

Rogers commuted to each gig by train. It was taxing for any performer, but especially for Rogers, who was using a horse in his act. Traveling with a two-thousand-pound animal slowed things down considerably, but Rogers considered it necessary. He tasked his boyhood friend Buck McKee with the job of getting the beast in and out of each theater and down to the rail yard for the next gig. Booking agents needed to ensure the venues could accommodate cattle. Each gig required a backstage area to tie the horse and water it, a freight elevator up to stage level, and a stage door wide enough for the animal to pass. Other popular horse acts in vaudeville included Professor Buckley's Curriculum, Rossi's Musical Horse, Madame Etoile's Society Horses, and the Five Lloyds—a group of white guys from Britain who did a pseudo–Native American shtick while affixing feathered headdresses to their steeds.

Occasionally a Rogers rope trick would miss its intended target, and it was in those moments that comedy developed. Rogers pioneered a method used decades later by Johnny Carson. When a joke fell flat during Carson's opening monologue on the *Tonight Show*, the late-night host referenced the failure of the gag—getting a big laugh at his own expense and, in essence, saving the failed joke. Sixty years earlier, Rogers was doing "savers" whenever a rope trick went awry. "I'm handicapped up here," Rogers told the crowd. "The manager won't let me swear when I miss." After a year on the road, he had several pages' worth of savers, and the transition from cowboy to comedian had begun.

Onstage he wore a red western shirt, buckskin pants, and a Stetson hat. It was a familiar look in Indian Territory, and he billed himself as the Cherokee Kid. "Cherokee ranching culture influenced the way he presented himself," wrote Rogers biographer Amy M. Ware. "In the end, Rogers's self-representation as a cowboy limited the public's recognition of him as an Indian. . . . He was both a cowboy and an Indian, a conflation that baffled and titillated his urban fan base."

There were forty-five vaudeville theaters in New York City in 1905. The most common acts were blackface performers, comic jugglers, dog acts, dialect comedy teams, schoolroom acts, magicians, tap dancers, and tramp comedians. Rogers ascended quickly in the vaudeville ranks. He signed with William Morris (not just the agency, but the man) and hired a tailor to make intentionally rumpled suits to match his down-home persona. Rogers grew friendly with the Three Keatons and their boy wonder, Buster Keaton, and the comic-juggler W. C. Fields, who referred to him as "injun."

Rogers did interviews with the show-biz press and spoke frequently of his background: "Well, I reckon I'm about as real an American as you can find. I'm a Cherokee . . . and they're the finest Indians in the world. . . . We are civilized and educated. Why, the government don't allow the Cherokees to go to Carlisle and the other big schools for Indians. They're for the ignorant kind." His ethnocentric patter was common in an era in which Natives were conditioned to have shame. "Such tribal supremacist talk goes a long way in unearthing Rogers's role in his own typecasting," wrote Amy M. Ware. "As he describes it, he and other members of the Cherokee Nation were 'good' Indians . . . superior to those . . . living on fenced-in reservations across the country." Then again, Rogers didn't have much positive to say about non-Natives either. "I [have] just enough white in me," he said, "to make my honesty questionable."

Indian Territory was absorbed into the new state of Oklahoma in 1907, and Rogers changed his billing from the Cherokee Kid to the Oklahoma Cowboy. Privately he lamented the changeover, pining for the days of his five-thousand-acre ranch with nary a white settler in sight. "We had the greatest territory in the world," he said. "They ruined it when they made it a state."

As his Keith contract came to a close, he briefly entered burlesque, where the stakes were low, in order to develop a new act. Armed with new material, he returned to vaudeville in 1908, signing with the Orpheum Circuit, the other vaudeville monopoly. An Orpheum performer could bring their contract into any bank and use it to secure loans or mortgages. It was a guaranteed income and a good one, enough to get married and start a family, so Rogers proposed marriage. "The ceremony was performed at my mother's home, November 25, 1908," Betty Rogers said in her memoir. "Will had to play a few weeks' engagements in the East, and then, in early spring he was booked for a tour on the Orpheum Circuit. This would be our honeymoon." Two and a half years later they welcomed their first child—Will Rogers Jr. A gift of beaded moccasins arrived in the mail from the proud grandfather. A week later, Clem Rogers dropped dead.

Rogers looked glumly at his bank account and realized he couldn't provide for a wife, child, horse, and horse wrangler all at the same time. He fired his friend Buck McKee and purchased an advertisement in the trade papers: "Will Rogers—the Droll Oklahoma Cowboy—In His New Single Offering, ALL ALONE, NO HORSE."

He continued to twirl rope, but almost as an afterthought. It was a secondary prop, like Henny Youngman's fiddle or George Burns's cigar. He structured his new act the way many road comics did, padding it with local references and getting laughs with regional specificity. As soon as he arrived in a new town, he would study the local paper and grill the bellboy about local affairs. In this modest manner, Rogers became a political comedian.

Gene Buck, the head writer of the Ziegfeld Follies, recommended the vaudevillian to his boss, Florenz Ziegfeld. The Ziegfeld Follies were Broadway's bourgeois version of vaudeville, famed for clever comedy sketches and sexy dancing girls. Vaudeville had always been considered working-class, if not low-class. The Ziegfeld Follies allowed wealthy Broadway patrons to see the top vaudeville acts without having to mingle with the great unwashed. Ticket prices were four times as much as a Keith or Orpheum vaudeville show. Higher prices meant higher budgets. Higher budgets meant higher pay. And a residency on Broadway meant Rogers would no longer have to crisscross the country. With this in mind, Betty and Will welcomed more children—a son, Jim, and a daughter, Mary.

A stint on Broadway also meant fame. Major newspaper columnists covered the shows, and the names of Broadway stars were known to those who would never attend in person. But despite the fame and notoriety that came with a Ziegfeld show, Rogers learned that the showgirls were the main attraction and the comedians mostly filler. "A male actor's monolog in a girl show is just like an intermission," he said. "My little old act with the lasso was just put into the Ziegfeld Follies to kill time while the girls were changing from nothing to nothing."

No longer making jokes about small-town mayors, he zeroed in on national affairs. He spoke about foreign policy, the specter of war, and legalized graft. Much like the late-night television monologues of today, he provided immediacy with jokes based on that day's news. If the jokes bombed, he'd deliver a saver: "I guess I'm a couple [newspaper] editions ahead of you folks."

Will Rogers joined the Friars Club in 1916, becoming its first Native American member. The great show-biz fraternity was known for its star power, and Rogers joined Irving Berlin and George M. Cohan at the annual Friars Frolics, a variety show that toured the Eastern Seaboard. When the show came through Baltimore, Rogers was mortified to learn President Woodrow Wilson was in attendance. Most of his material ridiculed the administration. While the roasting of politicians is commonplace today, it was unheard of in 1916. "It was the first time in theatrical history that the president of the United States came just to see a comedy show," said Rogers. "I don't think anyone else had ever heard of a president being joked personally in a public theatre about the policies of his administration. The nearer the time come, the worse scared I got. . . . Finally, a warden knocked at my dressing room door and said, 'You die in five minutes.' "

The president loved the performance. The comedian who joked about the headlines was now making news himself. The fact that Rogers wrote his own material, the fact that he made fun of the president, the fact that he was Native American, all of this made him a real curio. It was inevitable that the film industry would try to cash in.

The future Hollywood mogul Samuel Goldwyn was just a budding producer when he approached Rogers about doing a series of silent movies. The films were "rube melodramas," fish-out-of-water scenarios in which a country hayseed struggled to adapt to the big city. But the magic of Will Rogers was lost without his main attribute: words. Critics agreed that other than the written titles that provided the exposition, the films were duds. Rogers made thirteen films for Goldwyn and hated them all. He witnessed Charlie Chaplin, Douglas Fairbanks, and Mary Pickford going into business for themselves with the creation of United Artists and decided to take charge of his own cinematic destiny. He mortgaged the family home and established Will Rogers Productions. It was a resounding failure. He lost his life savings—approximately half a million dollars. Betty had just given birth to their fourth child, and now Rogers was desperate. He started pimping himself out to any private organization that would have him. He played for the Chamber of Commerce, the Grand Rapids Retail Furniture Association, and the National Association of Waste Material Dealers. Modern stand-up parlance refers to this as a "corporate gig."

He was hired to speak at a campaign rally for a congressional candidate of whom he'd never even heard. Rather than turn down the cash, he adjusted his words to roast the stranger: "I don't know the candidate and don't want to. That's the reason I have been chosen to talk about the candidate . . . if a speaker knew him he couldn't say anything favorable."

The *New York Times* covered the event, quoting some of his better lines. The McNaught newspaper syndicate was impressed. In late 1922 they offered him a thousand dollars a week to write a political humor column. In the days before radio and television, a syndicated newspaper column was the most powerful force in media. Will clawed back up from failure and once again had money, fame, and respect, finally transcending his tragic past. So he thought.

Rogers was packing a suitcase in New York, preparing to cover the Republican National Convention in Cleveland, when he got word from his wife in California that the children had all come down with diphtheria. Forty-eight hours later, his newborn was dead. Rogers was crushed. Those same feelings of anguish and helplessness that had crippled him after the death of his mother came rushing back. He was never one to expose his emotions, burying himself in work in order to avoid reality. His written output was enormous and people wondered how he could be so prolific, but those closest to him knew that he used the typewriter to escape his feelings.

"I don't make jokes," said Rogers. "I just watch the government and report the facts." Five days a week for the next thirteen years Will Rogers cranked out the most widely read newspaper column in the world. Political bon mots made it stand out. Of the two-party system, he wrote, "If we didn't have two parties, we would all settle on the best men in the country and things would run fine—but as it is, we settle on the worst ones and then fight over 'em." Of political investigations, he wrote, "We are always saying, 'Let the law take its course.' But what we mean is 'Let the law take *our* course.'" On the military-industrial complex, he commented, "I have a scheme for stopping war. It's this—no nation is allowed to enter a war till they have paid for the last one." And of foreign policy, he joked, "We could never understand why Mexico wasn't just crazy about us, for we had always had their good will, and oil and coffee and minerals, at heart."

News editors found his commentary more incendiary than anticipated. To distance themselves from his words, the *Times* ran a disclaimer noting that the opinions of Rogers did not reflect the views of the paper. For his next column, Rogers composed a disclaimer of his own:

> I would like to state to the readers of the *New York Times* that I am in no way responsible for the editorial policy of this paper. I allow them free rein as to their opinion, so long as it's within the bounds of good subscription gathering. But I want it distinctly understood that their policy may be in direct contrast to mine. Their editorials may be put in purely for humor, or just to fill space. Every paper must have its various entertaining features and not always to be taken seriously, and never to be construed as my policy.

Rogers wrote in a colloquial manner, intentionally using bad grammar and poor punctuation. By employing "dident" instead of "didn't," he adopted the persona of the common man. Comedian Fred Allen, who worked with Rogers in vaudeville, observed, "He seemed to speak for the little man, the man with no collar on, and the ungrammatical man. Will was not an ungrammatical man himself, but he spoke in words that would be used by people who were untutored."

Most of the politicians Rogers ridiculed took it in stride, but some called for censorship. After he made fun of the cronyism in the Harding administration, a White House aide showed up at the Ziegfeld Follies and presented him with an ominous message at the stage door: "Stop making jokes about the president." Rogers acquiesced out of fear. After President Harding's sudden death in 1923, his successor, Calvin Coolidge, invited Rogers to the White House to make amends, but the Cherokee comic believed it was an attempt to neutralize jokes about a Coolidge presidency before it even began.

At a time when the population of the United States was 120 million, Rogers was averaging 40 million readers every day. There had never been a Native American personality so influential among the white population. He held serious sway, and his influence was disturbing to his literary colleague H. L. Mencken: "He alters foreign policies. He makes and unmakes candidates. . . . Millions of Americans read his words daily, and those who are unable to read listen to him over the radio. . . . I consider him the most dangerous writer alive today."

Rogers responded to Mencken directly: "Come on, now, Henry, you know that nobody with any sense ever took any of my gags seriously." Mencken shook his head: "They are taken seriously by nobody except half-wits . . . in other words . . . 85 percent of the voting population."

Rogers returned to Hollywood in 1922 to give silent film another try. The money was enormous and the deal made at the last minute. Comedy star Fatty Arbuckle was suddenly embroiled in a high-profile rape and manslaughter case, his half-filmed comedies put on hold. Rogers was hired as an emergency replacement, reshooting all the scenes that had previously featured Arbuckle. He took the opportunity to reestablish his roots in California, purchasing a Beverly Hills estate and making it the family home. Situated directly behind the Beverly Hills Hotel, it was equipped with a bowling alley, a projection room, horses, tennis courts, and a library of Cherokee history and Osage literature. Rogers referred to it as "the House that Jokes Built." But a few months into his stay, the neighbors started to complain. The Beverly Hills Hotel led the push to get the Rogerses ejected from the neighborhood. They said the family's home smelled like shit.

"There was a protest against the horses," recalled Will Rogers Jr.

"The Beverly Hills Hotel was stopping its breakfast. . . . They didn't like . . . the smell of the horses. . . . They were beginning to push the old man and his horses out."

Rogers was fortunate that he could afford another property. He was making $2,500 a week for his newspaper column, $10,000 per film short, and a minimum of $1,000 per public appearance. Pretty good money in an era when the average three-bedroom apartment was $30 a month. He was wealthy, but sometimes had trouble relating to his class. At a Bankers Association banquet in 1923, he addressed the dais in a manner similar to the way comics today stir controversy at the White House Correspondents' Dinner:

> Loan sharks and interest hounds. I have addressed every form
> of organized graft in the United States, excepting Congress. So
> it's naturally a pleasure for me to appear before the biggest.
> You are without a doubt the most disgustingly rich audience I
> ever talked to, with the possible exception of the Bootleggers
> Union. . . . I understand you have ten thousand here, and with
> what you have in the various federal prisons, that brings your
> membership up to around thirty thousand.

The new medium of radio was more important with each passing year. In the early 1920s it looked like it might be a massive educational tool devoted to the common good. But by the late 1920s major corporations had taken control of the airwaves for advertising purposes. Oil companies, tobacco interests, and military contractors donated large sums of money to political campaigns to ensure favorable legislation and approval of broadcast applications. Rogers was lured to radio by the American Tobacco Company, hired to write and deliver twenty-six radio commercials for their Bull Durham line. In contrast to the stark seriousness of cigarette advertising to come, Rogers made light of the endorsement. He told listeners that

Bull Durham Tobacco was *probably* good, but he wouldn't know because he had never smoked. The underhanded pitch became a Rogers trademark. Hired to deliver ads for a piano manufacturer, he confessed to the listening audience that he didn't know how to play one, but the company made "the best pianos I ever leaned against."

The rise of radio coincided with the collapse of the stock market. Rogers blamed the Wall Street crash on "irresponsible financial speculation by the wealthiest segments of the nation's population" and dismissed those who traded stocks as freeloaders who expected "to get something for nothing and had by their folly and greed undermined the nation's financial structure." He wrote in his column of November 1, 1929, "There is one rule that works in every calamity, be it pestilence, war or famine—the rich get richer and the poor get poorer." He sounded more and more like a political radical. "You will say, what will all the bankers do? I don't care what they do. Let 'em go to work, if there is a job any of them could earn a living at."

He said it was time to tax the rich—like himself. "People want *just* taxes more than they want *lower* taxes. They want to know that every man is paying his proportionate share according to his wealth." And he condemned the hollow strategies of politicians: "When a party can't think of anything else they always fall back on lower taxes. Presidents have been promising lower taxes since Washington crossed the Delaware . . . but our taxes have gotten bigger and their boats have gotten larger until now the President crosses the Delaware in his private yacht."

When Rogers tired of Wall Street and its political enablers, he took shots at the oil industry. "Frank Phillips of oil fame was out the other day . . . going to Washington. The oil men were going to draw up a code of ethics. Everybody present had to laugh. If he had said the gangsters of America were drawing up a code of ethics, it wouldn't have sounded near as impossible."

Rogers reprimanded the media for championing optics over policy. "I think the camera has done more harm for politics than any other faction. Everybody would rather get their picture than their ideas in the paper." And he complained about the divide-and-conquer strategy of the ruling class. "It just shows that if you can start arguing over something, and get enough publicity to keep the argument going, you can divide our nation overnight as to whether spinach or broccoli are the most nutritious." His forecast for the Great Depression was bleak. "Last year we said, 'Things can't go on like this.' And they didn't. They got worse."

Jackie Curtiss Breaks Ed Sullivan's Foot

Jackie Curtiss was a child of the Great Depression, born shortly before the stock market crash of 1929. By the time he entered show business, America was on the rebound. Curtiss belonged to the glamorous nightclub era, a period in which comedians wore tuxedos and were employed by organized crime.

Today his tuxedo permanently hangs in the closet of his small, one-story home in North Hollywood. A large American flag waves above the entrance, casting a shadow over his front lawn. Curtiss purchased his house in the 1960s while working full-time as the house emcee at the Playboy Club on the Sunset Strip. He was known for his fast quips, madcap physicality, and violent pratfalls. He appeared on most of the major television shows as one half of the comedy team Antone and Curtiss.

Today, suffering from severe physical pain, he has limited mobility. The pratfalls have caught up with him at the age of ninety-four. He winces as he moves, but the pain can't stop him from showing off the many framed photos hanging on the wall. "Here I am on *The Steve Allen Show*. This is my good friend Dave Madden. You probably know him from *The Partridge Family*. Here I am with Ed Sullivan. We timed a routine in advance where I was going to jump into his arms. He missed his mark and I ended up stomping on his foot. I broke Ed's big toe. I figured that was the end of my career."

As he digs through a closet for a VHS copy of the appearance in question, he name-drops old comedians like Lenny Bruce and Redd Foxx and reminisces. "Ed Sullivan took a liking to me. I think it was because we had a similar past. We were both orphaned at a young age." From the room down the hall, his wife can be heard shouting, "Tell him about the Zieglers! Tell him about the Zieglers!"

Curtiss was born at the end of the vaudeville era to a Mohawk mother. "In the late eighteen hundreds, white families could *buy* Indian children if they passed a certain standard," he says. "They used the word 'adopt,' but white families would actually pay for Indian children—and the biological parents didn't have much say in the matter. My mother was from the Mohawk Nation. She wasn't an orphan, but someone from the government facilitated her 'adoption.' She was purchased by a man named Ziegler. He was a tobacco salesman. He bought her, brought her back, and made her part of the family. He had three daughters who toured vaudeville as the Ziegler Sisters—Myrtle, Valma, and Adelaide. Old man Ziegler paid three hundred dollars for my mother when she was just a little girl. That was the going price to 'adopt' an Indian child. Her name was Wiwa, but they gave her a new name and called her Marion Ziegler. They took her back to New York City and put her in a school where she learned to speak English. . . .

"My father was Jewish. He was working as a carny. That's how my mother first met him. She attended a carnival somewhere in Long Island where my father was working. They met, went on a date, and ended up getting married. My father got her a job at the carnival as a ticket taker. She had me not long afterward.

"I was born in the Bronx. I was raised around the carnival, and when I was quite young I taught myself how to do the high wire. People commented on my balance, referencing the Mohawk steelworkers in New York. I was six years old. With carnivals you worked x amount of months per year, and in winter you worked one spot. Certain carnivals would be linked up with circuses, like the World of Mirth. They would attach themselves so when you went through the fairgrounds, you'd go through the carnival and the circus would be behind. You'd have to pass by all the rides, all the concessions, and it was markedly a big deal. I worked as an acrobat for Ringling Brothers for many years. . . .

"My mother told me stories—whatever she could remember— about her father and mother being placed on a reservation. She told me about the Ziegler family. When they retired from vaudeville, they stuffed all of their money in a mattress. They never used a bank. They were unaffected when the stock market crashed. My mom would go and visit and they would go into the other room and grab money out of the mattress to give to her. I never met Mr. Ziegler. He died long before I was born. It's funny—they wanted to hide the fact that they were Jewish and at the same time tried to keep it a secret that my mother was Indian. . . .

"She was a very sweet lady. My mother was very loving and encouraging. My father was the opposite, very manipulative and cruel. They'd go into a restaurant, and when the waiter wasn't looking he'd push my mother off the chair and she'd fall to the floor and then he'd yell at the restaurant, 'I'll sue you! I'll sue you!' and they'd give him twenty dollars or something to shut him up. He was a real piece of work. I had to listen to him put her down all the time. 'Oh, she's just an Indian, what does she know?' He was an awful man. When I was nine years old, I came home from school one day and they had *moved*. They didn't leave a forwarding address. They deserted me. I don't blame my mother. I'm sure she had nothing to do with it. . . .

"When I got out of the service in 1947, I worked in the Bay Area as a big band singer. I sang with Jack Fina and some dates with Frankie Carle and Del Courtney. These were fairly decent bands. Fina was the pianist for the Freddy Martin Orchestra and then he went off on his own. He became very famous for 'Bumble Boogie' and 'Warsaw Concerto.'

"In the nineteen fifties, when big bands kind of faded, I went into comedy. I was with a guy named Al Bello and we were Bello and Curtiss for about six months. Al Bello was a real flake. A real wacko. I had to leave him. While we were working in Fresno, I saw this singer named Marc Antone. And then right around that time, my agent said, 'You ever heard of Marc Antone?' I said, 'I just met him.' He said, 'I'd like you two to team up.' So he put us together. I wrote a bunch of material for us, and it just clicked. The agency booked us and, boy, we just took off. We worked all of the major clubs. The Cave in Vancouver, the Tidelands in Houston, the Fontainebleau in Miami Beach, and the Copa in New York. We played Eddy's in Kansas City with a famous singer named Gretchen Wyler. She took a liking to us and she asked if we would go with her to Jack Silverman's International in New York. She was a big favorite of Ed Sullivan. We played Jack Silverman's International with her, and that's how we got on Sullivan for the first time. He was in the crowd and called us over to his table afterward. This was on a Tuesday night. We were on his show that Sunday. Antone and Curtiss did a lot of Sullivan shows. We worked all over the world, and when he passed on, I teamed up with a guy named Bill Tracy. Curtiss and Tracy. We were living in Los Angeles at a time when novelty records were everything. I wrote a song called 'The Ballad of Puppy Breath.' The guy I did it for was a front man for some hood. They put it out and [it] sold fast. They made a lot of money, and I went back to the office, and all of a sudden—closed! No office. No nothing. They just disappeared with the money.

"The Mob was an integral part of everything. I became a darling of the Mob years later. We were doing our act in [Phoenix] Arizona, Antone and Curtiss, at the KoKo Club with the DeCastro Sisters. The Mob came in and told me that we were going to be their guests at some show and we wouldn't have to perform that night. They were presenting a young singer that they were 'taking care of' because the kid's father was going to the penitentiary. In those days the Mob would take care of the family and get them a job if the father went to jail. Well, this kid was going to be a singer, so they had Buddy Bregman arrangements, Sy Devore clothing, but he was the *worst* singer. But he looked great. We were sitting at the table with the top Mob guys, and everybody there was connected to the Mob. So the cheers this singer got were unbelievable. I mean, they really cheered this guy who couldn't sing. When the show was over, the Mob guy goes, 'Well, whaddaya think?' I said, 'Um, well, uh, you see, how do I put it . . .' He said, 'That bad, huh?' The kid walked up to the table and asked the Mob guy, 'How'd I do?' He told him, 'Tomorrow you're a fighter.' And that was it. They made him a boxer!

"I used to babysit for Lenny Bruce. His wife, Honey, would have a club date and Lenny would have a club date and I'd take care of the baby. That happened a few times. He was a great guy. I would finish my last show and then we would meet for breakfast at the little coffee shop in the Thunderbird Hotel on Sunset Boulevard. People don't realize that Lenny didn't get high to get high. Lenny was in a lot of pain. He was addicted. Most of the time he was high he was still lucid. His mother was Sally Marr. After I did a show at the Playboy Club, she walked up to me and said, 'You know something, Jackie? You remember every joke in the world. You're not very funny, but you've got the greatest memory.'

"I wrote for a lot of comics, but not to get paid. I'd just give them something. I wrote a lot of stuff for Redd Foxx because he was my buddy. Redd would call me twice a week and run jokes by me to see if I thought he should put them in his act. He trusted me. . . .

"They were going to close the Playboy Club in Los Angeles because it was losing money. I flew to Chicago and begged Hugh Hefner, 'Don't close the room. Let me run the club. Give me six months to turn it around.' They stripped it down to hardly anything, but I ran it and got them out of the red. I ran it for fifty-six weeks and put them back in the black. I had this place jumping. I got Redd Foxx and Sammy Davis Jr. to go onstage for free. Joe Parnello, who was my pianist for a year, suggested I use this guy Kenny Colman because he was such a good singer. I heard him and he was fabulous.

So I booked him not knowing this guy has something in his brain that doesn't work right! He came along and just about ruined me with one show. Oh, God, he gave me a heart attack. Opening night he comes out and sings a song. It was great and everything. After he finished—I thought he got good applause—he stops. He said, 'How dare you fucking people not give me the applause I deserve! Don't you know what a great singer I am? Frank Sinatra tells everyone what a great singer I am! You fucking people!' I physically pulled him offstage and into the kitchen. I said, 'What the hell are you doing?' He said, 'Well, these fucking people don't even know what talent is!' I said, 'Well, this show is over. We'll talk about this later.' I ran up onstage and said, 'Ladies and gentlemen, I must apologize for Kenny. He's a great singer and a great guy, but he has just had a personal tragedy in the family. His dear, beloved mother died tonight and he really shouldn't have been doing a show. Please do not judge the Playboy Club based on what just happened, and I do hope you come back and see Kenny Colman another evening.' He was the most narcissistic guy I ever met. . . .

"When I was running the Playboy Club out here, I hired comics all the time. They gave me less grief than singers. Sammy Shore was a comedian from Las Vegas. He was an opening act for Elvis. He came in and saw that I was booking a ton of comedians. He said, 'Why the hell are you using so many comics?' I said, 'It's good to have a room full of comics!' He said, 'You shouldn't have so many comedians on one show.' A few months later, what does Sammy Shore do? Right down the street—he opens the Comedy Store.

"Joey Bishop was another good buddy of mine. He was the last of the Rat Pack. He always hung out when I had the Playboy Club. I remember once he came in limping, and I said, 'What's the matter?' He said, 'I hurt my back.' I asked, 'How'd that happen?' He said, 'I fell off my wallet.' I did Joey's talk show when his sidekick was Regis Philbin. I gave Regis one of his first jobs singing at the Playboy Club.

Will Rogers Takes a Fateful Flight
With a One-Eyed Pilot

"The Pilgrims were a very religious people," said Will Rogers. "They would shoot a couple of Indians on the way to every prayer meeting." Firmly established as a powerful voice in the culture, Rogers spoke about Native American issues with regularity. He wrote about the forcible removal of the San Carlos Apache from the Gila River to make way for the new Coolidge Dam in March 1930. "It's as I told you before, the Apache Indians owned the land the dam is built on . . . [they] fought to hold all they had, and most of them wound up in jail. . . . I expect if the truth was known . . . [they were] dedicating a dam to get water for white people [and] gradually take more Indian land away."

Rogers heard about a federally funded hospital being built in Claremore, Oklahoma, and griped that "it took 400 years for the Government to build a hospital for the Indians. Look what the Indians have got to look forward to in the next 400 years. They are liable to build us a cemetery."

He addressed federal hypocrisy in his columns. "The Government, by statistics, shows they have got 456 treaties that they have broken with the Indians. That is why the Indians get a kick out of reading the Government's usual remark when some big affair comes up, 'Our honor is at stake.' They sent the Indians to Oklahoma.

They had a treaty that said, 'You shall have this land as long as grass grows and water flows.' It was not only a good rhyme but looked like a good treaty, and it was—till they struck oil. Then the Government took it away from us again. They said the treaty only refers to 'Water and Grass,' it don't say anything about oil.' "

Addressing a Native American audience of three thousand in Asheville, North Carolina, Rogers railed against the late Andrew Jackson: "I got no use for him or any of his methods, for all he ever did was pounce on the Indians." He went into a passionate spiel about the Trail of Tears. "Well, to tell you the truth, I am not so sweet on old Andy. He is the one that run us Cherokees out of Georgia and North Carolina . . . Then he would go to Florida, and shoot up the Seminoles . . . and he would come back and sick himself onto us Cherokees again. . . . But old Andy made the White House. . . . Even the Indians wanted him in there, so he would let us alone for a while. . . . The Indians wanted him to serve a third term, but Andy had to get back to his regular business, which was shooting Indians."

A white reporter in attendance dismissed him as a hater: "His transformation was terrifying, and for three minutes, his astonished audience was treated to a demonstration of what primitive, instinctive hatred could be."

LIKE MOST COMEDIANS, Will Rogers could be hostile, morose, and depressed. The slightest criticism made him defensive. Famed cartoonist Rube Goldberg roomed with Rogers during one of the political conventions and said his companion spent most of the week in silence, staring at the ceiling in "abject misery." Rogers suffered from complex grief and trauma, haunted by the many tragedies in his family tree. His wife said he spoke of his mother's death only once: "He cried when he told me about it many years later. It left in him a lonely, lost feeling that persisted long after he was successful and famous." His friend Homer Croy said his demons stood in stark contrast to his public persona: "He was vastly reserved. There was a wall that no one went beyond; and there were dark chambers and hidden recesses that he opened to no one."

A bleak tone occasionally seeped into his column: "What all of us know put together don't mean anything. We are just here for a spell and pass on. Any man that thinks that Civilization had advanced is an egotist. Fords and bathtubs have moved and cleaned you, but you was just as ignorant when you got there. . . . We have got more tooth paste on the market, and more misery in our Courts than at any time in our existence. . . . Indians . . . were the highest civilized, because they were more satisfied . . . and took less from each other. The whole thing is a 'Racket,' so get a few laughs [while] you can."

As the country plunged into depression, Hollywood film studios transitioned from silent film to sound. While nearly half the population was thrown into unemployment, the Fox Film Corporation hired Rogers at a rate of $10,000 a week. Talking pictures gave him the success silent movies never could. One critic concluded, "Will Rogers is the man talkies were invented for."

Some of the features will still entertain any classic film fan. *Too Busy to Work* (1932), *Mr. Skitch* (1933), and *Life Begins at 40* (1935) feature a naturalistic acting approach unique for the era. Rogers wasn't really an actor, so with the permission of the director, he rewrote his lines to conform to his personal cadence and made each character an extension of his own persona. "He'd read his script and say, 'What does *that* mean?'" recalled director John Ford. "I'd say to him, 'Say it in your own words!' And he'd go away, muttering to himself, getting his lines ready, and when he came back, he'd make his speech in typical Rogers fashion, which was better than any writer could write for him."

In his film *So This Is London* (1930), Rogers debated a customs agent using a line of logic that first appeared in his written work:

CUSTOMS AGENT: If you don't have a birth certificate, then how are we to know of your birth?

63

ROGERS: Out in our country if you walked up and appeared
  before anybody in person, why, we'd take it as fairly
  positive proof that you must have been born. . . .
CUSTOMS AGENT: But you *are* an American citizen?
ROGERS: Well, I think I am. My folks were Indian . . . and I
  was born and raised in Indian Territory. Of course, I'm
  not one of those Americans whose ancestors came over
  on the Mayflower, but we met them at the boat when
  they landed. And it has always been to the everlasting
  discredit of the Indian race that we ever let 'em land.

Rogers became a huge movie star in the new decade. As one of
the top box-office draws alongside Clark Gable and Shirley Temple,
he was in demand and commanded a handsome fee. The Gulf Oil
Company hired him to deliver radio monologues on three different
variety programs—*The Gulf Headliners*, *The Good Gulf Program*,
and *The Shell Chateau*. Press and public feared that the giant oil
company would censor him, but the corporation insisted that for
$7,000 per shot, they wanted their money's worth. Gulf would not
"muzzle the monologist's comments."

Rogers walked up to the microphone on each episode and placed
an alarm clock on a stool by his side. Setting it for nine minutes, he
improvised a monologue based on the week's news, including asides
about how well the material went over. The lack of polish made
him unique in a radio era of slick, fast-talking vaudevillians. The
laughter was scattered. Some caught the references while others did
not, and sometimes there was no laughter at all. If he was in mid-
sentence when the alarm clock rang, he'd simply say, "Thank you
very much," and walk off. Speaking during a *Shell Chateau* broadcast, he told the audience, "Our record with the Indians is going
down in history. It is going to make us mighty proud of it in the
future when our children of ten more generations read of what we

did to them. Every man in our history that killed the most Indians has got a statue built for him."

Growing up in the Indian Territory shaped his sense of justice, but growing up in the South also created a blind spot. On *The Good Gulf Program* of January 21, 1934, Rogers introduced a song titled "The Last Round-Up." "The words to the song are cowboy all right," he said, "but the tune is really a nigger spiritual."

Some listeners thought they'd misheard. Others assumed it was a slip of the tongue. Both theories were discarded when Rogers proceeded to use the racial slur several more times.

"Will Rogers' description of the music in the popular song 'The Last Round-Up' as a 'nigger' spiritual, roused protests from all over the nation last night following his broadcast," reported the *New York Daily News*. "He repeated this three times during his broadcast. . . . NBC officials refused to discuss the matter until they had conferred with Rogers."

An NBC spokesperson explained that Rogers was "simply using a term which was common throughout the South and West." Roy Wilkins, the future leader of the NAACP, responded, "This excuse is not sufficient for you to permit it to be used over your network. Besides, it is not true. It may be true in Claremore, Oklahoma, where Mr. Rogers had his beginning [but] is the local standard of an Oklahoma town of 3,720 inhabitants to become the standard of a national broadcasting network?"

Reaction in the Black press was swift. The *Pittsburgh Courier* wrote, "Three times during his coast-to-coast broadcast Sunday evening Rogers used the word nigger. . . . The unwarranted and vicious insult to 12,000,000 Negroes also shocked countless thousands of white radio listeners." Rogers refused to apologize, explaining on the following week's episode, "I wasn't only raised among darkies . . . I was raised by them."

The *New York Age* responded with a curt commentary:

"Mr. Rogers . . . related that during his youth he not only lived with 'darkies' but was brought up by them. . . . We do feel that Mr. Rogers, so far as relating to his knowledge and personal regard to the Negro, lives more in the past than in the present. He still visualizes the race, with one or two notable exceptions, as he did fifty years ago."

His biographer Ben Yagoda wrote, "His attitude toward blacks was as patronizing and as unenlightened as you would expect from the son of a slaveholder and Confederate veteran. There was no overt contempt or cruelty. . . . The essential point here is that he showed no awareness that blacks in America might possibly have a grievance."

The *Philadelphia Tribune* suggested a boycott and divestment campaign. In an editorial reprinted around the country, the paper stated, "Will Rogers, by using a certain insulting epithet in referring to Negroes, offers an opportunity for colored Americans to prove to American business that it cannot insult them and get away with it. . . . This newspaper has heard the complaints. It has been asked what is [there to do] about the Rogers insult? Will Rogers is paid to advertise the products of the Gulf Refining Company. Good Gulf Gasoline is its chief product. . . . The effective protest is not then in writing letters to newspapers . . . but a refusal to make Will Rogers a successful sales promoter for the Gulf products."

Carita Roane, superintendent of the New York State Employment Service, organized the Gulf Oil boycott, publishing the name and address of every Gulf-owned gas station in New York, asking African Americans to withhold their patronage. The *New York Age* took it further, recommending that its readership "boycott every picture that Will Rogers appears in, even to picketing the theaters where these pictures are shown, especially when they happen to be in colored neighborhoods."

Black film critic Vere Johns lent his support to the cause: "Usually, I am against a form of boycott as I always feel that there are better ways of fighting back. . . . In the case of Will Rogers, however, a boycott if consistently carried out by Negroes all over the United States will have a marked effect on that actor's income. . . . Rogers will find out what his impudence has done to him when the time comes to renew his contract. In the meantime, let us keep up the good work and keep Will Rogers pictures out of Harlem theaters."

Harlem's Roosevelt Theater and the Harlem Opera House pulled the latest Rogers pictures from their screens, and the *New York Age* concluded, "The next thing to be done, failing some apologetic statement, is to widen the boycott to take in all the Fox pictures. If we can get the Harlem exhibitors and others throughout the country to decline to take the Fox Film products . . . and also impress on the country that is all due to Rogers, it will be a striking blow that will shake the entire movie industry to its foundations. . . . I appeal to all managers of the colored theaters to keep the very homely countenance of Will Rogers off their screens, and I entreat all self-respecting Negroes to turn their backs on any box office where they see a Will Rogers picture advertised. We are niggers to Will Rogers and he is trash to us!"

The wave of outrage was too great to ignore. Rogers addressed the issue on his next Gulf broadcast, but stopped short of correcting himself. "I want to say this . . . I think you folks are wrong in jumping too hastily onto someone or anyone who might use the word with no more thought or belittlement than I did. There is millions in the South who use that word, and if the race has more real friends among millions of people down there I don't know where it is."

WHENEVER THINGS GOT too stressful for Will Rogers, he jumped on a plane. Aviation was brand-new, and he used his clout to secure pleasure flights around the country. He tagged along with postal aviators and met with Wiley Post, the one-eyed pilot who held the record for the fastest round-the-world trip. Post was lauded for his achievements, but also notorious for his recklessness; one of the mechanics in his employ recalled of one occasion, "We were just barely over the trees when the engine quit. It came back on just in time. When we were on the ground, Wiley said, 'I took off on an empty tank.' He wasn't too bright."

From spare and scavenged parts, Post built a makeshift plane and asked Rogers to join him for a test run to Alaska in the summer of 1935. Rogers agreed. As they were about to depart, a technician at the Burbank Airport warned that the nose of the plane was too heavy. Rogers himself observed that the pontoons were out of proportion and not structured correctly. Wiley Post snapped at them both: "Do you hold a world record for flying around the globe?" Nothing more was said about it.

They flew out of Burbank, fueled up in Seattle, and headed to Juneau. As the plane chugged north, Rogers sat with a typewriter on his knees, writing dispatches about the trip for his column. When they landed in Alaska, Rogers stepped off the plane and told a local newsman, "If they can just keep [Alaska] from being taken over by the U.S., they got a great future." After a two-night stop in the Yukon Territories, the boys headed to Fairbanks. It was a road trip for the ages. Rogers wrote, "Was you ever driving around in a car and not knowing or caring where you went? Well, that's what Wiley and I are doing. We sure are having a great time. If we hear of whales or polar bears in the Arctic, or a big herd of caribou or reindeer, we fly over and see it."

They were flying out of Barrow, Alaska, on August 15 when Post lost all visibility and got stuck in a heavy fog. As they flew in circles, unsure of their direction, the engine failed, and the overweight nose sent them straight down. The plane crashed in the remote Iñupiat village of Walakpa Bay. The community was rattled by the explosion. Emerging from their homes, residents saw half the wreckage floating in the water. One of the wings was torn clear off. Inside the steaming heap of metal was a pair of charred bodies, their faces no longer recognizable. A witness named Clair Okpeah traveled fifteen miles to notify authorities in Barrow. Meanwhile, the people of Walakpa Bay gathered around the accident and sang a traditional song meant to honor the passing of a spirit from one world into another.

Rogers's death was the biggest news story of the year. Radio broadcasts, newspaper coverage, and magazine profiles recapped his life and presented tributes. Typical overstatement seeped into the obituaries, remaining long after the eulogies ended. The complex and nuanced Cherokee comedian was reduced to a simple, home-spun cowboy, representing God and country. An NBC tribute was typical of how the Will Rogers story was distorted to fit an American ideal. "The name of this program is *Man of the Year*," explained the emcee. "And today it tells the story of a humorist, philosopher, pro-fessional joy-giver, who is one of the most lovable and down-right decent human beings in all American history . . . the simple Amer-ican humorist. . . . Will Rogers himself had a good deal of Indian blood—mixed to be sure with Irish stock." Gone were his comments about Andrew Jackson. His rants condemning the allotment period vanished. A myth was created that has endured for nearly a cen-tury. References to his Native American lineage were downplayed or erased. The most successful Cherokee comedian of all time had been born in a Native community and died in a Native community—but the coincidence was barely noted.

Dakota Ray Hebert Listens to
Jeff Foxworthy on Her Walkman

Fifteen hundred miles from Oklahoma in a remote part of northern Saskatchewan, a future comedian was totally smitten with her collection of cassettes. "I was five years old and I would listen to tapes of Jeff Foxworthy and Bill Cosby on my Walkman," says Dakota Ray Hebert. "I would listen to them every single night. My reserve is the English River First Nation, a community of around fifteen hundred people. I'm Dené and we are cousins of the Diné and the Navajo Nation. I lived in Meadow Lake, a border town next to the Flying Dust First Nation." There wasn't much in the way of entertainment where Hebert grew up, but when her family acquired a satellite dish, her whole life changed. She became obsessed with Comedy Central, a channel that wasn't available on Canadian cable. High school drama turned into a passion she pursued after graduation, attending the Gordon Tootoosis Nīkānīwin Theatre Company, a Native theater collective.

"I was going through my angry phrase, which a lot of Native kids go through," she recalls. "At theater school I learned about things I should have learned in regular school, horrific things that were swept under the rug. When you start learning about these things, you get angry. You feel robbed of your culture. The artistic director gently taught me how to overcome that. Having an Indigenous mentor at school helped me get back into my culture. I've been advocating for things ever since—rights for our people, our education, and even just trying to help other funny Indigenous folks do stand-up."

Hebert bluffed her way into stand-up when Ryan McMahon, an Anishinaabe comedian from another rural Canadian reserve, was booked to do a gig nearby. "I heard that he was coming to town and was looking for an opener. Someone threw my name in the hat and he contacted me. When he arrived, he asked me, 'So, how long have you been doing stand-up?' I had some audacity. I said, 'Oh, gosh, at least three, maybe four weeks.' His face dropped. He let me do the show anyway, and he gave me this intro: 'When I come to a new community, I like to give people a chance. Maybe they don't have a whole lot of experience. . . .' This whole thing. I didn't bomb as hard as I should have because he asked the audience for support. There really weren't any places to do stand-up where I lived. I wasn't able to grind as hard as I wanted. But then I went on a theater tour for a few weeks, and in each town there were rooms where I got stage time. I did more stand-up in those few weeks than I'd ever done before. And I brought that confidence home. And then I went to Toronto for a few months because I wanted to hit every mic I could and get better at stand-up. I met another female Indigenous comic there, Courtney Skye, who is Mohawk, and since then we've had an influx of Indigenous comics that have grown up on the rez—and now there's a good scene."

Jim Thorpe Demands Only American Indians for American Indian Parts

Decades of film and television told us that Native Americans weren't supposed to be comedians. They weren't supposed to be funny. They weren't supposed to exist in the present. Native actors were shut out of show biz if they looked like an average human being. Representation was nonexistent. Native Americans were expected to fulfill the preconceived, stereotypical notions of casting directors. It was something Native peoples objected to immediately, in the earliest days of the film industry.

Missionaries presented weekly screenings of silent films in reservation chapels as early as 1910. A government agent working on a California reservation said the locals loved silent movies, but were "loud in their complaints" about insulting portrayals and inaccurate history.

The Essanay film company used an "injun" mascot. "The Indian's aim is true," explained the promotional advertising affixed to their Charlie Chaplin releases. "The Indian Head brand of photoplays always hits the mark. . . .There is a guarantee of worth-while entertainment in the photoplays which bear the Indian Head trademark."

Francis Boggs, one of the very first filmmakers to arrive in Hollywood, made a picture called *Curse of the Redman* in 1911. It resulted in the first wide-scale outcry against stereotyping in motion pictures. "Two delegations of Anishinaabeg from Minnesota arrived in Washington, D.C., to protest against Indian films in general and *Curse of the Redman* in particular," wrote Harvard professor Philip Deloria. "Their criticisms were pointed: white men too often portrayed Indians. Because Indian actors were not always involved, so as to correct or refute the portrayal, film producers were able to depict scenes that Indians, actors included, found 'grossly libelous.'"

The delegation met with President William Howard Taft and requested help in halting "objectionable features" that "distorted Indian life." The movement spread across the country. "Indians Protest Against Indian Pictures," reported *Moving Picture World* in March 1911. "A recent dispatch from the Northwest announces the fact that the reservation Indians of the West and Northwest are registering strenuous objections with the Indian Bureau at Washington regarding the portrayal of Indian life in the films."

Native movie patrons wrote to fan magazines, complaining about what they saw. Using the English skills they'd been forced to learn under the cloud of boarding-school violence, they pushed back against racist slander. *Motion Picture News* published a letter from a man named Red Eagle in December 1911:

Dear Sirs:

To the average child—and adult, too—the Indian is a
yelling, paint-bedaubed creature, reeking of barbarism and
possessing little or no intelligence. Whether the National
Board of Censorship is aware of the fact or not (probably
not), it is instilling an antagonistic germ in the mind of
the young American against the American Indian that if
continued may cause a bitterness. The finer sensibilities of
an Indian rise futilely at the grossly exaggerated and falsely
represented position to which his race is subjected. I know,

for I am a full blooded Milicete [Maliseet]. Not including the tribal rites and ceremonies, an act should be passed prohibiting the showing of the 'Indian' picture so prevalent to-day. By all means let the ceremonies live in picture and song, but let those who are capable of going through the ceremony without holding it up to ridicule and derision do the reproducing.

Film and makeup departments, following in the tradition of blackface minstrelsy, devised a method of turning white people into "Hollywood injuns." Caucasian actors dunked their face in buckets filled with red clay and water. The paste was known as bole armenia, a mixture originally devised as a cure for diarrhea. The bucket was eventually replaced with a new method—the airbrush—with bole armenia applied like a racist spray tan.

Moving Picture World ran the headline "Indian Criticizes Indian Pictures" and published a letter from a Carlisle graduate named John Standing Horse in 1911:

Dear Sir –

If the directors of the moving pictures knew how foolish their women and girls look in the Indian pictures, with three turkey feathers stuck in the top of their heads, they would be more careful. . . .

The [real-life] braves wear the eagle feather, one or two, after they are braves—but they have to earn them. The chief and council-chief have the war bonnet. Have also seen pictures with all the made-up Indian men with big war bonnets on their heads. Another big laugh, but don't think the managers know this; if they did, they would do different. Then again, they should get the real Indian people. There is about a hundred men, women and children in New York out of work most of the time. . . .

The magazine published an editorial of agreement: "From the standpoint of a student, most of the picture plays shown are ethnologically grotesque farces. Delawares are dressed as Sioux, and the Indians of Manhattan Island are shown dwelling in skin tipis of the kind used only by the tribes beyond Mississippi."

Luther Standing Bear, an Oglala Lakota scholar, fought historical inaccuracies and sloppy depictions in film. Standing Bear had worked as an interpreter for the Buffalo Bill Wild West shows at the start of the century and felt that now, a decade later, the time for stereotypes had passed. He pleaded with filmmakers and screenwriters to educate themselves about the differences between Native nations, but was essentially told by film moguls, "Audiences don't know the difference—so why should it matter?"

Oklahoma was oil-rich country by the 1920s, and enrolled members of the Osage and Cherokee tribes accrued handsome royalties. The Cherokee Nation used some of its oil revenue to campaign for positive film portrayals. The *Miami News* reported in 1921, "Cherokee Indians have turned to eradicating the stain of villainy placed upon the Indians by the cinema. The Cherokees met at Okmulgee, Oklahoma, raised a fund, and appointed a committee, to see that Indians become heroes and heroines in books, plays and films." When actor Monte Blue, an Osage and Cherokee descendant, was cast in a D. W. Griffith film as a Native villain in the early 1920s, the Cherokee Nation objected. The tribe "appointed a committee to negotiate with Blue to induce him to forgo all roles displaying him in an unfavorable light." They offered him oil money "for any financial loss he might suffer by such action." Blue ignored them.

A movement emerged, criticizing casting choices, historical distortions, and the use of racial slurs—several years before sound film even existed. The objections came together under one banner with the formation of the Hollywood War Paint Club in 1926.

Film studios pled ignorance when criticized for using white people to play Native American characters. They claimed they had no choice because there simply weren't any Native actors. The War Paint Club countered this argument, providing a full list, noting their tribal affiliations and special skills. Whenever a film with Native American characterizations was announced, the War Paint Club submitted its recommendations. The Associated Press reported, "Now as many as 150 Indians can be delivered on a set at short notice."

Jim Thorpe, the famed Sac and Fox Olympian, lent his voice to the cause in the early 1930s. He wanted a rule enshrined in the film code that all Native roles be played by Native people. He championed his cause with the slogan "Only American Indians for American Indian Parts."

The motion was welcomed by the U.S. secretary of labor, although for a completely different reason. *Variety* reported, "Murray W. Garsson, special assistant to the Secretary of Labor, has started an investigation of Hollywood 'Indians' to determine if they are in the country illegally. To avoid immigration difficulties, many Italians, Mexicans, Armenians, and other swarthy-skinned foreigners have been passing themselves off as Indians, figuring no one could then question their entry. . . . Garsson is checking over a list of real Indians compiled by Jim Thorpe. . . . He is assisting Garsson in picking out the real Americans from aliens."

Thorpe's campaign merged with the War Paint Club. Together they renamed themselves the Indian Actors Association and drafted a charter that forbade members from playing intoxicated characters or hostile villains. They insisted on accurate representation, respectful portrayals, proper pay, and better working conditions. Chief Many Treaties, an actor in several Hollywood westerns, explained, "Our present membership is seventy-seven. Fifty-two men and twenty-five women. Membership is open to any Indian, no matter where he's from. . . . Tribes represented in the Association are Blackfoot, Iroquois, Sioux, Osage, Pima, Creek, Nez Perce, Wiyot, Hope, Cherokee, Navajo, Ottawa, Mission, Pueblo, Apache, Comanche, Potawatomi, Delaware-Cherokee, Klamath, Papago, Sac-Fox, Kickapoo, Penobscot, and Arapaho. So you can see we can give producers just about any kind of tribal representation they want." Lobbying wasn't the group's only purpose. Many Treaties said it also helped create a sense of community and belonging for Natives in Hollywood. "Our association has had other very beneficial effects. For one thing, it has made us all even more conscious of our own Indianness. . . . We can perpetuate our Indian heritage and better prepare [ourselves] for jobs as technical advisors."

Despite organization and politicking, Hollywood largely ignored their concerns. There were objections to racial slurs like "redskin," "redmen," and "squaw," yet the media insisted on using them whenever reporting on the protests. "Hollywood's habit of casting palefaces in Indian roles while redman actors go jobless, provoked a protest yesterday from the Six Nations," wrote the *Rochester Democrat and Chronicle* in 1939. "They decided by unanimous vote to take the matter up with Hollywood after one of their leaders pointed out that in a new film on early American history all but one of the Indian actors are 'fake' Indians. They contend 174 genuine redmen are registered at the central casting bureau in the film capital."

Western movies were the main culprits, but the comedy films parodying the genre were a close second. White actors slathered in bole armenia chased after the Three Stooges in *Whoops, I'm an Indian!* (1936), the Marx Brothers in *Go West* (1940), and Abbott and Costello in *Ride 'Em Cowboy* (1942). Groucho Marx reportedly wanted to cast Native Americans in *Go West*, but MGM said it couldn't be done. "Honest Injuns—The Marx Bros. are hard at work on another picture," reported *Modern Screen*. "But they're running into snags, for the script calls for Indians and the boys are determined to have honest-to-goodness wild Injuns or none. A call to Central Casting would bring out hundreds of domesticated Hollywood Indians, but the studio is sending scouts to Nebraska and South Dakota reservations to round up the kind that will suit their stars." In the end, it seemed to be little more than a press agent stunt. *Go West* featured the same old white impostors.

Filmmaker Raoul Walsh convinced Warner Brothers to do what MGM would not. Walsh hired a large caravan of Lakota, Nakota, and Dakota actors to appear in *They Died with Their Boots On* (1941). When the actors from South Dakota arrived, they were appalled by the accommodations Warner Brothers had arranged. Rather than provide hotel rooms as they would for any other out-of-town cast or crew, the studio constructed an outdoor "reservation" with cliché imagery and phony tipis. When they weren't on set, the extras were forbidden to leave their quarters, day or night. Infuriated, after a week and a half they collectively quit and walked off the film.

Such protests were common. During the filming of Cecil B. DeMille's *Union Pacific* (1939), seventy-five Navajo extras staged a sit-down strike to protest the conditions in which they were expected to live. During the filming of a Gary Cooper western, twenty-four Seminole extras held up production, outraged by the makeup department's attempt to make them "look more Indian." Chief Thundercloud, the first actor to play Tonto on the screen, asked for script changes when he was cast as an intoxicated adversary in the Fritz Lang film *Western Union* (1940). Lang agreed after a meeting with the Indian Actors Association. The ongoing campaign by Native American actors was having an effect, and it looked like the worst of the stereotypes might just fade away.

From Meteorology to the Upright Citizens Brigade with Joey Clift

As a member of the popular Upright Citizens Brigade in Hollywood, Joey Clift has been pushing the theater to present a Native comedy showcase for several years.

"I'm an enrolled member of the Cowlitz Indian Tribe," says Clift. "The Cowlitz are based out of Washington and northern Oregon. Mount Saint Helens is our original land. A deal was made with the U.S. government in the 1850s when there was a mass dying-off of Cowlitz people. We went from something like eight thousand Cowlitz to two hundred in less than a decade. That's why we never had a reservation. The U.S. government decided, 'There's not enough of you to keep you as a federally recognized tribe.' So for a hundred and fifty years, Cowlitz tribal members were gathering records, making them aware of enrollment numbers, trying to prove to the government that we are a thriving people. In 2000, we finally got our federal recognition, and in 2009 we finally got what is called trust land. For some tribes, if you purchase land that exists in your Aboriginal territory, even if they don't have a reservation, they can make the land into trust land, with legal benefits. We used that to open a casino-resort. I grew up on the Tulalip Indian Reservation, and not for any cultural reason but because my mom found cheaper housing there. I went to their tribal-run schools, but it wasn't my tribe and I felt a little disconnected.

My mom was a passionate Native and made all efforts to explain that this was part of my culture too. That made me more passionate. At school, I was doing morning announcements, like a little news broadcast for the school, and I developed this love for making people laugh. I got the comedy bug from doing this little weather program. I wanted to do comedy, but I had no idea what that really meant. Growing up on a reservation, I didn't really see a path. I went to Washington State University for broadcast news to be a television meteorologist. I was a mentor at the university's Native American Student Center and did a canoe journey with my tribe from southern Washington to northern Canada where every day we'd stop at a different reservation or Aboriginal land. Every reservation that we stopped at, people from that tribe would join us for the rest of the journey. By the time we got to the end of it, three weeks later, a hundred tribes were represented. When I got back, I wrote a thing for our college TV show, and it ended up winning a nationwide college comedy award. It beat out people at Harvard, but at the time I still thought, 'Well, this will be a cool trophy to put on my meteorology desk in Post Falls, Idaho.' My professors pulled me aside and said, 'You should do the comedy thing.' That led to me moving to Los Angeles and getting involved with the Upright Citizens Brigade. UCB led to me getting a bunch of writing jobs. I wrote for a Looney Tunes reboot, and I wrote and worked at Nerdist. I've been trying to convince UCB to put on a showcase of Native comedy for years. I started pitching the idea of this show when I first joined UCB, but I was new and untested and they weren't going to listen to me. Over the years I have done a lot of shows there, and people trust what I bring to the table. And really, it's only recently that we have had enough Native performers who are far enough along in experience." Clift eventually mounted the very first UCB showcase of Native comedy in November 2018, and it has since become an annual event. "It's a tricky thing because everybody is new," he says, "but this is an untapped area of comedy."

Will Rogers Jr. Hated Analogies to His Father

In January 2019, Deb Haaland of New Mexico and Sharice Davids of Kansas were sworn in as the first Native American women in U.S. congressional history. They followed a long line of male Indigenous representatives who'd attempted to change things from within the halls of Congress. Among those who came before was Will Rogers Jr.

Born in 1911, he lived in the shadow of his famous father. It didn't help that he looked exactly like the old man. With his soft-spoken drawl, people expected him to rattle off witticisms every time he opened his mouth, but he would never be able to satisfy the expectations. "I deliberately tried not to be humorous or funny," said Will Jr. "There seemed to be a feeling on the part of a lot of people that, 'This is Will Rogers' son. He'll tell a few jokes and be funny.' I was dismayed by being asked to live up to the model of my father. I was expected to sparkle and be witty. Well, I just didn't have it."

But he did inherit his father's interest in politics. After studying journalism at the University of Arizona in the early 1930s, Will Jr. was hired by the McNaught Syndicate to file dispatches from the Spanish Civil War. When he returned to the United States, he started a progressive newspaper with his brother Jim called the *Beverly Hills Citizen*. Jim was eventually lured to the Hal Roach Studios to star in a series of westerns, leaving Will to run the paper on his own. As an editorial writer, Rogers found the voice that prepared him for a congressional run in 1942. Elected to the House of Representatives, he became the prime adversary of Congressman Martin Dies, the political precursor to Senator Joseph McCarthy.

Dies saw a communist conspiracy behind every liberal cause. Rogers listened as Dies demanded the firing of forty government employees who had criticized his un-American activities committee. Rising from the floor of the House for the first time, Rogers condemned his colleague: "I should like it to be known that I disagree with the sentiments expressed, the flamboyant manner of expression used, and the use of this forum as a means of what we in Hollywood would call personal publicity."

Most Democrats were too timid to criticize one of their own, but Will Rogers Jr. had no problem speaking his mind. He was lauded by the *York Gazette and Daily*: "We like him, not because of his father . . . but because he has what it takes. He can spot a fascist when he sees one and he knows how to throw hooks in him. It was young Will's job Monday to shame the rest of the House of Representatives by telling off Martin Dies [who] had been . . . doing the same sort of job on the floor of the House that Goebbels and Goering were doing in Germany last Saturday. . . . We hope young Will Rogers makes a career of showing up Martin Dies and his kind in Congress."

As World War II raged on, Rogers resigned from Congress and joined the army. He served as a second lieutenant in the U.S. Seventh Armored Division, fighting with a tank battalion in France. He was awarded a Purple Heart for his part in the Battle of the Bulge. After the war he ran for a Senate seat and lost, but remained engaged, using his celebrity to advocate for Native rights. His first high-profile campaign was waged on behalf of Isabel Crocker, a gift shop manager forced from her Hollywood home by six racist neighbors. "A mother and three daughters of American Indian descent today were under court order to move from their Hollywood home because of racial restriction in property deeds," reported the Associated Press in 1947. "The order issued by Superior Judge gives Mrs. Isabel Crocker and the daughters . . . a month to vacate. . . . The complaining witnesses were neighbors. Their complaint stipulated that Mrs. Crocker and her children were excellent neighbors but non-Caucasian."

Will Jr. joined with the American Civil Liberties Union and the National Congress of American Indians for a rally. He delivered a speech condemning the "violation of the State Constitution and the 14th Amendment" before leading a march of a thousand Native Americans from Hollywood High School to Beverly Hills. He recruited movie stars Johnny Mack Brown, Linda Darnell, Richard Dix, Ann Sheridan, Jay Silverheels, and Monte Blue, all of whom claimed Native lineage, to pledge financial support for Crocker's legal defense. Tom Humphreys, a Hopi veteran, told the assembled crowd, "A lot of us are veterans—and we're beginning to wonder what we fought for." Pima war hero Ira Hayes also gave a speech: "The court hasn't served the woman the eviction papers yet because they're afraid of what we might do. If she's tossed out, we'll take the case to the State Supreme Court, and I'm sure we'll win. The outcome of the case can establish a precedent. It's the first time in California that the word 'Indian' has been mentioned in a discrimination case."

Rogers started advising the Truman administration on Native issues, but lived to regret his recommendation of Dillon Myer as the commissioner of Indian affairs. Myer was considered a good candidate because of his bureaucratic experience in managing unwieldy projects—namely the Japanese internment camps during the war. A biography of Myer published years later was titled *Keeper of the Concentration Camps: Dillon S. Myer and American Racism.* Myer's prejudice informed the Termination Act, which he helped ghostwrite between 1950 and 1953.

The Termination Act voided the government's long-standing treaty obligations. The Feds kept the land and resources, but stopped paying out the compensation various Native nations were contractually owed. The Flathead, Klamath, Menominee, Potawatomi, and Turtle Mountain Chippewa lost their federal recognition under termination. Several other tribes in California, New York, Florida, and Texas suffered the same fate. The government no longer recognized these tribes as a nation, ending tribal sovereignty. Since they were no longer recognized, the government absolved itself of all further legal obligations. Schools and medical clinics were shuffled from the BIA to other departments or eliminated altogether. Facilities that employed locals were shut down, throwing hundreds of Native Americans out of work. Nearly every Native nation resisted the termination policy, but Myer's office rammed it through. "We must proceed," said Myer, "even though Indian cooperation may be lacking in certain cases."

Will Jr. rescinded his endorsement of Myer and condemned congressional plans for termination. "After World War Two we had the idea that it [termination] was the answer," he said. "But it does not work. You must strengthen a person in his own culture."

In 1949 Rogers became a lobbyist for the Navajo Nation and the National Congress of American Indians. The NCAI was the leading Native American advocacy group at the time. Founded in 1944, it was partially inspired by the Congress of Racial Equality, which made inroads with the first antisegregation lunch counter sit-ins. The NCAI used similar methods to secure the rights of Native Americans. Rogers worked for an NCAI division called ARROW, which stood for Americans for Restitution and Righting of Old Wrongs. "Through this organization, the American Indian speaks for himself," said Rogers. "This is not someone else speaking for him, saying what should be done. . . . This congress is the voice of the Indians themselves." As president of ARROW, Rogers traveled to reservations around the country, oversaw the distribution of antibiotics, implemented a reservation-wide eye-care program, and devised alternatives to failed BIA programs. He tried to interest fellow

Democrats, but their knowledge of, and concern for, Native issues was limited. To his surprise, he received support from right-wing politicians representing states with substantial Native populations. "Senators Paul Fannin and Barry Goldwater [of Arizona] are excellent on Indian matters," noted Rogers. "It is interesting that some eastern liberals are our worst opponents."

The NCAI effected a shift in attitude if not in deed. By the mid-1960s, President Lyndon Johnson acknowledged what the Native nations had been saying all along: "Both in terms of statistics and in terms of human welfare, it is a fact that America's first citizens, our Indian people, suffer more from poverty than any other group in America. That is a shameful fact. Unfortunately, many Americans live on the outskirts of hope—some because of their poverty, and some because of their color, and all too many because of both. . . . We must pledge to respect fully the dignity and the uniqueness of the Indian citizen. . . . We must affirm the right of the first Americans to remain Indians while exercising their rights as Americans."

It was a nice speech, but Will Rogers Jr. had lost faith in both Democrats and Republicans alike to do right. The damage of termination was already done, and Rogers discouraged Natives from participating in party politics. Instead he encouraged everyone to read a new book called *Custer Died for Your Sins* by Vine Deloria Jr.

Charlie Hill Orders a Ventriloquist Dummy

"When I was eighteen, Vine Deloria's book *Custer Died for Your Sins* came out," said Charlie Hill. "I saw him on *The Dick Cavett Show* and I thought, 'Wow, this guy is the real deal!' He was wearing a T-shirt and jeans and he was so funny, and his humor was real biting. I thought, 'This is what I'm going to do.'"

The book was a rarity in American literature: a bestseller about Native America written by a Native American author. Typically such books were written through the distorted lens of white interpretation. *Custer Died for Your Sins* was a game changer, providing a perspective on allotment and termination that had been excised from American textbooks. It also circumvented a familiar stereotype in a chapter titled "Indian Humor."

"The Indian people are exactly opposite of the popular stereotype," wrote Deloria. "I sometimes wonder how anything is accomplished by Indians because of the apparent overemphasis on humor within the Indian world. Indians have found a humorous side of nearly every problem and the experiences of life have generally been so well defined through jokes and stories that they have become a thing in themselves. For centuries before the white invasion, teasing was a method of control of social situations by Indian people. Rather than embarrass members of the tribe publicly, people used to tease individuals they considered out of step with the consensus of tribal opinion. . . . Whether Indian jokes will eventually come to have more significance than that, I cannot speculate. Humor, all Indians will agree, is the cement by which the coming Indian movement is held together."

Custer Died for Your Sins had a tremendous influence on Charlie Hill, the first Native American comedian to do stand-up on network television. Hill grew up in Oneida, Wisconsin, ten miles west of Green Bay, down the road from a government building named after his father. The family name was well-known long before he was born. Lillie Rosa Minoka-Hill, Charlie Hill's grandmother, was born in 1876. Her mother passed away shortly after she was born, and, despite protests from her biological family, a government agent placed her with a family of white Quakers in Philadelphia. She described her strict upbringing as that of "a little wooden Indian who hardly dared look right or left."

After attending Catholic school, Minoka-Hill attended the Women's Medical College of Pennsylvania, becoming the second Native female physician. She fell in love with an Oneida man, a graduate of the Carlisle school, Charles Hill. They were married in 1905 and moved to the Oneida reservation he was from, where Minoka-Hill would open her first practice. Together they had three daughters and a son. The son, Norbert Hill, had a broad, athletic build that came in handy when he and his siblings attended high school in Green Bay.

"There was a lot of racism in Green Bay in those days, but nobody messed with them," Charlie's brother Norbert Hill Jr. says of their father. "His sisters said it was like going to school with a bodyguard. Old-timers told me they felt safe around my father. If there was ever any trouble, he would take care of it." Defending himself from racist threats, Norbert Hill Sr. developed a talent with his fists. It led to a brief boxing career and a Golden Glove title. "He fought in Green Bay, where there was so much anti-Indian sentiment," said Charlie Hill. "He would go there and he would just smoke these guys."

Norbert Hill Sr. moved to Detroit during the Great Depression, where he landed a job as a union machinist for a company called C. M. Smile. He formed the North American Indian Club, a friendship society for urban Natives. "It was an Indian meeting ground for the Indians who were sort of lost around Detroit," explains Norbert Jr. Similar clubs sprang up across the country during the urban relocation period. "They were often abandoned by the federal bureaus, with little knowledge of city agencies, left on their own, uncomfortable with urban life, separated from their tribes," wrote Stan Steiner in his book *The New Indians*. "The Indian center might be a tiny, dreary storefront, or an elaborate and well-equipped community hall. But, whatever it looked like, it was run by and financed by tribal Indians, for tribal Indians."

The North American Indian Club held weekly dances, and it was there that Norbert Hill met a Cree woman from Lake Athabasca, Alberta. Her name was Eileen Jonston. They would marry and have four children. Their second was named Charlie Hill.

Born in Detroit on July 6, 1951, Charlie grew up watching a steady stream of sitcoms, variety shows, cartoons, and old movies on local television channels WWJ and WXYZ. He was obsessed with the images on the screen. His older brother, Norbert, recalls, "We watched Jackie Gleason and *The Amos 'n' Andy Show*. There was *Who Do You Trust?* hosted by Johnny Carson before he got his talk show. And Soupy Sales, who was real big in Detroit at that time." When Charlie was playing outside, he re-created the characters he loved. "He'd find a black shirt and a navy hat and role-play Popeye," says Norbert Jr. "He'd pretend to be Davy Crockett and wear a coonskin hat when it was ninety-five degrees outside." He even went so far as to play the Lone Ranger, forcing his younger brother, Rick, into the menial role of Tonto, the Native American sidekick. "I didn't realize until later what kind of brainwashing was being done to us," said Hill. "The irony of Indian kids playing cowboys and Indians."

One of Hill's favorite programs was hosted by Paul Winchell, who, with his smart-aleck dummy Jerry Mahoney, was one of the top ventriloquists of the 1950s. The program advertised a child-size ventriloquist doll available by mail order. Hill desperately wanted one. "I was eight years old and I sent away for this dummy. I saved all my money, and my dad helped me. And the dummy came—it was Jerry Mahoney. *Fucking great*, man. And my brothers and sisters who were older than me—they told me I was playing with a *doll*. And I got really mad. I tore the head off and the arms. I was so pissed off. I still had the book—*How to Be a Ventriloquist*—and the next day I took it to school. And the nun took it away! Man, I got no encouragement at all being a ventriloquist. So when I wanted to be a comedian—I just kept my mouth shut. Fuck."

Charlie Hill was eleven years old when his father moved the family from Detroit back to Oneida, Wisconsin, where Norbert Hill Sr. immersed himself in tribal politics. "He had grown up watching his mother, a doctor, doing community health work in Oneida, so he decided to move us all back so that he could get involved," says Norbert Jr. "He would drive my grandmother around the reservation in a Model T when she was doing community health work. He ran for tribal council and became chairman. He grew up on the reservation and had been in the navy—so he knew how to navigate both worlds, socially and politically. But we went from a middle-class existence in Detroit to an existence of no running water and no central heat in Oneida."

Norbert Sr. was the vice chairman of the Oneida Nation and led the Great Lakes Inter-Tribal Council. He had a reputation for being amusing, although his wife stole his best jokes. "He would tell jokes and my mom would just stare at him," said Charlie Hill. "And then when my mom would be around a gathering of family people, she'd repeat the joke—and get a big laugh with it."

They gathered around the television each weekend and watched comedy as a family. "As a kid, on Saturdays, after all the work was done, we would go up the hill to the Oneida Mission because they had showers," said Charlie. "You'd pay the guy a quarter and we'd take a shower and we had to stand in the water of the previous family. But we were glad to have it. And we'd come home and my mom would make chili or something and we would watch Jackie Gleason. That's when it kind of set in. . . . I *loved* watching Jackie Gleason. I'd sit on my dad's lap. I couldn't wait for Saturday night. When I got a little older, I'd stand behind the door late at night because I couldn't stay up and my mom would be watching Jack Paar. . . . I thought, 'How do I get in there? How do I learn how to do that? How do I get in that box?' "

According to Charlie's mother, her son was already writing in a notebook, devising ideas for a nonexistent act. "Reading and writing were his main things. He used to go up on the roof and knock the ladder away so no one would know where he was. And he liked to make kids laugh. He always wanted an audience."

Brian Bahe Goes Onstage Twelve Times a Week

"I usually go up twice a night and get onstage around twelve times a week," says Brian Bahe. "There's so much stage time in New York that, if you want it, you can go up four or five times a night."

There are hundreds of stand-ups in the New York comedy scene. Bahe is one of the only Native American comedians among them. "I'm Navajo–Hopi–Tohono O'odham," he says. "I was always aware of my tribal affiliations. That informed my life. My dad is Navajo and grew up on the reservation. My mom is Hopi and Tohono O'odham, and her mom, my grandmother, still lives on the reservation by the Mexico-Arizona border. I grew up as an urban Native kid wandering around West Phoenix, and we visited the reservation multiple times a year. My dad was a sheet-metal construction worker and my mom worked as a social services representative for the Bureau of Indian Affairs. Growing up, I was obsessed with everything on TV. I loved comedy—30 Rock, The Office, Community—those television shows really influenced me. Going into college, my friend took me to see an improv team, and I was blown away. I had no idea this existed in Phoenix. There was a place called the Torch Theatre, and I immediately enrolled in improv classes. And then during my senior year of college, I dipped my toe into stand-up at a handful of open mics around town. I did a bar that was attached to an ice rink, and it was bad—really bad. And *I* was bad—really bad. I moved to New York to commit to comedy full-time. I knew some things about New York comedy from listening to the podcasts hosted by Pete Holmes and Chelsea Peretti. I enrolled at UCB and did the whole Upright Citizens Brigade thing, but realized I didn't want to do improv, I just wanted to do stand-up."

At a popular club called the Stand, he takes to the stage and tells the crowd, "I dyed my hair blond a few weeks ago and I ended up burning my scalp in the process. It felt like the universe was trying to send me a message. I guess when I was like, 'I'm going to bleach my hair,' my ancestors were like, 'Bitch, how about you *avenge our deaths first?*'"

Davy Crockett Brainwashes the Kids

From sitcoms like *I Love Lucy* to cartoons like *Yogi Bear*, Charlie Hill watched whatever the three television networks had to offer. And every time he turned on the set, he watched as Natives were defamed.

During the medium's earliest years, TV stations were desperate for content. In order to fill the void, stations bought old films—mostly B westerns—and aired them in vacant time slots. The old stereotypes came straight into the American living room, misinforming a whole new generation of viewers from the comfort of their own homes.

The western genre enjoyed a resurgence thanks to the old films. They were so popular that Hollywood production companies cranked out new westerns by the dozens, resulting in the first major trend of early TV. Television westerns were geared toward children, marketed in the form of cap guns, board games, comic books, breakfast cereals, lunch pails, and BB rifles. TV shows like *Hopalong Cassidy*, *The Cisco Kid*, *The Lone Ranger*, and *Davy Crockett* were largely responsible for children role-playing cowboys and Indians.

Davy Crockett starred Fess Parker in a hat made from a raccoon pelt. It created a schoolyard fashion trend. Conformist children across the country hoarded coonskin hats as they enthusiastically re-created genocide during recess. An activist named Charlie Blackfeet complained to the *Orlando Evening Star*, "These false impressions have been delivered one year after another. Generations of children have grown up to gain an entirely false idea of what Indians are [and now we have] television coming in, buying up all those hideous old films and compounding the slander in the eyes of the youngsters today."

Television sitcoms picked up on the trend. In an early episode of *I Love Lucy* titled "The Indian Show," Ricky Ricardo auditioned actors for a new "Indian routine" in his nightclub act. His neighbor Fred Mertz wants to play a part in the show, but Ricky explains, "They've got to be *real* Indians." Lucy Ricardo, unaware that her husband is holding auditions in their home, answers the door when a pair of sitcom Native Americans arrive on her doorstep. She screams in terror and runs around the living room in a spell of racist paranoia, convinced the two men are there to scalp, steal, or murder her newborn baby. With the help of her friend Ethel Mertz, Lucy bashes them over the skull with a flower vase and knocks them unconscious. Ricky explains the mix-up to his wife and a mortified Lucy helps the beleaguered men to their feet.

LUCY: Mr. Indian, oh, me heap sorry me smack-um on coco.
ACTOR: Huh?
LUCY: Oh, you speak English?
ACTOR: [in Bronx accent] Soitenly, I speak English! Whaddaya tryna do? Murder me?

With sponsorship from a powerful tobacco company, *I Love Lucy* turned Lucille Ball and Desi Arnaz into a formidable, profitable force. They incorporated their own company, Desilu, and became landlords to a busy soundstage. Desilu fingerprints were on most major Hollywood sitcoms. *The Danny Thomas Show*, *The Andy Griffith Show*, *Gomer Pyle USMC*, *My Three Sons*, *The Real McCoys*, *The Joey Bishop Show*, *That Girl*, and *The Dick Van Dyke Show* all had a Desilu logo affixed to the closing credits. One of their sitcoms made mockery of Native Americans its primary premise.

Guestward Ho! was essentially a western version of *Mr. Blandings Builds His Dream House.* In this now forgotten Desilu production, a couple leaves the big city to lead a rural life—unaware that their new home is on unceded Native land. The program starred Irish character actor J. Carrol Naish. *Variety* announced, "J. Carrol Naish will figure prominently as the feathered Redman, who would sell out the tribe to make a buck. Naish, an Irishman, now goes from Italian to Cherokee and will be the main cog." Italian to Cherokee—Naish's specialty was portraying other races. Even at the time, such practices were not without controversy.

Naish had starred in the 1940s radio sitcom *Life with Luigi* at a time when ethnic angles were common—from the phony Black dialect on *Amos 'n' Andy* to the exaggerated Jewish dialect of Mr. Kitzel on *The Jack Benny Program.* But as radio comedy gave way to the television sitcom, many of the old stereotypes were phased out. Things considered okay in 1940 were not necessarily acceptable in 1950.

Life with Luigi moved to television in 1952, directly following *I Love Lucy.* The stereotyped portrayal by J. Carrol Naish was immediately controversial. "*Life with Luigi*, despite high ratings—helped along by the fact that it follows *I Love Lucy*—may be fading from television soon," wrote TV critic Art Cullison in the *Akron Beacon Journal.* "There have been too many complaints from viewers, and not all of them Italians, that the show is objectionable. It does tend to perpetuate the Italian stereotype and put such immigrants in a bad light." The program was pulled from the air, but Naish soon returned, sporting a massive headdress and slathered in bole armenia.

Blackface was taboo and Italian stereotypes objectionable, but when it came to the racist portrayals of Native Americans, network television didn't care. *The Beverly Hillbillies, The Lucy Show, Get Smart, Green Acres, Dennis the Menace, Julia, Petticoat Junc-*

tion, *Mister Ed*, and *The Munsters* all presented racist stereotypes with white people grunting in feathers. Chester Diablo, a Mohawk member of the North American Indian Brotherhood, was tired of it. "We're getting sick of the kind of Indians on TV," he said. "If television is so enamored with the Indian, why not dramatize the Mohawk steelworkers revered for their construction of Manhattan's tallest skyscrapers? . . . Television Indians stand around with a sour look. . . . Real Indians are happy. They've all got troubles, sure, [but] they laugh at everything."

Syndicated television columnist Charles Mercer joined the chorus: "Having taken away the Indian's lands, we persist—with a few notable exceptions—in belaboring the Indian's character on television filmed programs. Too often there is no good Indian but a dead Indian. Too many of our television Indians say nothing but ugh."

There were some white actors who made a living playing only Native American roles. John Lupton, costar of the television western *Broken Arrow*, had a typically racist justification. "We tried to use genuine Indians in feature roles when we started making the series, but oddly enough, they weren't convincing. They didn't have enough strength of face or figure or character."

Famed newsman Edward R. Murrow urged television to drop the insults and replace them with factual information: "Instead of showing so many Hollywood Indians, television should go after real Indians and talk about them. . . . Some courageous soul with a small budget might be able to do a documentary telling what, in fact, we have done—and are still doing—to the Indians in this country."

The only program to use actual Natives on a regular basis was a game show that featured Johnny Carson as a semiregular. Hosted by the veteran emcee Bud Collyer, *To Tell the Truth* presented three contestants posing as the same news-making personality. It was up to the celebrity panel to figure out who was the real subject and which two were impostors. The program is best remembered for its catchphrase, "Will the real [so-and-so] please stand up." Under these auspices, several Native artists, tribal leaders, and musicians—including a young Buffy Sainte-Marie—appeared as contestants in the 1950s and '60s. While the booking practices were forward-thinking, the Native guests were usually dehumanized once they got on the air. Panelist Hy Gardner, scanning three Native contestants, said, "I voted for [contestant] number two. I think I met number one once at Macy's during a parade. Number three looks like he posed for the radiator cap of a Pontiac." In response, the host chuckled and quipped, "He looks more like a nickel to me." Dolores Short, a Mohawk contestant, appeared alongside Nez Perce and Navajo guests, posing as the winner of the Miss Indian America pageant. The pageant was held in Wyoming every year, and unlike the bathing suit competitions of Miss America, contestants were judged on their knowledge of tribal practices. Panelist Polly Bergen asked one of the contestants where she lived, and when she answered, "Brooklyn," Bergen was aghast: "Boy, I tell ya, they get around, don't they?" In a moment of righteousness, Bergen's fellow panelist Kitty Carlisle snapped, "They've got a right."

"Television's portrayal of the Indian is not justified, not fair, and not decent," said Floyd E. Maytubby, governor of the Chickasaw Nation in 1960. "We want to impress upon producers and writers that television has not presented the true history nor character of the American Indian. We're simply trying to make a dignified and diplomatic approach to the situation without condemning or censoring television."

Stereotypes had only amplified since the major protests of 1911. Among the worst culprits were animated cartoons. In most local markets, packages of cartoon shorts were introduced by a weatherman pulling double duty, usually dressed as a policeman, a sailor, a train engineer, or an "Indian chief." Popeye cartoons like *Big Chief Ugh-Amugh-Ugh* (1938) and *Wigwam Whoopee* (1948) were common. There was *Big Heel-Watha* (1944) directed by Tex Avery, *Two Little Indians* (1953) featuring Tom and Jerry, and *Rhythm on the Reser-*

vation (1939) starring Betty Boop. Everyone took a turn. Gumby starred in *Indian Trouble* (1956), *Indian Country* (1957), and *The Indian Challenge* (1957). Terrytoons released *Indian Pudding* (1930), *The Last Indian* (1938), and *The Wooden Indian* (1949). The Van Beuren studio contributed *Molly Moo Cow and the Indians* (1935), while Columbia Pictures unveiled *Wacky Wig Wams* (1942). Racial slurs were used in the titles of Paramount cartoons like *Slip Us Some Redskin* (1951), *Sight for Squaw Eyes* (1963), and *The Squaw Path* (1967). Some cartoons went so far as to demean specific tribes. Warner Brothers released *Sweet Sioux* (1937) and *Sioux Me* (1939), while the Walter Lantz studio produced *Syncopated Sioux* (1940) and *Boogie Woogie Sioux* (1942). And just in case your children didn't get the point about the apparent peril, there was Porky Pig in *Injun Trouble* (1938), Mighty Mouse in *Injun Trouble* (1951), Lippy the Lion in *Injun Trouble* (1963), and Cool Cat in *Injun Trouble* (1969). One of the last Looney Tunes shorts ever made was *Hocus Pocus Powwow* (1969), which swapped Wile E. Coyote for a beleaguered Native American falling from cliffs and his body transformed into an accordion after being leveled by an anvil.

Native parents complained that television was warping the minds of their children. A Dakota mother told the *Boston Globe* in 1961, "I have a three-year-old son. He just loves these programs. And when they're over he runs through the house pointing his cap gun and shouting, 'Bang-bang! I'm killing Indians.' It can be very embarrassing when we have visitors."

Cartoon stereotypes contaminated the minds of their viewers, courting ignorance and distorting perceptions. "Writers and producers know nothing of Indian life or history and find it easier to deal in stereotypes than search for the truth," said Clarence Wesley, president of the NCAI in 1960. "Even my own kids are getting a warped version of history."

Throughout the 1950s, at the end of the broadcast day, a test pattern appeared on most television screens. The frozen tableau aired while most of America slept. It featured an image reminiscent of the old Buffalo nickel and became known as "the Indian Head." Comanche television historian Dustin Tahmahkera explains, "By the late 1940s and 1950s, this Indian's ongoing appearances during early-morning and late-night hours on television screens across North America garnered him far more airtime than small-screen stars Milton Berle, Ed Sullivan, Jack Benny, Martha Raye, Lucille Ball, and Jackie Gleason combined. TV's first Indian superstar [was] the Indian Head test pattern."

Such imagery was common. TV stations like WHIO in Dayton; KWWL in Waterloo, Iowa; WJW in Cleveland; KOLO in Reno; WEBC in Duluth, Minnesota; KSWO in Lawton, Oklahoma; and WBRE in Scranton all used a headdress mascot as a logo.

Several Oklahoma-based tribes joined forces in 1960 to fight televised defamation. The Associated Press reported, "Leaders of 19 Oklahoma Indian tribes met at the state capitol to protest the television 'savages,' and called on President Eisenhower to help solve the ticklish problem. . . . 70 Indians present unanimously passed a resolution. It was directed to Mr. Eisenhower, various officials of the state and federal government, and to the three major television networks. 'We believe that no valid excuse exists for some producers of television pictures to ignore the harm which may be done to the children of America by repetitious distortion of historical facts pertaining to the way of life of any race or creed, including and especially the American Indian.'"

Cherokee attorney Earl Boyd Pierce complained, "Television has painted the American Indian as a sadistic, irresponsible killer. It is going to mis-educate a whole generation of American children . . . by its persistent, erroneous portrayal of the true facts."

Choctaw leader Jack Davidson added, "Television makes the younger generation think that Indians were only savages. The Indians only protected their homes. Television never tells about [that side] of the American Indians."

Harry J. W. Belvin, a senator from Oklahoma and leader in the Choctaw Nation, said, "There is no excuse for TV producers to ignore the harm that may be done to the children of America by repetitious distortion of historical facts pertaining to the way of life of any race or creed. They're portraying us as blood-thirsty marauders and murderers and it's hurting us."

When the press covered Native protests of this sort, they employed the very same racist stereotypes that were the source of objection. A UPI wire story was typical in its ignorance: "Indian war drums are sounding again in Oklahoma, protesting the white man's electronic 'Big Medicine'—Television. Modern Indian leaders, who wear white collars and ties instead of buckskin and feathers, say television has painted their ancestors as a race of wild savages dedicated to killing and plundering. They fear the younger generation will take this portrayal as historical fact. . . . Tribal leaders from throughout the state have organized a modern war party to carry a protest to the Great White Father in Washington."

Vine Deloria Jr. argued that reducing Natives to stereotypes fulfilled a definite purpose. "Politically, it is convenient to have Indians not as people because then what you do to them doesn't matter."

Lucas Brown Eyes Sells a Sitcom Pilot

"There are huge stereotypes that every one of us deals with," says sitcom writer Lucas Brown Eyes. "The stoic, not-laughing, black-and-white photo—that's what people think Native Americans are. The reality is the exact opposite. We are constantly joking around. I'm from the Pine Ridge Indian Reservation where the average life expectancy is forty-five years old. It is known as one of the poorest places in America. I grew up in that context. My family is Oglala Lakota and I'm an enrolled member of the Oglala Sioux tribe. There was this dichotomy of being on Pine Ridge where everybody was Native American, and then going outside the reservation, where *nobody* was Native American. It gave me this skewed vision of reality. I think that's why I gravitated toward comedy. I had a huge family and we were tight. It was my mom, my grandma, my aunt, my four cousins, and my brothers, all living under one roof, in one house. It was loud, but there was a lot of love there. When I was thirteen, my older brother committed suicide—and that tore my family apart. My grandmother kind of withdrew. My other brother went sort of crazy, partying as a form of coping. And my aunt had to leave because she didn't want to be around this stuff. I had this huge family and it just dwindled down to me and my mom. My mom felt she had to do something drastic, and she asked me, 'If we could go anywhere and start all over—where would it be?' I was thirteen and I said, 'Hollywood!' I had always wanted to go because, growing up, television was the escape. That was where I really grew to love comedy. Making television was something I wanted to do. We went to Hollywood in 2003 with nothing. I got into university and looked up Native American writers in television. I discovered there were two—Jason Gavin and Sierra Ornelas. I found out that Jason and Sierra had both gone through the ABC television writing program. It was a yearlong program where they take writers and train them and send them out to be staffed on a television show. I pinned all my hopes on that. My mother and I just went down there on hope, and I got into the program. They staffed me on a new show called *Young and Hungry*, a sitcom on ABC Family. I worked on that show for twenty straight months, and then my contract was picked up and I spent five more seasons writing that show. I rose through the ranks and ran the joke room. . . . I got an agent and a manager and met with a production company about my idea for a Native American sitcom. The story was based on my life, leaving Pine Ridge with my mother and coming to Los Angeles with no prospects. I met with Twentieth Century Fox in 2017. They loved it. They bought the idea right in the room. No one suggested anything hacky or cliché. When you come from such a hard place, you either laugh or you cry—and many of us choose to laugh."

Charlie Hill Is Inspired by Bob Newhart and Other Political Radicals

Charlie Hill saw all the sitcom stereotypes growing up and he watched as his father yelled at the screen, "Those aren't Indians! Look how dumb they are! Indians—they're not like this!" As he entered his teenage years, Hill was openly critical of what he saw on TV, and not just stereotypes. He became a discerning critic of comedy. "I would watch this comedy team called Allen and Rossi, a fat, dumpy Jewish guy and a handsome Italian singer. Even when I was eleven years old, I thought, 'These guys are *awful*. They suck! They're so bad.' They made me so angry." But if Allen and Rossi could land on *The Ed Sullivan Show*, then perhaps, Hill thought, there was a chance for the kid from Oneida. "I wanted to be a comedian," he said. "It was like a secret wish."

It was a revelation for Hill when he saw Dick Gregory on an episode of Jack Paar's *Tonight Show* in 1961. Gregory was a political comedian and an African American activist. He participated in civil rights marches and joked about lunch counter sit-ins, Bull Connor, and the Ku Klux Klan. And to Hill's surprise, he delivered a line about Native Americans on *The Tonight Show*:

"About three months ago I worked up in Minneapolis, Minnesota, and everybody told me, 'Greg, you'll love the state of Minnesota. We have terrific civil rights laws. And in this state you'd never know you're Negro.' That's true—because they're too busy picking on the Indians. If the Indians ever pack their bags and leave the state of Minnesota, I'll be getting on the next train out of there."

Hill watched the performance through a crack in his bedroom door, and it convinced him to do stand-up. He whispered quietly to himself, "I'm going to go for it. I'm going to find a way. I'm going to learn how to do it." It became an obsession. When his fifth-grade teacher handed out a "What Did You Do on Your Summer Vacation?" assignment, Hill formatted his essay like a Bob Newhart routine. From then on, his every move was done in service of furthering his dream. "I didn't want to get drafted, and I didn't want to work in the goddamn paper mill here [in Green Bay, adjacent to Oneida]. I thought, 'I'm gonna find a way to do this. I don't know how I'm going to do it, but that's what I'm gonna do.'"

When he was sixteen, he learned that the comedian Irwin Corey would be performing in a Minneapolis nightclub. Hill had seen Corey do his absentminded professor routine on *The Jackie Gleason Show* and desperately wanted to attend. He borrowed a fake ID from his brother Norbert and dressed in an Edwardian suit, the fashion worn by well-to-do men during World War I, in the hope it would fool the bouncer. The ruse worked, and Hill was enchanted by his first live comedy experience. After the first show ended, he hid in a bathroom stall so that he could catch Corey's act a second time.

The protest movement of the 1960s was dominating the news when Hill moved to Menomonie, Wisconsin, to enroll in the Clyde Warrior Institute. From a classroom at the University of Wisconsin, the Clyde Warrior Institute taught methods of nonviolent, direct action protest. Warrior was a respected Ponca activist. "For the past hundred years Indians have been held back and told they cannot be both Indians and Americans," said Warrior. "We refuse to accept that definition. We will be Indians *and* we will be human beings." The institute taught methods of organizing, emphasized the importance of ceremonial life, and advocated "respect for American Indians' right to embrace, celebrate, and maintain their unique identities."

Clyde Warrior joined with Paiute activist Mel Thom in the acts of civil disobedience staged by the National Indian Youth Council. The NIYC's mandate was to do for Native Americans what civil rights organizations like the Student Nonviolent Coordinating Committee had done for African Americans. Warrior spent a summer with the SNCC, participating in voter registration drives, civil rights marches, and organizing the poor. In the early 1960s when the state of Washington violated the terms of a federal treaty with the Tlingit Nation, the NIYC sprang into action. The legally binding contract had guaranteed the Tlingit Nation the right to fish the Quillayute River in any area at any time, as they had done for hundreds of years. But by 1964, state police were arresting Tlingits who cast nets beyond the reservation. Clyde Warrior, inspired by the lunch counter sit-ins in the Deep South, applied the concept along the Quillayute River with a series of organized "fish-ins." Alerting the media, the NIYC arranged a caravan of boats to fish defiantly. In an act of solidarity, more than a thousand Natives from fifty-six different tribes staged fish-ins across six different rivers, while game wardens and state troopers awaited orders.

"You could feel there was a squaring off," recalled Mel Thom. "The riverbanks were crowded. The tone of the crowd was rather tense. You could feel the hostility build up against the game wardens; [they] were really mad at us for being there. We knew the game wardens would make arrests. They did. . . . And then a funny thing happened. The Indians began to enjoy it. They were happy to see some direct action. Then the tenseness broke . . . and laughing. And some of the Indians took out their cameras and began taking pictures of the game wardens. Most times you see white people taking pictures of Indians, but this time it was Indians taking pictures of *mad* white people. That made them madder. It was our turn . . . the first time in recent history that we were publicly demonstrating what we privately felt."

Gonzo journalist Hunter S. Thompson covered the protests for the *National Observer*. "Throughout the country, Indians are doing battle with the Federal and state governments over a variety of causes," wrote Thompson. "And even though last week's 'fish-in' and assorted protests here resulted only in a stand-off, the attitudes they represented could have wide-ranging repercussions. . . . Among the important results were: A new feeling of unity among Indians. . . . Plenty of publicity for the Indian cause [and] the emergence of a new, dynamic leadership in the form of the National Indian Youth Council."

From Charlie Hill's time with the institute, a political philosophy emerged. "Whether an Indian writes a letter or brushes his teeth," he said, "in America that is a political act."

Hill was enamored with author Vine Deloria Jr. and his afore-mentioned book *Custer Died for Your Sins*. The 1969 bestseller was serialized in *Playboy* and educated non-Native readers about the negative impact of government policies like allotment, termina-tion, and urban relocation. Deloria promoted the book on *The Dick Cavett Show*, one of the only places on network television where Native issues were discussed.

Marlon Brando appeared on *The Dick Cavett Show* to discuss his interest in Native American issues during a 1973 appearance. "I read a book called *Indians of the Americas*," said Brando. "I realized that I knew nothing about the American Indian and that everything we are taught about the American Indian is wrong. . . . Our school-books are hopelessly lacking, criminally lacking, in revealing what our relationship was with the Indian. When we hear . . . that we are a country that stands for freedom, for rightness, for justice, for everyone—it simply doesn't apply. . . . We were . . . murdering and causing mayhem among the Indians. . . . Indians have been tragically misrepresented in films and in our history books and in our attitudes and in our reporting. And we must set about to reeducate ourselves."

Charlie Hill was impressed and inspired. When he wasn't taking notes at the Clyde Warrior Institute, he spent his time playing comedy records on his turntable. Lying down on his back between two speakers, he absorbed the dirty jokes of Redd Foxx, the timing of the Smothers Brothers, and the monologues of Bob Newhart. When he learned that Newhart got his start as a Chicago radio personality, he applied for a gig at Radio WBAY in Green Bay. Between vinyl cuts, Hill filled the airtime by reciting gags from "My Favorite Jokes," a weekly column from the newspaper supplement *Parade*. By studying their structure, he devised an act of old-fashioned jokes, rewriting them to include Native references. All of it was good experience, but he had yet to try the stage. He wasn't exactly sure how one started a stand-up career, so instead he joined the Broom Street Theater, an avant-garde collective at the University of Wisconsin. One day while perusing the bulletin board in the theater mezzanine, he came across a sheet tacked to the wall:

About the American Indian Theatre Ensemble Company

The American Indian Ensemble Company is the first all-Indian theatre troupe in America. The company has been in residence at La MaMa since its formation in February of this year. The 16 members were recruited from all parts of Indian Country and have been studying theatrical concepts and techniques in a special nine-month program since their arrival in New York City. Organizers of the company are Ellen Stewart of La MaMa and Hanay Geiogamah, a Kiowa-Delaware Indian from Oklahoma.

Says Mr. Geiogamah, "We want to do plays about the Indian past, Indian present, and Indian future. We believe that the American Indian Theatre Ensemble Company can function as a component of the overall movement to achieve true equality and self-determination for American Indians. Eventually we want to organize a performing arts group within every Indian tribe that is large enough and viable enough to sustain one. If we can do this, there is no question that Indian culture will thrive and evolve in the future."

Hill was floored by the prospect of an all-Native theater troupe. He recalled, "I kept writing them letters that I wanted to come to New York and wanted to be in this group." A few days later, he received a response:

Thank you for your letter of February 12th, and your interest in La MaMa. Am forwarding you a copy of our current *La MaMa Newsletter* and a packet of information on the American Indian Theatre Ensemble. Since you state that you are Oneida, thought you might be interested in that troupe and their activities. Would appreciate receiving more information about your interests and talents. Please let us know if you play any instruments, do you dance, and do you sing. As you are currently enrolled in the University of Wisconsin, we would like to know when and if you will be free and if you are interested in the American Indian Theatre Ensemble, or otherwise. . . .

THE THEATER ENSEMBLE reflected the mood of the growing protest movement, which Charlie Hill was increasingly involved in. He explained, "We started going to ceremonies. People started dressing Native. On campuses, we started growing our hair." Minneapolis became ground zero after the American Indian Movement (AIM) was founded in response to racial profiling. The Minneapolis police department operated under a quota system that required a certain amount of arrests each week. To keep their numbers up, police prowled Fourth Street and targeted Native Americans.

Founded by a generation of boarding-school survivors and inspired by the Black Panthers, AIM operated as a self-defense organization. AIM leader Dennis Banks said, "Police had to arrest a certain number of Indians. Usually about two hundred every week—to provide unpaid labor for the workhouse and various city projects. The cops concentrated on the Indian bars. They would bring their paddy wagons around behind a bar and open the back doors. . . . The police raided only the Indian bars and never the white ones."

Dennis Banks and his friend Russell Means were the media-savvy front men for the group. Behind the scenes, it was women who did much of the organizing. Mary Jane Wilson, Madonna Thunder Hawk, Anna Mae Aquash, and Mary Crow Dog participated in bold acts of civil disobedience, occupying government facilities and honing strategies to maximize the impact of their message.

A similar movement brewed in South Dakota, where two Lakota women, Lizzy Fast Horse and Muriel Waukazoo, initiated a protest with symbolic meaning. They took over Mount Rushmore in the name of the Treaty of Fort Laramie of 1868, which guaranteed ownership of the Black Hills to the Lakota people. The federal government honored the treaty for its first six years until gold was discovered in the Black Hills. White settlers then flooded the area, while the government did little to curtail them. Illegal settlements displaced the Indigenous population, and the government claimed ownership of the Black Hills in violation of its own treaty, eventually carving Mount Rushmore on the side of the mountain.

News cameras caught the activists patrolling George Washington's head as they unfurled a large bedsheet spray-painted with the words RED POWER. AIM pledged solidarity and sent fifty people to camp along the trail leading to the monument. "That mountain is part of the sacred Black Hills," said Dennis Banks. "Within the Black Hills are some of the holiest sites of both the Lakota and Cheyenne. To have the mountain defaced with the likenesses of Washington, Lincoln, Jefferson, and Roosevelt has been like rubbing salt in our wounds. For us, the giant faces were the images of our conquerors, planted in the very heart of Indian country to mock us."

For some, AIM represented a voice for the voiceless. For others, it represented a national security threat. Brandishing rifles and armaments, AIM members struck an imposing image, but Banks refuted the idea that they were dangerous. "We never went [anywhere] to cause any trouble—the trouble was already there."

In other parts of the country, another organization, the Indians of All Tribes, staged a series of occupations in BIA offices in Chicago; Cleveland; Gallup, New Mexico; Littleton, Colorado; and Washington, D.C. The Bureau of Indian Affairs maintained a bureaucratic stranglehold on Native nations, keeping them from exercising sovereign rights. The Indians of All Tribes refused to move until granted the autonomy to determine their own affairs. For the first time in a century, the whole country was talking about Native issues. Johnny Carson mentioned the protests on *The Tonight Show*: "Did you read about that in Washington? The Indians occupied the Bureau of Indian Affairs building. I guess because they're a little hot. They did not get a good deal in this country—did they? Not at all. They used to have the whole country, and now all they have is an alligator handbag concession in the Everglades."

Will Rogers Jr. considered the BIA occupations a perfectly logical action for those Natives "sick and angered" by the "stiff, unresponsive, white-dominated bureaucracy maintained by the Bureau of Indian Affairs and its area offices." He was especially livid when Louis Bruce, the first Bureau of Indian Affairs commissioner of Mohawk descent, was neutralized for implementing changes. "He had done something really astounding—staffed the BIA with dynamic, brilliant young Indian graduates—and they went to work in that area of control that is so important. They had lawsuits going all over the country over water rights and mineral rights . . . lawsuits going in the area of timber leases. . . . They were authorizing funds not for roads and ski lifts and hotels but to buy back the lands which had been sold generations before to whites." For his efforts, Bruce was fired, and, in Rogers's words, "the same types of ineffectual white bureaucrats phased back in and the anti-Indian status quo restored."

Lehman Brightman of the activist group United Indians of all Nations complained, "Eighty-nine percent of the top executives are non-Indian, which means we don't run the Bureau of Indian Affairs. We don't even select the commissioner of Indian affairs—he's selected by the president. We are the only group of people in this country who have a *bureau*. They don't have a bureau of Black affairs or white affairs."

The most ambitious of the occupations occurred when fourteen activists took control of Alcatraz Island on November 20, 1969. Among them were Richard Oakes, LaNada War Jack, Adam Fortunate Eagle, Stella Leach, and Grace Thorpe, the daughter of Jim Thorpe. They announced their plans to turn Alcatraz Island into an ecology center, training school, and Native American museum. The notorious prison had been lying vacant since 1963. The U.S. Department of Justice was trying to sell the property when Richard McKenzie of the Indians of All Tribes filed a claim based on the 1868 Treaty of Fort Laramie, which promised that dormant federal lands would automatically revert to Native ownership. The California attorney general ignored them and instead entered negotiations with *Dragnet* star Jack Webb to turn it into a permanent filming location. Director Victor Beaumont was promised use of the facility to film *Baked Apples*, an all-nude sex comedy.

The occupation of Alcatraz captured nationwide interest. Hundreds of Natives from around the country poured into the Bay Area in solidarity. Santee-Dakota poet John Trudell dropped out of Valley College in San Bernardino and joined the movement. He wrote a satirical manifesto that conveyed the feelings of the occupation:

> We, the Native Americans, re-claim the land known as Alcatraz Island in the name of all American Indians by right of discovery. We wish to be fair and honorable in our dealings

with the Caucasian inhabitants of this land, and hereby offer the following treaty: We will purchase said Alcatraz Island for twenty-four dollars in glass beads and red cloth, a precedent set by the white man's purchase of a similar island about 300 years ago. We know that twenty-four dollars in trade goods for these sixteen acres is more than was paid when Manhattan Island was sold, but we know that land values have risen over the years. Our offer [is] $1.24 per acre. . . . We will give to the inhabitants of this island a portion of that land for their own, to be held in trust by the American Indian Government—for as long as the sun shall rise and the rivers go down to the sea— to be administered by the Bureau of Caucasian Affairs. . . . We will further guide the inhabitants in the proper way of living. We will offer them our religion, our education, our life-ways, in order to help them achieve our level of civilization and thus raise them and all their white brothers up from their savage and unhappy state. We offer this treaty in good faith and wish to be fair and honorable in our dealings with all white men.

Trudell's humor impressed people like Charlie Hill but alarmed the FBI. The bureau opened a file on Trudell and noted in an internal memo, "He is extremely eloquent—therefore extremely dangerous." An Indians of All Tribes spokesman stood on the steps of the San Francisco courthouse and spoke to a KPIX reporter about the federal government's "turning over surplus facilities right and left to white profit-making corporations. Lytton, Philco, Ford, RCA, Westinghouse. They've all gotten surplus federal facilities—free of charge—that they can use to make money. The federal government has not seen fit to turn over any such facilities to Indian people so that Indian people can run their own educational programs. Alcatraz is such a facility—it's available, no one's using it right now . . . and there are others around that can also be obtained for that purpose."

Members of the Hopi Nation joined the protest. Eighty years

earlier, U.S. troops had forcibly removed Hopi children from their homes and sent them to residential schools against their will. Hopi parents who resisted the child separation policy were imprisoned at Alcatraz. For them, their participation in the Alcatraz occupation was symbolic.

The image of a raised red fist adorned the entranceway, and the phrase PEACE AND FREEDOM was spray-painted on a water tower. A wooden sign greeted boats approaching the island: WARNING—YOU ARE ON INDIAN LAND. Lumbee activist Dean Chavers operated a mainland headquarters from a cluttered San Francisco storefront. "Chavers answers telephone calls, sorts correspondence and greets a steady stream of well-wishers bringing food and other aid," reported UPI. Financial support arrived from the International Longshoremen's Association, the Warehousemen's Union, the Painters Union, the United Auto Workers, and comedian Jonathan Winters. "I don't know many people in or out of show business who are doing much for the Indian," said Winters. "My goal is to help make the tremendous strides the Indian needs to catch up with the rest of his country easier."

Winters was one of the top stand-up comedians of the 1950s and 1960s and another of Charlie Hill's heroes. He had come out of the same coffeehouse circuit that made a star of Dick Gregory. In the late 1960s, he contributed money to a variety of political causes. "Not many are aware of Jonathan's active participation on behalf of the Indians," reported the *Baltimore Sun* in 1969. "During the past two years he has been visiting reservations throughout the country." A year before the Alcatraz occupation, the National Congress of American Indians presented Winters with an award "in recognition of his long-standing interest in the welfare of the Indians."

Winters secured permission from the Indians of All Tribes to visit Alcatraz. After meeting with John Trudell and LaNada War Jack, he pledged financial aid and solicited donations from film producer Jerry Adler and actor Anthony Quinn. They staged a number of benefits for the occupation, some of which featured Janis Joplin with Big Brother and the Holding Company. The state government cut off all water and power to the island in an attempt to end the occupation, but the UAW sent a flotilla of plumbers and electricians to help reactivate the most basic necessities. Jane Fonda donated an expensive generator, which John Trudell used to broadcast *Radio Free Alcatraz*, a fifteen-minute daily update that was heard in Berkeley, Los Angeles, and New York.

The occupation of Alcatraz was among the most famous protests of the twentieth century. It entered the mainstream culture, referenced in Bob Hope films and the nightclub acts of comedians like Pat Buttram, who joked, "I don't understand why the Indians want to squat on Alcatraz. I had an uncle who lived there and didn't like it at all."

After eighteen months, the state of California had no choice but to negotiate. It was announced that the occupiers would vacate Alcatraz in return for several hundred acres of land near Davis, California, which would be used to build Deganawidah-Quetzalcoatl University, the first Native-run postsecondary institution.

John Trudell declared victory: "The significant thing that's been accomplished by Alcatraz—we never sold ourselves out. . . . No, man, there's no such thing as defeat. When they start kicking you around, you just gotta learn to bandage up the bruises and stand up again."

Paul Littlechief's Only Ambition Is to Be the "First American Indian Comedian"

"If Bob Hope can take talent to Vietnam, then I can go to Alcatraz," said Paul Littlechief. Flanked by a pair of dancing girls, Littlechief was a Kiowa-Comanche performer who brought wild costumes, corny jokes, and relentless energy to a circuit of lounges in midcentury Nevada. He combined Native American pride with Vegas-style kitsch, and the result was a dazzling spectacle. It was all part of his grand strategy to become, in his words, "the first Indian American comedian."

Paul Littlechief was born in Lawton, Oklahoma, on June 25, 1935, to a Comanche mother and a Kiowa father. His great-grandfather Kath-Tia-Shun, loosely translated as "Little Chief," was killed by federal troops at Fort Sill. The outpost had been established for the purpose of subjugating Kiowa, Comanche, and Cheyenne peoples in the Indian Territory. His grandfather John Littlechief joined the very same troops. It was his only viable option when given the choice of jail time, execution, or enlistment.

In the 1950s, Paul Littlechief's parents were mystified by his passion for the new fad of rock 'n' roll. He was enamored with the music and became a quick study on the guitar. He mastered the pedal steel at a young age and regularly played with a local country band on KSWO-TV. He was eighteen years old when he had his first son, Brock. A daughter named Jocelyn followed in 1955, and a second son, Lance, in 1957. His parents helped raise the children while Littlechief toured honky-tonks from Bondurant, Wyoming, to Terre Haute, Indiana, eventually trading country licks for a rockabilly sound. He billed himself as Chief Little Chief, but his father hated the name and pleaded with him not to subscribe to stereotypes.

Littlechief moved to Hollywood and hustled songs to the many music publishers around Vine Street. He convinced a small label, 4 Star Records, to release two songs—"Come On Darlin'" and "It's for Certain (That I'm Hurtin)." He hoped it would lead to some live gigs, but Los Angeles had recently banned rock concerts within city limits, disturbed by reports of "teenage race mixing." Young music fans were forced east of town, where disc jockey Johnny Otis presented Black and Latino rockers like Lil Julian Herrera, Hank Ballard, and Little Willie John at El Monte Legion Stadium. Littlechief patronized the shows in El Monte and was blown away by an R&B group with coordinated dance moves, fast-paced songs, and outrageous outfits. The effect was sheer excitement. They were called the Ike and Tina Turner Revue.

A few weeks later Littlechief did a gig with a former Miss Wisconsin who was singing under the stage name Baby Rae. They developed an act together based on the Ike and Tina format. Landing a yearlong engagement at the 49er Club in El Monte, they tested new ideas and new wardrobes, six nights a week. Their costumes were Indigenous-themed—but remembering what his father had told him years earlier, he was careful to avoid western movie clichés. Littlechief started collecting one-liners and introduced comedy into the act, trying out jokes between songs. Romance blossomed during the run, and Baby Rae accepted his marriage proposal. Expecting yet another child, Littlechief needed a larger income. There was only one logical place for a lounge act to make a good amount of money in a short amount of time.

Thanks to healthy gambling profits, the cities of Las Vegas, Lake

Tahoe, and Reno paid performers twice as much as anywhere else. When Littlechief and Baby Rae rolled into town in 1965, Reno was part of a circuit nicknamed the Silver Circle, comprising hundreds of small lounges throughout the region. At the time, the Silver Circle was in the throes of a go-go dancing trend. A familiar theme was seen on marquees all over town—Action a Go-Go, Casino a Go-Go, Buffet a Go-Go—everywhere you looked, women in knee-high boots were demonstrating the Frug, the Swim, and the Watusi. At the entrance to the Mapes Hotel a sign read: MAPES A GO GO WITH PAUL LITTLECHIEF AND HIS WATUSI WARRIORS. As Baby Rae's pregnancy advanced, a second woman was added to the act to pick up the slack. Together the trio was an impressive sight, with matching buckskin jackets, winged sleeves, and a fringe that flailed as they got into the groove. The *Reno Gazette-Journal* raved, "The show is one of the fastest-paced on the nitery circuit. Paul Littlechief has a peripatetic personality. The distaff of the show, Baby Rae, ranks in a class by herself when it comes to beautiful dancers. The finely proportioned young beauty and her equally blessed partner go through a dance history. . . . Littlechief handles the emcee chores with timing and aplomb."

The act caught the attention of Sam Boyd, manager of the Mint Hotel in Las Vegas. Originally from Enid, Oklahoma, he was intrigued by the concept of a Native American lounge act. He summoned Littlechief for a six-month residency at the Mint, advertising the act as "a music comedy group featuring Paul Littlechief—the First American Indian Comedian."

Littlechief had aspirations beyond the lounge. The ambitious comic wanted nothing less than headliner status. "I refused to accept any more bookings in the downtown lounges and pushed hard for a booking on the strip," he said. "There is a longtime feeling of a 'status' difference between the strip and downtown lounges."

He was offered a better deal at the Aladdin, one of the few Las Vegas venues showcasing minorities as headliners. African American comedians Redd Foxx and Godfrey Cambridge had just finished runs at the venue when Littlechief was booked for twenty-eight weeks. "The Indian-flavored revue is attracting sizable crowds here nightly since it's one of the unique lounge shows on the glittering strip," reported the *Lawton Constitution*. "The 34-year-old Kiowa-Comanche Indian's popularity has spread so fast in this gambling resort city that he now gets top billing. . . . His pretty blonde blue-eyed wife, billed as 'Baby Rae,' does an exotic dance attired in a brief loin cloth and Indian headdress. . . . Littlechief's routine is spiced with a variety of quips, some of which are too blue for print. . . . A couple of his jokes fell flat. . . . A take-off on TV's *Laugh-In* is a highlight."

His daughter Jocelyn saw the show when she was a teenager. "It was for my thirteenth birthday. I was living with my mother in Tustin, California. He flew me to Vegas and had a car pick me up at the airport. I got to sit in the light booth and watch the show. . . . It was really high-energy, and everything was completely choreographed. A lot of the comedy was largely visual." Reporters noted that "the fine comedian" was dressed in an "unorthodox mod Indian costume with a Tom Jones–type blouse with stars and bell bottom oatmeal slacks, designed especially for him." The clothes were the product of a burgeoning designer. "All of their outfits were made in Vegas by a woman named Suzy Creamcheese," says Jocelyn Littlechief. "She designed all kinds of fringe and capes and all of these things. Shortly after that, she started outfitting Elvis. All the wild things you saw Elvis wear later were first worn by my father."

The Landmark Hotel lured Littlechief away for even higher pay. He did three shows a night—midnight, 2 a.m., and 4 a.m.—for $10,000 a week, the equivalent of $70,000 today. Littlechief reflected on his success: "It's a wide-open field since there are no real Indian comics. Most people think of Indians as being shy and introverted, you know, and I feel I can help overcome this impression, and in the process, might help my people."

Littlechief infused his act with lounge-friendly Red Power. A fan letter from a Native couple on vacation gave a sense of his effect: "The thing that really got to us was the reality of self-determination you displayed before the public and the pride and joy you instilled within us while watching you perform. Also, we really felt the brotherly feeling you shared with us during the breaks of the show. We feel that it is leaders (and you are indeed one) such as you who will throw a whole new light upon the Indians to non-Indians everywhere and will do more good to erase the old established image of the drunken Indian and do more good towards helping our people. We especially feel that you will be a great influence upon our youth . . . not only for your great talent as an entertainer but for the pride, leadership qualities, and the self-determination you show and communicate to us—your brothers."

A wealthy Las Vegas attorney who drank in the lounge every week was one of his biggest fans. He bankrolled an LP of politically themed tunes for Littlechief titled *The Real American*. It featured two songs written by his son Brock.

Paul Littlechief thought songwriting might keep his son out of trouble, but he was unable to acknowledge that his son had behavioral problems. "Brock was schizophrenic," says Jocelyn Littlechief. "My dad couldn't come to terms with it. He didn't want to send Brock off to an institution, so he sent him to live with my grandparents—but I don't think he understood that this wasn't going to help him get well."

Inspired by the occupation of Alcatraz, Littlechief became more politically minded in the early 1970s. He took on Native-specific gigs—the Kyi-Yo Indian Youth Conference in Missoula, Montana; an intertribal convention in Sparks, Nevada; an AIM fund raiser in Denver—and he used his position to secure work for other Native American performers. He enlisted the Cree actor Cody Bearpaw to help with an open audition for a new Native revue, and was certain it was just a matter of time until Native Americans secured proportional representation in show biz. "It'll all work out," he said. "It just takes time."

Going through a transitional period, Littlechief committed himself to making a difference beyond the lounge. "My dad quit alcohol, and then he quit Vegas," recalls Jocelyn Littlechief. "He was selected to work on Indian policy and serve on a committee about Indian drug and alcohol abuse in Washington, D.C. He was going to be gone for a year, so he drove across the country with a trailer filled with all his equipment and stopped in Oklahoma to visit my grandparents. My brother Brock was still living with them, constantly arguing or yelling to himself."

And then on November 12, 1975, the *Lawton Constitution* reported the news. "Brock Littlechief, 22, was charged in district court here Tuesday with second degree murder in the Monday night shooting death of his father. Paul Littlechief, a Las Vegas comedian and vocalist since 1964, was dead on arrival at an Anadarko hospital [with] a single bullet wound to the head. Brock Littlechief walked out of a bedroom in the home with a .22 caliber rifle in his hands, walked up to his father and shot him once by the left ear as the victim's parents, wife, and small child, watched."

"[Brock] was sent to a federal prison in Missouri," says Jocelyn Littlechief. "But because it happened on Indian land, the local DA fought it and they threw it out. The police who arrested and charged him didn't have jurisdiction over Indian land." The appeals court elaborated: "It is conceded that the land where the alleged murder took place is what is commonly referred to as Indian Trust Land. It is part of an original Kiowa Allotment and is held in trust for the Kiowa Tribe by the federal government." Littlechief's son was placed in permanent psychiatric care. The ruling led to the formation of a tribal police force and court system within the Kiowa Nation. It was an unexpected legacy for a man who had wowed them in Vegas, slayed them in Reno, and would never have the chance to fully realize his dream of being "the First American Indian Comedian."

The Trickster Figure Causes People to Fart When They're Most Keen to Impress

A whole infrastructure of Native American media emerged in the wake of the Alcatraz occupation. Operating with limited resources, Native American newspapers covered news stories ignored everywhere else. Charlie Hill's earliest press came from the American Indian Press Association, a Native wire service formed in early 1972. One of AIPA's initial reports concerned Charlie Hill's first professional performance:

> New York, NY—(AIPA)—Two new Indian musicals performed by the Native American Theater Ensemble will open here at the La Mama Theater in the East Village on the night of Oct. 25. The two musicals are "Foghorn," a biting and humorous account of Indian experience in the late 1960s and 1970s by Kiowa playwright Hanay Geiogamah, and "The Coon Cons the Coyote, Etc.," a dramatization of a classic Nez Perce coyote tale written by the entire company.

The Coon Cons the Coyote was renamed *Coyote Tracks* and based on a Nez Perce trickster figure that caused people to "fart when they're most keen to impress." The ensemble turned the tale into an outlandish piece of experimental theater with Charlie Hill in the title role.

Accompanied by the sound of a beating drum, Hill entered the scene shouting, "My eyes! My eyes!" An actor addressed the audience and explained, "This is Coyote. The powerful and foolish Coyote. There are two things which fascinate him. One is playing with his eyes and the other is eating. He is always hungry and will do just about anything for food." Approached by a character named Farting Girl, Hill as Coyote stole her possessions, including a red arrow. Coyote was pleased until he started experiencing brutal gas pains, failing to realize his flatulence was caused by the arrow in his grip. The performance climaxed with Hill screaming, "How do you stop farting! How do you stop farting! Tell me! Tell me! How do you stop farting!"

Foghorn was the ensemble's second production. Geiogamah called it "an examination of all the false stereotypes about Indians done within the framework of Indian history, tracing the Red Power movement from Alcatraz Island . . . a dramatized lobotomy on the mind of a Middle American white man." It opened with Hill and the cast sitting in a circle, the Alcatraz foghorn bleating in the distance, as each character told a story about a modern tragedy, from residential boarding schools to termination. Between soliloquies the cast broke into song, performing famous stereotype numbers: "Kaw-Liga" by Hank Williams, "Indian Giver" by the 1910 Fruitgum Company, and "Indian Love Call" from the musical *Rose-Marie*. Hill portrayed an activist who questions the wisdom of the Alcatraz occupation:

CHARLIE HILL: No unity! There is no unity here! We are pretending! Pretending we have a common purpose! Pretending to get along! Instead we are always fighting with each other!

CAST MEMBER #1: Charlie, it is good to fight. . . . In families, you fight. . . . What we need here is a *family* of

Indians. . . . Here we are, all different tribes, and we are
trying to get together! Right now, Charlie!

CHARLIE HILL: Every old person back home disagrees with
everything we do. Every political move we have, this
occupation, they don't care what we're doing. I don't
think they even know why we're here on this island.
Sometimes I think those old people live in a different
world than we're in . . .

CAST MEMBER #2: The old people do, in a sense, live in
a different world, but I think it's because they have a
deeper understanding about things than we do. The white
man's government has tried to control their thinking
for so long. They tried to force them to believe that they
don't deserve a respectful place in America. . . . Think
about that, Charles, before you say they don't understand
what we're trying to do here!

CHARLIE HILL: My grandfather told me to get off the
island. . . . I'm starting to wonder what the hell we're
doing here. . . .

The ensemble set out on an ambitious six-week tour of Germany,
but infighting and Geiogamah's inability to pay his performers led
to its implosion. By the time Hill returned stateside, the troupe had
disbanded—but he found himself in the epicenter of a burgeoning
comedy club scene. Greenwich Village was the testing ground for
the newest stand-up comics, and Hill was within walking distance of
two early comedy clubs: Catch a Rising Star and the Improvisation.
He started to spend all of his time leaning against the back wall ob-
serving future stars. "Jay Leno had long hair and glasses," recalled
Hill. "Elayne Boosler [was] seating people. At the end of the show
she'd stand up there and read jokes off of cards." Hill needed to get
up there; he just wasn't sure how. Johnny Carson had just moved

The Tonight Show from New York to Burbank, and most of the New York comedians were migrating to Hollywood for that reason. Hill figured it was time to go west.

The country's second all-Indigenous theater troupe, the Red Earth Performing Arts Company, formed in Seattle in 1974. *Foghorn* was its first production, and Hill was asked to come work with the actors and share his experience. So Charlie packed his bags and brought along a hand drum his father had given him for good luck. He spent a month in Seattle and then made his way down to California, where he crashed on an aunt's sofa. The next night he went down to the Sunset Strip and showed up on the doorstep of a Hollywood nightclub that would change his life. It was called the Comedy Store.

F Troop Represents the F-Word

Minority activism in the late 1960s altered perspectives in the body politic. The Palm Springs *Desert Sun* reported in September 1967, "A firebrand Kiowa, Amos Hopkins-Dukes, filed suit in federal court asking for an injunction against ABC-TV to 'halt discriminatory practices against American Indians.'"

Hopkins-Dukes was the national executive director of the Tribal Indian Land Rights Association and one of many activists who took on television stereotypes. In response, some sitcom writers turned their stereotyped characters into activists themselves. Influenced by the news reports of fish-ins and occupations, Native activism was parodied in the popular secret-agent comedy *Get Smart*.

When a fictional activist group called Red Feathers insists that their stolen land be returned, agent Maxwell Smart, played by comedian Don Adams, is assigned to infiltrate the group as an informant. His boss, the Chief, played by Edward Platt, convenes an emergency meeting with the heads of the American military to plan a strategy to suppress the activists:

GENERAL ONE: Exactly what do these Indians want?
THE CHIEF: They demand the return of all territory we took from them.
GENERAL THREE: Well, give it to them.

GENERAL TWO: But, Harry—it's all theirs! The whole country.

GENERAL THREE: Everything?

GENERAL TWO: Everything.

GENERAL ONE: Wait a minute, wait a minute, now. Maybe we can make a deal. They might be able to accept less. Say . . . New Jersey?

GENERAL TWO: Would *you*?

An honest moment crept into an episode of *The Beverly Hillbillies*. When the Clampetts trace their lineage and learn they qualify for "high society," Jed Clampett and Cousin Pearl engage in a sly exchange:

COUSIN PEARL: Well, Jed, now that we's high society, I can't be seen riding around in that old truck.

JED CLAMPETT: Since when is we high society?

COUSIN PEARL: Since that historical lady found out that your ancestors come to this country on the *Mayflower*!

JED CLAMPETT: What has that got to do with me?

COUSIN PEARL: That's the way society works, Jed. The earlier your kinfolk got here, the higher up that put ya.

JED CLAMPETT: Well, I reckon the highest-society folks is the injuns.

COUSIN PEARL: No, it don't work that way.

JED CLAMPETT: How come?

COUSIN PEARL: I don't know how come.

JED CLAMPETT: Well, they was here before anybody else.

COUSIN PEARL: Now, now, now, Jed. Let's not try to change the rules.

The Andy Griffith Show reflected evolving interpretations of American history in the 1966 episode "The Battle of Mayberry." Andy's son Opie, played by child actor Ron Howard, is writing a history paper on the founding of their town. He hears conflicting stories from local residents about what exactly happened during the Battle of Mayberry, a fight between white settlers and the Indigenous population. Andy suggests that his son might get some good information from Mayberry's Cherokee resident, Tom Strongbow. Andy and Opie find Strongbow, played by white actor Norman Alden, doing work in his yard, wearing contemporary jeans, a work shirt, and a cowboy hat:

STRONGBOW: It was my revered ancestor Chief Strongbow that led the Cherokee in the defense of their original hunting ground. It was fifty braves against five hundred settlers. . . . . Bows and arrows against muskets—the Battle of Tuckahoosie Creek.

ANDY TAYLOR: Tuckahoosie Creek? We're talking about the Battle of Mayberry, Tom.

STRONGBOW: Well, that's what the settlers called it. But to us Indians, it's still the Victory of Tuckahoosie Creek.

ANDY TAYLOR: Victory?

STRONGBOW: Yeah, that's right. Us Indians forced them settlers and their cattle off our hunting grounds.

The activism of the late 1960s was altering perceptions. It looked as if years of vocal agitation might finally be having an effect. But then ABC announced a new sitcom called *F Troop*. It was set at a U.S. Cavalry fort where soldiers were stationed to keep the fictional Hekawi tribe from leaving the reservation.

Had it been proposed just a few years later, it would have been rejected. Comedy would turn to a more realistic, satirical approach in the wake of *All in the Family*, *National Lampoon*, George Carlin, Lily Tomlin, and Richard Pryor. *F Troop* got in just under the wire. It was an old-fashioned and unapologetic stereotype sitcom with an enormous budget for bole armenia.

The Native American characters were played by Don Diamond, a mainstay of the Yiddish theater; Edward Everett Horton, a legend of 1930s Hollywood; Ben Frommer, once featured in Ed Wood's *Plan 9 from Outer Space*; and Frank DeKova and J. Pat O'Malley, Italian American and British character actors, respectively. Celebrity guest stars like Don Rickles, George Gobel, Paul Lynde, and Milton Berle were eager to do the program. It became a major ratings hit thanks to its place on the schedule, airing immediately after the popular *Batman*, starring Adam West.

The name of the Hekawi tribe and the title *F Troop* were derived from a dirty joke that Redd Foxx had once used in his stand-up act:

"Two Indian braves from the Fakawi tribe. Two of these Fakawi Indians were out hunting in the woods, had their moccasins and stuff on, and they were creeping up on some game. They were creeping and creeping and pretty soon . . . they were lost. Both of them were on the mountaintop looking over, trying to find out where their tribe was. This one Indian looked at his buddy, said, 'You brought us out here, you get us back home. You know we're lost.' His buddy looked at him and said, 'Don't worry. I know where we are.' And his buddy looked at him and said, 'Well, where the Fakawi?'"

F Troop obviously couldn't use *fuck* on the air, so the *fuh* was replaced with a *heh* and the Fakawi became the Hekawi. According to 1960s comedy producer George Schlatter, the *F* in the show's title represented "the missing fuck."

F Troop escaped without major protest, but a year later when ABC announced a new series that would frame General George Armstrong Custer as an American hero, the network was immediately condemned. "General Custer was a madman, the Indian's worst enemy," explained Amos Hopkins-Dukes. "We are lodging a complaint to ABC, petitioning sponsors of the series to boycott it. We hope the nation's 600,000 Indians and all persons interested in the welfare of Indians will protest the Custer series."

The series avoided using Custer's actual words. Writing in his autobiography, Custer had said, "The Indian [is] a creature possessing the human form but divested of all other attributes of humanity, and whose traits of character, habits, modes of life, disposition, and savage customs disqualify him from the exercise of all rights and privileges, even those pertaining to life itself."

But producer Frank Glicksman justified the series by ignoring Custer's own words. "From my reading and from people we consider authorities," he declared, "I judge that Custer was a man of heroic proportions." Wayne Maunder was cast in the title role and said any criticism of Custer was a lie: "I don't believe Custer did those things this Indian [Hopkins-Dukes] is talking about. I mean massacring village after village of Indians. I'm sure he was not as bad as people have been led to believe."

Lawyer James Hovis of the Yakama Nation filed a motion that the various Native nations be granted "equal time" under the FCC's fairness doctrine to counteract the prevailing point of view. Vine Deloria Jr. wrote, "As tribes in different areas began to move, ABC, through its affiliate board, arranged a trip to California to discuss the program with the NCAI [National Congress of American Indians]. Several tribes filed against local affiliates of ABC and did receive some airtime to present the Indian side of the Custer story during the brief run of the show. Later we heard that it would have cost ABC some three thousand dollars per complaint if every tribe had gone ahead and demanded FCC hearings on the controversy." During the show's ten-episode run, ABC ran a spoken disclaimer over the credits: "Tonight's episode has been a fictional drama."

Williams and Ree Perform for Thirteen People at the Holiday Inn

Standing onstage in Custer, South Dakota, a pair of men in matching white suits and panama hats entertain a small crowd inside a revolving restaurant decorated with garish orange drapery. With a stylized pompadour and a wide, disarming smile, the Lakota half of the duo cracks a joke about President Ford and then stares at the thirteen patrons in the crowd and says, "You're probably wondering why we invited so few people."

A man in a paper chef's hat pushes a metal cart into the showroom. As he unveils a steel tray of simmering roast beef, the thirteen patrons abandon their seats and walk toward him with plates in hand. The comedy team onstage continues with their jokes and novelty songs, pretending they haven't just been abandoned by an apathetic crowd. A cardboard flyer on each table reads: "Tuesday— Prime Rib Special—Holiday Inn Starlite Room—with South Dakota's Favorite Comedy Team—Williams and Ree."

"I WAS BORN in Huron, South Dakota, about a hundred miles from the Crow Creek Reservation," says Terry Ree, the burly half of Williams and Ree. "My mom and dad were in one of the original relocation programs. They took a bunch of Natives from Fort Thompson, put them in the back of a military truck, drove them a hundred miles away, and dumped them in the middle of the street. 'Find a job and live here.' Within a couple of days all the Natives went right back. My mom and dad stayed. We became the only Indian family in Huron. I was known as 'the Indian kid' and dealt with a lot of racism. I wasn't allowed to join the Cub Scouts or the Boy Scouts. You just had to live with racism—but I learned to find humor in those situations."

Ree was the son of a mechanic, the youngest of eight children. He was a small boy when his fifty-three-year-old father died suddenly. Television became his babysitter, and he gravitated toward comedy programming. "I started watching comedians on *The Ed Sullivan Show*," he says. "I watched *The Jackie Gleason Show*. I loved it." He lost himself in music. By the age of thirteen he had mastered the electric guitar, emulating plugged-in country stars like Buck Owens, performing standards at local dances and legion halls. "My cousin had a band, and he was sort of like the Native Glen Campbell. He had so many gigs around South Dakota that he couldn't play them all. So he gave me some of those jobs, and I would do these shows—just me—from Belle Fourche to Huron. I was thirteen when I formed a group called the Terry Ree Combo, and we'd play my reservation, Crow Creek, doing dances and stuff. I really didn't know enough songs, so I would talk in the middle and tell jokes or make fun of someone in the crowd. And that's how I started to develop comedy. I was stalling for time."

Ree attended Black Hills State College in Spearfish, South Dakota, where he met his future comedy partner, Bruce Williams. Williams was a bespectacled, nerdy white boy with a knack for guitar licks. He was employed by Upward Bound, a program under the auspices of the U.S. Office of Economic Opportunity for which Buffy Sainte-Marie was an advisor. "Upward Bound was a series of government programs that helped Native kids reach college," says Ree. "The high school dropout rate on the reservation was *ninety* percent. Bruce was involved with Upward Bound, and I was involved with a similar program, going to every school on every reservation, putting on a little show and talking about the importance of education." Williams and Ree took an immediate liking to each other. With a pair of college classmates, they formed a band the same year the Bill of Rights was first extended to Native Americans—1968. They became regulars at a steak house called Taylor's El Cochero near Mount Rushmore, and it was there that they devised their earliest routines. Another recurring gig was at the Deadwood Elks Lodge, a three-story venue that required them to haul their equipment—including a five-hundred-pound Hammond organ—up and down three flights of stairs. It was a completely different trajectory from those comedians developing at the Comedy Store in Los Angeles or Catch a Rising Star in New York. A big break in one of those cities meant a recurring spot on a TV show. A big break for Williams and Ree meant a residency at a truck stop.

Their first steady gig was at the Phil-Town Truck Stop in Sturgis, every Wednesday through Saturday, competing with the growl of idling tractor-trailers outside. "The Phil-Town Lounge was a gigantic truck stop right on the interstate with a motel connected to it," says Ree. "We played in its basement, which they called the Fiesta Room." The audience consisted of truck drivers who got lost searching for the bathroom.

The Phil-Town had a Googie-inspired, space-age design; its mid-century roof came to a triangular point on one side, resembling a Chevy Impala. On the west side of the building, three cylindrical tanks dwarfed the parking lot where rows of motorcycles lined up in unison. Biker gangs used the Phil-Town Truck Stop as their last respite before landing at the nearby Hog Heaven, a biker campground off Interstate 90.

Williams and Ree enjoyed a brief rest when the Phil-Town booked an out-of-town comedy team named Dennis and Cree for one week. Marv Dennis and Ed Cree had just finished a run along the dense circuit of nightclubs, casinos, and lounges throughout Nevada known as the Silver Circle. Dennis and Cree were indicative of the Silver Circle style: frilly blue tuxedos, a trunk filled with props, and routines cribbed from dime-store paperbacks like *2,000 Sure-Fire Jokes for Speakers* by Bob Orben. Ed Cree was a hulking presence, a former state wrestling champion with a walrus mustache. His gawky partner, Marv Dennis, made him carry their trunk of feather boas, thrift-store hats, and rubber chickens in and out of every gig. A review in Reno called Cree "a master rubber-faced mugger [and] baggy-pants comedian who plays an unbelievably good banjo." Williams and Ree had a similar sensibility to Dennis and Cree and were informed by their style. "Dennis and Cree had a drummer and a Cordovox [accordion] player backing them up," says Terry Ree. "They would play an instrumental and get the audience built up, and then go into this up-tempo thing: 'Ladies and gentlemen! Please welcome . . . Dennis and Cree!' And then Dennis and Cree would come *running* onto the stage and jump right into their act. It made it feel like something exciting was happening, so we started doing the same thing."

Marv Dennis was impressed when he saw Williams and Ree and helped arrange a tour for them along the Silver Circle. Ree says, "The railroad went right through all these little stops with hotels and casinos—this whole circuit in Nevada—all places you could work. Wendover and Wells and Elko and Lovelock and Carson City and Reno and Tahoe and Sparks and Jackpot—you could keep working every lounge for years and never once have to leave the state." Most of the comedians along the circuit never did.

To patronize the Silver Circle venues—from the Holiday Hotel in Reno to the Thunderbird Motel in Elko—was to be exposed to comedians whom you'd never heard of before and whom you'd never hear from again: Blackie Hunt, Rummy Bishop, Red Coffee, Frankie Ross, Lou Mosconi, Antone and Curtiss, Davis and Reese, Tepper and Nelson, Nelson and Palmer, Crandall and Charles, Skiles and Henderson, Deedy and Bill, Sherman and Lee, Stanton and Peddie, Romer and Howard, Ford and Mercer—and now Williams and Ree.

Time stood still along the Silver Circle. It was a region unaffected by hippies, Black Panthers, or women's lib. Social unrest was limited to drunken middle-aged gamblers. Long after the rest of the United States had evolved, the Silver Circle was frozen in time like a cryogenic caveman. Every now and then a Silver Circle act tried modern material, but the results were generally pathetic. The comedy team of Red Coffee and Karen DeLuce was a typical case. The *Reno Gazette-Journal* reported in 1971, "Show business pros Karen and Coffee mix vaudeville with the 'now' generation. A blending of the old with the new." DeLuce told the paper, "We give 'em a bit of Jolson . . . play a lot of banjo . . . and the hot pants portion of the show is a take-off of the current 'hot pants' fashion fad."

Comedians who toured the Silver Circle long enough might get lucky and land a long-term residency at Harrah's on Lake Tahoe or Harold's Club in Reno, opening for a celebrity singer. And if the management liked you, anything you asked for—food, drink, gambling money—was yours. "Harrah's was the big time," recalls ninety-four-year-old comedian Jackie Curtiss. "Harrah's bought the traffic lights and programmed them so that you'd have to wait for the light a long time right in front of their marquee. You'd be waiting and waiting for the light to change, so you had no choice but to stare at this giant sign that told you who was playing. They really knew how to advertise the Silver Circle in those days, and everything had the word 'gold' or 'silver' in the name."

But even if the gigs paid well and the surroundings were glamorous, the audience usually hated the comedians' guts. They were there to see Vikki Carr and Barbara McNair sing the hits—not some fucking comedy team with funny hats. Still, a successful residency could lead to television bookings on a summer replacement like *Dean Martin Presents the Golddiggers* or *Allen Ludden's Gallery*. Talent scouts from those television programs could be found getting blotto in one showroom after another, lording their drunken power over comedians whose names they couldn't remember.

Many of the performance spaces were "stage bars," venues with a raised platform directly behind the bartender. "The stage bars were all over Nevada," says Terry Ree. "They had a stage on the bar in casino after casino—and they were *great* acts. Rowan and Martin worked all the stage bars." But such opportunities were reserved for the chosen few. New comedians paid their dues in the roughshod bars, trying to entertain chain-smoking degenerates, most of whom had just lost it all at the tables. In these venues it didn't matter how well-polished your jokes, how perfect your tuxedo, how wide your grin—inevitably some devastated soul would throw a shot glass at your head.

Marv Dennis sent Williams and Ree to Elko in 1974. An old mining town two hours east of Las Vegas, known for Basque cuisine and run-down motels, Elko was routinely mocked with throwaway gags in Rocky and Bullwinkle cartoons and whenever Don Rickles wished to reference a hick town. Williams and Ree played an extended engagement at the Commercial Hotel as the opening act for an ancient musical comedy team with the worst toupees in the business.

Walt, Gene, John, and Emil Matys performed as the Matys Brothers. Back in the 1950s, they'd had a hit song in their hometown of Philadelphia called "Who Stole the Keeshka?" By the 1970s, they were stuck in the purgatory of Elko with their best days behind them. But for Terry Ree, the atmosphere was exciting, with the feel of big-time show business. "That whole circuit was a comedy college in the early seventies. We were opening for the Matys Brothers, and there was nobody—*nobody*—in the room. We did our act for an empty bar, but as soon the Matys Brothers were introduced—it was packed. They were four Polish guys from Pennsylvania and the drummer had an anger problem. He would become enraged and kick over his drum kit. We studied their comedy every night and learned how to direct and misdirect and how to do callbacks." While they learned tricks from the Matys Brothers, they picked up on the rhythms of the comedy teams they saw on television. Ree says, "In those days, the Smothers Brothers were real hot. We would watch them on TV on Sunday nights, and then go up onstage and *be* the Smothers Brothers. Bruce did the Tommy Smothers role and I'd be the aggravated straight man."

One night they decided to capitalize on the most obvious idea of all. "Everywhere we played, people called me the big Indian. I'd hear 'the big Indian this' and 'the big Indian that.' So we decided to use it." Accentuating the physical differences between the little white guy and the towering Lakota man became their essence, as they took turns insulting each other's ethnicity, running down a list of every possible racial stereotype. The new formula clicked, and Williams and Ree were well on their way to realizing their goals. A journalist from the *Reno Gazette-Journal* captured the atmosphere:

When I drifted through the Commercial Hotel in Elko last Friday, I caught a few words of what sounded like a raunchy act featuring an Uncle Tom Indian. Since they were followed by a bunch of old guys in wigs and polyester suits looking even more foolish, our group drifted out as fast as in. But after a hot day watching Basquos lift weights we returned to the Commercial, and sat down to an act so funny that the calories consumed in chorizo that day were probably laughed off by the second set. The act was Williams and Ree of Spear Fish, South Dakota. . . . From the start, Terry Ree, a Sioux Indian, lets loose with a string of "tipi creeper" slurs that could embarrass any redneck. Then the two warn the audience that "we are all the same," and if ethnic humor is offensive, leave. They roundly attack gays, handicapped, Mormons, Mexicans, Chinese, Scots, ugly women, blacks, and—in order not to leave Bruce Williams unscathed—Norwegians. . . . The act gets raunchier by the show, disintegrating in the early morning to, as Ree says, "total smut." Why is it funny and not offensive? . . . Maybe because it's an Indian up there laughing at stereotypes of himself and at people who make those stereotypes. . . . Ree simply credits the delivery, saying the material is weak.

The acts of the Silver Circle were expected to do several shows a night. It was a grueling routine, but it helped new comedians get better fast. "Three shows a night, sometimes four, even five shows a night," says Ree. "Those were the days of twenty-four-hour entertainment, but that swing shift was tough. It was only attended by the gamblers who ran out of money."

Like the Smothers Brothers, Williams and Ree would perform a straight song until Williams veered off script, butchering the lyrics or making a derogatory remark about his partner. Ree would stop and shoot Williams an angry look, staring him down with an indignant deadpan. It was the reaction on Ree's face that got the biggest laughs, although someone could always be found laughing for the wrong reasons. Williams and Ree had to clarify that while they played off stereotypes onstage, in real life they despised "prejudiced human beings, card-carrying, flag-waving bigots, and low, scum-sucking leeches." Bruce Williams said, "Our routine, our satire, happens onstage. When prejudice happens offstage, it's not funny."

They were held over at the Commercial Hotel, but not because of popularity. They'd been paid well, but blew it at the tables and ended up owing the casino money. It was a wise move to take care of your gambling debts. Nevada was still largely controlled by organized crime. "Being from South Dakota, we didn't realize the Mob was running these venues," says Ree. "It wasn't until after *The Godfather* came out that I thought, 'Wait a minute . . .' "

The death of Lake Tahoe casino operator Richard Chartrand was a typical Silver Circle story. *Variety* reported, "Chartrand was killed Tuesday morning when a bomb, secreted on the underside of his car, exploded as he was leaving his home. Chartrand's body was shattered by the explosion. . . . The force of the blast blew a hole in the pavement."

If you got on the Mob's bad side, you might be tortured or killed—but if you were a professional comic who kept your mouth shut, you were treated like a king. Ree says, "When the Mob ran things—those were fun days. Anywhere you went in Nevada you could get a breakfast for fifty cents or a steak dinner for a dollar. The Mafia was laundering money, running skimming operations, but it was fun. They took care of you. They gave you rooms. They gave you food. They gave you drinks. There was backstage catering and people to serve you whatever you needed. There were shows going on everywhere, all night long, all Mafia."

For their next engagement, Marv Dennis booked the boys at a gaudy casino-hotel 230 miles west of Elko. The Eldorado in Reno was surrounded by small motels with blinking neon lights. The Reno Royal Motor Lodge, the Bonanza Inn, the Keno Motel, the El Rey Motel, and the Star Dust Lodge all had magnetic marquees with missing letters. The Eldorado had a gold motif and atmosphere provided by rows of elderly women huffing on portable oxygen tanks, plunking coins into the nickel slots. Performing for the blue-hairs was tough, but it made the duo immune to impossible situations. Their ethnic references often enraged the crowd, but also garnered attention. "Sometimes we bomb," said Williams. "But even when we do bomb, people are still talking about us."

Williams and Ree took to the stage at 9 p.m., 11 p.m., and 1 a.m. six nights a week, with an extra show at 2:30 a.m. on the weekends. Logging a remarkable twenty shows every seven days, they received four times as much experience as any comedy contemporary playing the more sought-after rooms in Los Angeles.

Charlie Hill and a Bearded Comedian in a Rusty Red Truck

Charlie Hill arrived in Los Angeles at the end of 1974 with one goal in mind: stand-up. Perusing the entertainment section of the *Los Angeles Times*, he came across an advertisement for the Garden Theater Festival. The three-day event in East Hollywood's Barnsdall Park was developed by the son of Richard O. Linke, the wealthy talent manager who produced *The Andy Griffith Show, Gomer Pyle USMC*, and *My Mother the Car*. The festival featured experimental rock bands, counterculture street mimes, and young comedians. Hill stretched the truth and told the person on the other end of the line that he was a comedian who had just returned from a European tour. Sight unseen, he was granted ten minutes on the outdoor stage. He joined then-obscure performers like Danny Elfman and Al Franken, the former fronting a band called Oingo Boingo and the latter in the comedy team of Franken and Davis. Charlie Hill went onstage at 10 p.m., but the audience thought he was a roadie fiddling with the mic stand. "I figured I'd just get up there and talk," recalled Hill. "But I found out right away why they call it an *act*. It was frightening—staring at the microphone and seeing all those strange people drinking and staring at me." Nobody laughed, and Hill bombed hard.

Deflated but not defeated, he found a number of open mics in the

San Fernando Valley, including Tynes in Studio City, mainly patronized by jazz musicians, and the Palomino Club in North Hollywood, mainly patronized by country singers. Argus Hamilton was one of Hill's open-mic contemporaries. "Charlie worked the Palomino Club talent night when he first started, and it was a rowdy cowboy crowd," says Hamilton. "They got a big kick out of him because it was literally cowboys and Indians." But neither of those open mics were the place Hamilton and Hill were aiming for.

The Comedy Store had opened in May 1972, and it quickly became a scouting ground for major network television shows. Stand-up hopefuls lined up along Sunset Boulevard in the late afternoon, waiting to audition for Comedy Store matriarch Mitzi Shore. While the amateurs loitered, they got to know one another—forging bonds that lasted a lifetime. Hill stood in line behind a tall man with an orange beard and introduced himself.

"Hey, man. Charlie—from Oneida, Wisconsin."

"Hey. Dave from Indianapolis."

They chatted about their mutual *Tonight Show* dreams and became fast friends. Hill rode shotgun as Dave drove them around in a dented red truck, searching for any open mic they could find. "Letterman used to pick me up in this pickup truck and we'd go to all these gigs," said Hill. "I'd get on at two o'clock [in the morning] and he'd get on at two-fifteen. He'd always say, 'What are we doing this for?'" But the reason was obvious. The more shows you did, the better you got. They gained experience working for free, but Letterman was growing short on gas money, and Hill could no longer afford groceries. "I never knew true poverty until I became a comedian," said Hill. "There were times when I wouldn't have *anything*." In order to feed himself, he hung around the Echo Park United Methodist Church, where the famed Mohawk actor Jay Silverheels was running the Indian Actors Workshop, a theater that helped young Native actors break into the industry. Hill said that when he was starving he would "go to the Indian Actors Workshop [whenever] they'd have a . . . party and I'd take all the candies and pies and put them in my pockets for something to eat the next day."

Hill was also hanging out at the Native Friendship Center downtown, and it was there that he saw Buffy Sainte-Marie perform for the first time. The popular Cree singer-songwriter had the type of career in music that Hill wanted in comedy. A contemporary of Joni Mitchell with an unapologetic Native point of view, Sainte-Marie enjoyed crossover success as a socially conscious folk-pop hybrid. Hill said, "I met her at the Indian center in 1975. She took to me right away. She said, 'Well, give me a tape of what you're doing.' So I sent it to her, and a week later she called me up and she talked to me for two hours. . . . Then she came back to L.A. and I got to open for her."

Hill was extremely green, with barely ten minutes of material, but Sainte-Marie knew that the handsome, affable goofball would go over big with her audience—most of whom had never even heard of a Native comedian. "It was a real easy decision," she says. "I liked him and I thought the audience would love him—and they did."

Hill was delivering gags based on the collection of "My Favorite Jokes" clippings he'd used on Wisconsin radio, but merely mentioning he was Oneida made his performance a minor revelation. The audience delivered loud laughs of recognition. "His Great Lakes Indian look in itself broke stereotypes," says Sainte-Marie. "A little scruffy—just rez enough—good-looking and hip. He looked like where he came from." Here was a comedian with whom they could identify.

When Hill finally secured an audition at the Comedy Store, he was surprised to find Mitzi Shore's office decorated with Green Bay Packers memorabilia. Shore was delighted to learn that the handsome young man was from an area just down the highway from the house where she grew up. They spent an hour talking about Oneida, the University of Wisconsin, and the Broom Street Theater. Completely charmed without even seeing his material, she gave him plenty of stage time and full creative freedom. "We hit it off right from there," said Hill. "When I started playing some clubs, a lot of people were offended by my point of view. They didn't want to hear it. 'Do you *just* do Native material?' But Mitzi always let me do whatever I wanted onstage."

Shore was a loving mother to her collection of stand-up ne'er-do-wells, and the comedians bonded as they crammed the back hallway before and after their sets. "We were running in a posse of young comedians that all hung out together, partied together, wrote jokes together, did everything together," says Argus Hamilton. "We were—if you will pardon the expression—a tribe of comedians. That tribe included Ollie Joe Prater, a tremendous mountain-man type of comic; Vic Dunlop, a big, round, mustachioed comic with a tremendously funny face; Dave Tyree, an African American comic fresh out of Vietnam; Michael Keaton; and Robin Williams. It was essentially a pledge class, the Comedy Store pledge class of 1976. We'd go to Vic Dunlop's house off of Melrose Avenue and sit in his living room and get high. We would sit around that coffee table, smoking pot, writing jokes together. It was a very creative time. There was about a dozen of us. And Charlie Hill, this beautiful Native American man, handsome by every definition, was the most welcoming of all."

Occasionally Hill ditched his pot-smoking posse to join Buffy Sainte-Marie on the road. It was a different dynamic when he was with fellow Native artists, and he cherished every moment. Native audiences loved him, and he loved them right back. Hill always said, "When you do stand-up comedy in front of a Native crowd, you are performing in front of royalty."

During their long commutes from gig to gig, Sainte-Marie regaled Hill with stories of the fundraisers she had done in the 1960s with Stokely Carmichael, Muhammad Ali, Flip Wilson, and Charlie's hero, Dick Gregory. Sainte-Marie explained, "I brought Dick Gregory to Saskatchewan for an event defending Native land rights. It was an early turning point for him. I brought him to my reservation and, riding in the back of the plane, Dick was crying. He told me he thought he had seen poverty and abuse—until now. He already had a huge heart regarding marginalized people, but up until then he hadn't equated it with Indians."

Charlie and Buffy bonded on the road. "We had a mutual liking of each other's material and observations," says Sainte-Marie. "We also shared similar perspectives in being outsiders in show business, a foot in each of two canoes: grassroots/urban life and show-biz/traveling life. When we'd hang out, we would share our experiences about being the only Indian on the bill and sometimes the only Indian in the room."

Charlie and Buffy played fundraisers, rallies, and powwows together, but the conditions were not particularly conducive to stand-up. Charlie's brother Norbert Jr. recalls, "Some Indian gathering would have him come to a reservation where there was no microphone and no marketing. He would explain to them afterward, 'You *have* to have a microphone! You *have* to have chairs!' Stand-up comedy was all new in Indian Country."

Charlie recalled, "When I would do an AIM benefit—it'd be a bullhorn on the back of a porch. They took the blows for us. Everybody started asserting their treaty rights. Everybody started asserting their pride. Everybody just started talking the talk more."

Whether you were in favor of the American Indian Movement or directly opposed to their brash tactics, AIM brought Native issues to the mainstream press that otherwise would have been ignored. Dick Wilson, chairman of the Oglala Lakota tribe, was accused of using a private militia to intimidate residents and rig elections in 1973. AIM got a phone call from some of the locals requesting help. One hundred AIM members descended on Pine Ridge, and the result was an armed standoff between Wilson's self-proclaimed Guardians of the Oglala Nation (GOON) and AIM. The FBI lent support to Wilson, providing military-level firepower. Massive amounts of gunfire were exchanged in both directions during the seventy-one-day impasse, and images of the siege were broadcast around the world. It came to symbolize the bitter and strained relationship between the federal government and Native America. "Things won't ever be the same again—and that's what the American Indian Movement is all about," said AIM member Birgil Kills Straight. "We are the shock troops of Indian sovereignty. We intend to raise questions in the minds of all—questions that have gone to sleep in the minds of Indians and non-Indians alike. AIM is the new warrior class of the century, bound by the bond of the drum, who vote with our bodies instead of our mouths."

For white liberals, it became a cause célèbre. Eric Burdon, lead singer of the British rock group the Animals, had a typical hippie obsession and superficial understanding of Native Americans. "If you look at that AIM situation, there was a lot of the hippies [who were] being influenced by the Indian movement," said Burdon. "And although the Indians weren't that happy about that . . . to see these young kids copying their dress styles and getting to sweat lodges and all of that kind of stuff . . . All they needed was a definite power and a definite force to rally people to their cause—and [Jimi] Hendrix would have definitely been the guy for that."

Will Rogers Jr. endorsed AIM's armed insurrection. "There was nothing else they could do. In the long run, I think it'll be seen as beneficial. Indians thirty years from now will be able to look back and say, 'They stood up and said they were through being used.' It'll be a rallying point for constructive change." Rogers warned that armed standoffs were likely to occur again until control of natural resources was given back to the Native nations. "The stark naked fact is that all the other problems will stay with Indians as long as they don't control the resources and use of the lands which are supposed to be theirs. Indian business is big business. Oil, copper, timber, coal, all are on reservations in vast quantities—and they're being exploited by whites. In the West particularly, extensive water rights are held, or supposedly held, by Indians. In the Dakotas, rich grazing and farming land supposedly on the Sioux reservation is actually owned by white ranchers. Some of the most difficult and long-range work in the area of Indian rights is in the courts, fighting for control of the lands Indians are supposed to own by treaties. . . . Effective change in social conditions takes years of hard work. Russell Means and the other AIM leaders are very intelligent men, and they're not going to be talked down to."

In 1975, AIM leader Dennis Banks was placed on trial for inciting a riot in Custer, South Dakota. Charlie Hill played a fundraiser for his legal defense in San Francisco. A group of hippie spillovers from the Haight-Ashbury area were in the crowd and invited Hill to do a set at their temple a few blocks away. When he got there, Hill learned it was the People's Temple, run by the notorious cult leader Jim Jones. "He liked my goddamned act," said Hill. "Jim Jones thought I was funny."

Playing reservations, friendship centers, and community events, Charlie Hill slowly shed the crutch of jokebook material and replaced it with an earnest, personal point of view. "Dick Gregory did a lot of material on civil rights and Black issues," said Hill. "He also talked about experiences we have in common. That's what I'm doing from a Native American viewpoint to defuse that traditional John Wayne mentality."

Hill returned to the Comedy Store in early 1976 and walked into the greenroom to scan the sheet of paper taped on the wall to see what time he was going on. Scrawled in jiffy marker, the rundown said:

> *8:30 Argus Hamilton*
> *8:45 Howie Mandel*
> *9:00 Mike Binder*
> *9:15 Barry Diamond*
> *9:30 Ronny Kenney*
> *9:50 Jeff Altman*

10:10 *Jimmie Walker*
10:30 *Larry David*
10:50 *Allan Stephan*
11:10 *Jimmy Brogan*
11:30 *Jay Leno*
11:50 *Joe Restivo*
12:10 *Charlie Hill*
12:30 *Paul Mooney*

Hill took to the stage with the hand drum his father had gifted him before he left Wisconsin. He used it to re-create the cliché sound heard in hundreds of western movies, a tom-tom rhythm that went: *dum-dum-DUM-dum, dum-dum-DUM-dum, dum-dum-DUM-dum*. Hill looked out to the audience and asked in rhythm, "Hi-how-are-ya? Hi-how-are-ya? Hi-how-are-ya?" Hill then scanned the crowd and pointed at a college student: "How-high-are-ya? How-high-are-ya? How-high-are-ya?"

Hill asked the audience to imagine what it would be like if the world's most famous comedians were Native American. As examples he presented Rodney Dangerfoot ("I tell ya, American Indians get no respect"), Henny Youngblood ("Take my land—please!"), and a Native version of the Three Stooges: Geroni-Larry, Geroni-Curly, and Geroni-Moe.

"He'd do all these 'I get no respect' jokes, one line after another, and have the crowd on the floor," says Argus Hamilton. "Then he would break into his normal routine, complaining about sports teams like the Cleveland Indians, wondering why there were no teams named the Kansas City Caucasians." Hill joked about his activist friends who ranted against the white man. "When you say 'white man,' it's always singular. The white man this. The white man that. I'm wondering—who is this guy? Because he's screwing it up for everybody."

Sometimes Hill walked onstage carrying a picture frame concealed by a blanket. It was a visual gag based on an old street joke. "He'd lay the picture down on a chair and then go into his Rodney Dangerfoot routine," says Hamilton. "At the end of his act he walked over and revealed this thing. It was a big four-by-three painting of a meadow, this pastoral landscape. It showed a cow with a halo over its head. On a hillside were fifty Native American men having sex with fifty elderly white ladies." As the crowd looked up in bewilderment, Hill said, "I call this painting *Custer's Last Words*: 'Holy cow—look at all those motherfucking Indians.'"

Hill was onstage doing this routine one evening while Redd Foxx stood at the back of the room, buzzing from a combination of marijuana, cocaine, and cognac. He flagged Hill down as he left the stage and lavished him with compliments, suggesting they collaborate. "He was making a big deal about it," said Hill. "I was embarrassed 'cause I'd only been in Hollywood for [a few] months and I was just green." Foxx told Hill to phone him in a few days to talk about potential projects. "I called him up," said Hill. "He didn't even remember who I was."

The Comedy Store had three locations in the late 1970s: a flagship location on the Sunset Strip in Hollywood, a club in the Westwood area of Los Angeles, and one in San Diego's La Jolla district. Argus Hamilton says the Westwood room was one of the best places to perform. "It had been an old two-hundred-thirty-five-seat room called Ledbetter's. It had once been the main room for the New Christy Minstrels [folk group]. Mitzi bought the lease and refashioned it into a comedy club, but she couldn't afford another liquor license. She made it like a little restaurant instead, and this meant eighteen-year-olds could attend. Suddenly all the kids from UCLA were coming there on the weekends. Mitzi sent us to Westwood to develop, and in Charlie Hill, she saw a superstar. Charlie played Westwood every single night—and the laughter just bounced off the walls." Hill would open his set by counting the heads of people in the audience to the tune of "Ten Little Indians": "One little, two little, three little whiteys . . ." He went over big in La Jolla as well. His fellow comic Allan Stephan says, "Charlie killed a lot of places, but down there in La Jolla he *killed*-killed. We worked that room a lot together. He was a pot smoker and I was a pot smoker. We'd get high and laugh and laugh."

Westwood and La Jolla had superior acoustics, but it was the flagship location on the Sunset Strip that Richard Pryor used as his workout room. Whenever he was developing new material, getting ready for a *Tonight Show* appearance, or prepping for a stand-up special, Pryor dropped by. Hill was onstage one night when Pryor walked in. Pryor loved the way Hill roasted the white people in the crowd. He ran up to Charlie afterward and dragged him into the parking lot to smoke a joint. Pryor told him, "We have to get together, motherfucker! You talk to these white people like they're *dogs!*"

Hill said Pryor had "an incredible respect for Indian people. Every time I saw him he had time for me. He took me to the movies and he took me to his house. He asked, 'You ever been on TV?' I said, 'No, I'm just starting out.' He said, 'I'll get you on.'"

Comedian Paul Mooney was in the process of casting *The Richard Pryor Show*, a new sketch comedy program for NBC. And whenever Mooney was onstage at the Comedy Store, Charlie Hill's loud, Ricky Ricardo–esque laugh could be heard echoing through the room. "The Indians were here first," Mooney told a late-night crowd. "If I was an Indian? I would hate *every-body*. . . . The Indians were here and it was cool. And then they started sending all the riffraff from Europe. It's true! They sent the *riffraff*."

For Mooney, getting a rise out of his audience was just as good as getting a laugh. He was the comedian as provocateur. For *The Richard Pryor Show* he wanted a cast of comedians who could do the same. He brought in the cocky Sandra Bernhard, the manic Robin

Williams, and the pre–Venus Flytrap stylings of Tim Reid, although none of them did stand-up on the program. *The Richard Pryor Show* was strictly sketch comedy—with one notable exception.

"Charlie Hill, the 26-year-old Oneida, now living in Los Angeles, will be appearing on . . . *The Richard Pryor Show* next Tuesday," reported the *Green Bay Press-Gazette*. "It's the biggest and most exciting step in the budding comedian's career."

Williams and Ree Are Desperate
to Get on Carson

Williams and Ree were in a hotel room watching *The Tonight Show* the first time they heard Johnny Carson mention the Comedy Store. After playing the Silver Circle for more than a year, they returned to South Dakota to consider their next move. Terry Ree was at home when he received a visit from a local television personality who wore a sailor's hat and introduced Popeye cartoons on KELO-TV. "There was a knock on my door one morning and it was this guy, Dave Dedrick, a TV announcer on Channel Eleven, who had his own kiddie show called *Captain Eleven*. He told me, 'I have a friend who runs the Holiday Inn in Sioux Falls. He'll take care of you guys if you want to give him a call.'"

The Holiday Inn in Sioux Falls resembled a parody of the 1970s. Six nights a week, Williams and Ree were surrounded by its garish aesthetics. "It was a revolving dining room," Ree recalls. "The room went around on a big wheel. At the start of the show, the audience was right in front of us. Halfway through the show, they were on the other side of the room."

Richard Pryor, Cheech and Chong, and George Carlin were having great success with comedy records in the 1970s, so Williams and Ree decided to make one of their own. They plugged a tape recorder directly into the amplifier and released a cheap vanity pressing called *Buck Fuffalo*. They sold the album after each gig, but the audio was largely inaudible. "Williams & Ree follow the usual pattern of such teams on the outskirts of the big town," wrote *Variety*. "Pair have an album and hawk it from the stage, a desperate play that doesn't seem to fire up too much reaction or sales."

They'd been playing the lounge scene for seven years, making a passable living, but with no opportunity for advancement.

"We were getting tired of working for the drunks at the Holiday Inns and the Sheratons and the Ramadas. When we were on the road, we'd watch Johnny Carson in our hotel room, and whenever he had comedians on, he would always mention the Comedy Store. We figured it out. The Comedy Store led to an appearance on *The Tonight Show*. We decided that if we were going to make it, we'd have to go to where it's at—so we drove to California."

Williams and Ree arrived in Hollywood at a time when the Comedy Store favorites included Gallagher, Jimmie Walker, David Letterman, Jay Leno, and Charlie Hill. But for their first gig, they shared the lineup with a parade of losers. "I called Mitzi Shore, and she told us to come in Monday night at nine o'clock," says Ree. "It was an open mic free-for-all with all these weird people getting up, none of whom were funny. The crowd was booing. Mitzi came in right at nine and sat at a table with Robin Williams and Richard Pryor. We went up and did our five minutes. It was probably just luck—but we killed." As they left the stage, Bruce Williams joked about Hollywood's penchant for casting white people in Native roles: "The part of the Indian was played by Bob Bergland."

The other comics wondered where the hell these guys had come from. "It looked like they had a lot of experience," remembers comedian Jeff Altman. "You got the feeling they had arrived from some dive in Las Vegas. When they showed up at the Comedy Store, they were a pretty polished act." Terry Ree admitted, "Bruce and I have ten years together. If we're not funny, we're certainly professional."

Mitzi Shore added them to the Comedy Store rotation even though a lot of their material was designed for the patrons of South Dakota truck stops and Nevada mining towns. Some of the material was an obstacle to TV. "In the middle of the act, Bruce would hold my hand," says Ree. "He'd say [lisping], 'Let's go do something!' and I would shake him off and say, 'What the hell are you doing?' We lost The Merv Griffin Show because of that. They didn't like the gay stuff."

The Comedy Store was the place to be seen by television scouts, but the road was where Williams and Ree made their money. Mitzi Shore didn't pay any of the comedians at her venue. In her opinion, the chance to meet a Tonight Show booker was payment enough. "We'd work at the Comedy Store for two weeks and then do the road for two weeks," says Ree. "We did that for three years."

They were sent to La Jolla to open for David Letterman, who had just been signed by the Management Consultant Company, a firm started by comedian Jimmie Walker with his agent Helen Kushnick. "Walker would watch the acts, and if he liked them, he would sign them to his company," says Ree. "He signed Jay Leno and he signed David Letterman, and sure enough, he signed us too." Their management pushed them on Norman Lear, who was preparing In the Beginning, a sitcom starring McLean Stevenson as a priest in charge of a halfway house, but the project failed and Williams and Ree were dropped by the agency. "Our agents started jacking us around," said Williams. "Some flimsy story about us not being funny."

With or without a manager, Williams and Ree got work. They were booked on the first regular stand-up series, Norm Crosby's Comedy Shop, and played a week on the comedy game show Make Me Laugh. They shared the panel with Henry Winkler on Dinah

PIONEER PERILS IN THE EARLY DAYS OF THE ORIGINAL DEADWOOD STAGE COACH
AN ATTACK BY HOSTILE INDIANS AND RESCUE BY THE COW BOYS

The traveling road show of Buffalo Bill did much to establish the racist stereotypes that turned into western movie clichés. *Harry Ransom Center, the University of Texas at Austin*

After being forced to learn English at the Carlisle Indian School, Chauncey Yellow Robe became one of the most outspoken critics of the boarding school system, Wild West shows, and racist stereotypes in silent film. *Cumberland County Historical Society, Carlisle, PA*

Chauncey Yellow Robe at the Carlisle Indian School, where students were exploited by the government for the purpose of propaganda. *National Anthropological Archives, Smithsonian Institution*

MASTER KARLH WAYNE

OF

Clifford Wayne Trio

Alexander Posey of the Muscogee Creek Nation was the first Indigenous humorist of the twentieth century. *Oklahoma Historical Society*

Master Karlh was a child comic with the Clifford Wayne Trio. His impish comedy act made him one of the top Indigenous acts in vaudeville when he was only four years old. *1923 National Vaudeville Artists' Year Book*

Cherokee humorist Will Rogers (left) with a childhood friend in the 1890s.
Image courtesy of the Will Rogers Memorial Museum, Claremore, OK

The wardrobe of Will Rogers was informed by Cherokee ranching culture. *Image courtesy of the Will Rogers Memorial Museum, Claremore, OK*

Will Rogers was one of the most famous personalities of the early twentieth century, but his status as a proud Native American has been obscured over the years. *Image courtesy of the Will Rogers Memorial Museum, Claremore, OK*

Will Rogers was famous for the rope tricks he learned from an African American cowboy. In his left hand he holds his first child, Will Rogers Jr., while roping with his right. *Image courtesy of the Will Rogers Memorial Museum, Claremore, OK*

Will Rogers Jr. lived in the shadow of his famous dad. "I was dismayed by being asked to live up to the model of my father," he said. "I was expected to sparkle and be witty. Well, I just didn't have it." *Photo by Marie Hansen/The LIFE Picture Collection via Getty Images*

Jackie Curtiss was born into the circus where his Mohawk mother worked as a ticket taker. After several years as a child acrobat, he became a big band singer, stand-up comedian, and booker of the Playboy Club in Los Angeles.
Jackie Curtiss

Jackie Curtiss holding Ed Sullivan like a baby. He appeared on *The Ed Sullivan Show* several times as part of his comedy team, Antone and Curtiss.
Jackie Curtiss

Jackie Curtiss remained active as a cruise ship comedian in the 1970s and '80s.
Jackie Curtiss

Paul Littlechief
got his start as a
rockabilly musician
under the name
Chief Little Chief.
Jocelyn Littlechief

Paul Littlechief was considered one of the most exciting
performers along the Silver Circle in Nevada, a dense circuit
of nightclubs around Reno and Lake Tahoe.
Jocelyn Littlechief

Vine Deloria Jr. authored *Custer Died for Your Sins* in 1969. The influential book had an effect on comedian Charlie Hill and featured a chapter called "Indian Humor." *Denver Post via Getty Images*

Poet and political activist John Trudell used sarcastic humor in *We Hold the Rock,* a manifesto explaining the purpose of the Alcatraz occupation.
Photo by Michelle VIGNES/Gamma-Rapho via Getty Images

Charlie Hill was the first Native American comedian of the comedy club era. His appearance on *The Richard Pryor Show* in 1977 was a galvanizing moment.
Nasbah Hill Collection

Oneida comedian Charlie Hill got his start with the American Indian Theatre Ensemble in the early 1970s. Headquartered at the La MaMa Theatre in Greenwich Village, the name was eventually changed to the Native American Theater Ensemble. Hill is on the left with a bandana on his head and a clenched fist in the air. *Couresty of the LA MAMA Archive. Photo credit: Amnon Ben Nomis*

Charlie Hill wearing a
Comedy Store shirt circa 1980.
Hill's stand-up contemporaries
at the Comedy Store included
Michael Keaton, Jay Leno, and
David Letterman.
Nasbah Hill Collection

Comedy Store regulars Charlie Hill, John Witherspoon, and Robin
Williams. *Louie Anderson*

Richard Pryor handing the mic to Charlie Hill for his 1977 television debut on *The Richard Pryor Show*.
The Richard Pryor Show

In 1978, Charlie Hill became the first Native comedian to do *The Tonight Show Starring Johnny Carson*.
The Tonight Show Starring Johnny Carson

Charlie Hill appeared on *Late Night with David Letterman* in 1985.
Late Night with David Letterman

Williams and Ree have played thousands of shows in small taverns, roadhouses, truck stops, and county fairs. They moved to Hollywood to try their hand at the Comedy Store in 1977 because they got "tired of working for the drunks at the Holiday Inns and the Sheratons and the Ramadas." After a remarkable fifty-two consecutive years on the road, they are the longest-running comedy team in show business.
The Argus Leader

Larry Omaha was one of the most polished Native American comedians of the 1980s comedy club boom. *Larry Omaha Collection*

The 1491s backstage before a live show. Christopher Columbus arrived in 1492, hence the name "the 1491s." *Photo by Shane Brown*

From left to right: Thomas Ryan RedCorn, Dallas Goldtooth, Sterlin Harjo, Migizi Pensoneau, and Bobby Wilson onstage as the 1491s. Fans travel hundreds of miles to see them in person. *Photo by Shane Brown*

Jonny Roberts balances stand-up with family responsibilities in the Red Lake Nation. A comedy fan his entire life, he wonders if and when his big break will occur. *Courtesy of Jonny Roberts*

Adrianne Chalepah formed the Ladies of Native Comedy to expand female representation in the scene. *Courtesy of Matthew Williamson*

Brian Bahe, a Navajo-Hopi-Tohono O'odham stand-up, does an average of twelve gigs a week in Manhattan. Some of his Indigenous contemporaries only get to do twelve gigs a year. *Photo by Jordan Ashleigh*

Craig Lauzon's performance on the Canadian television special *Welcome to Turtle Island* inspired several future Native comedians to get into the business. *Denise Grant Photography*

Dakota Ray Hebert from the English River First Nation says there has been an "influx of Indigenous comics that have grown up on the rez—and now there's a good scene." *Tenille Campbell, Sweetmoon Photography*

Cree comedian Howie Miller was something of a novelty along the comedy club circuit as the only First Nations comic doing impressions. *Ryan Parker*

Jackie Keliiaa produces Native comedy events. The Paiute-Washoe comic called her initial exposure to Charlie Hill "transformative." *Katy Karns*

Saulteaux/Cree comedian Vance Banzo stars in the sketch comedy show *TallBoyz*. He was mentored by Bruce McCulloch from the Kids in the Hall. *Matt Barnes*

Cowlitz comedian Joey Clift produces events at the Upright Citizens Brigade theater in Hollywood. *Robyn Von Swank*

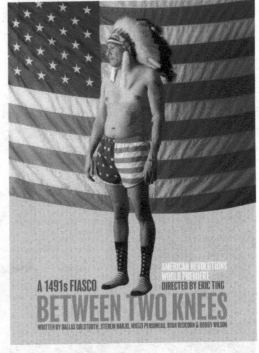

The critically acclaimed *Between Two Knees* played to sold-out crowds at the Oregon Shakespeare Festival. The sketch comedy opus from the 1491s addressed residential schools, genocide, and other bleak topics using a joke-driven narrative reminiscent of Mel Brooks's *History of the World, Part I.*
Thomas Ryan RedCorn

AMERICAN REVOLUTIONS
WORLD PREMIERE
A 1491s FIASCO   DIRECTED BY ERIC TING
BETWEEN TWO KNEES
WRITTEN BY DALLAS GOLDTOOTH, STERLIN HARJO, MIGIZI PENSONEAU, RYAN REDCORN & BOBBY WILSON

Jiles Turning Heart and Bobby Wilson joking around at a powwow as part of Thomas Ryan RedCorn's photography project "Under the Powwow Bleachers."
Thomas Ryan RedCorn

Charlie Hill's career slowed down in his final years just as his influence on a new generation of Native comedians became apparent. *Photo by Chris Felver/Getty Images*

Shore's daytime talk show and appeared on an episode of *Don Kirshner's Rock Concert* with Black Sabbath. Television exposure increased their value on the road. "When you get the TV credits, you become a recognized draw in a Reno-Tahoe-Vegas situation, which is where the money is," said Ree. "If you have a recognized name . . . they pay you that ridiculous salary to work." Charlie Hill might have been the most respected Native American comedian in town, but Terry Ree was the wealthiest. They shared a mutual respect. "We met at the Comedy Store, and we did a lot of Native shows together over the years," says Ree. "His act would absolutely slap white people in the face. I did the same thing, but delivered it a lot more gently. Charlie's tone was: 'You sons of bitches *did this*.' We became good friends."

But the most important television appearance eluded Williams and Ree. To get on *The Tonight Show*, a comedian first had to impress the fussy gatekeeper. Jim McCawley was the show's talent coordinator in charge of comedians. He watched Williams and Ree destroy at the Comedy Store and spoke to them afterward about their potential. McCawley told them to prepare three different routines for *The Tonight Show* to choose from. As requested, they honed three six-minute sets over and over, week after week. And then they waited. And waited. And waited. Whenever they followed up with McCawley, he was in no condition to talk business. "He was *wasted* every time that I saw him," says Ree. "He would come into the Comedy Store to watch, but the guy was an alcoholic. Finally after months of this, I called McCawley and asked him, 'Jim, are we ever going to get that shot at *The Tonight Show*? We have our three six-minute sets ready to go.' He said, 'Nah, there's two of you—and Johnny doesn't like that. Neither of you are funny—and *I* don't like that. You'll never do *The Tonight Show*.'"

It signified the end of their Hollywood adventure. "We had a good time, but we didn't do anything," said Ree. "So now we're

Charlie Hill Asks Barney Miller
to Free Leonard Peltier

Mitzi Shore left the Comedy Store for the afternoon to attend a taping at the NBC facility in Burbank. She was sitting in the front row with Argus Hamilton to witness a breakthrough in Native American representation. Charlie Hill's dream was realized on October 20, 1977, when he had his network television debut on *The Richard Pryor Show*. "I was twenty-six years old and I was thrilled," said Hill. "I couldn't believe it."

Richard Pryor and Paul Mooney had hired him to perform in sketches like the rest of the cast, but when Hill scanned the script, he found the material insulting. "They wanted me to be in a sketch . . . called 'White for a Day,' and it was real demeaning. I didn't want to do it. I said, 'I can't do this sketch, this is too racist.'" Pryor nodded. "Okay, well, how about I give you five minutes and you just do whatever you want?" Hill wanted to do stand-up.

The art department worked overtime to create an incongruous "Indian backdrop" that bore no relation to Oneida. Hill said, "They had the scenery set up like it was out in the desert, a big rock there and everything. They wanted Richard to come out dressed like Custer and he'd fall down with these arrows in his back. I thought that was real stupid, and so did Richard. He refused to do it, but they already had the scenery out there, so he just brought me on."

Pryor delivered his introduction in a hushed tone: "I'd like to introduce now a new talent on the show. He's an Indian brother. Iroquois Nation. Mr. Charlie Hill—please welcome." Hill took to the stage in a red shirt and blue jeans, long black hair down to his shoulders, a snappy-looking kerchief tied around his neck:

Hi-how-are-ya, hi-how-are-ya, hi-how-are-ya, hi-how-are-ya? I usually have problems doing my act, you know, 'cause I know a lot of you white people have never seen an Indian do stand-up comedy before. Like, for so long you probably thought that Indians never had a sense of humor. [*pause*] We never thought you were too funny either. [*laughter and applause*]

[*Hill points*] There's people back there putting their chairs in a circle.

[*laughter*]

My name is Charlie Hill. Sekoli. I'm Oneida. I'm from Wisconsin—it's part of the Iroquois Nation. My people are from Wisconsin. We used to be from New York. We had a little real estate problem.

[*laughter*]

Ah, Indians. Y'know, people come up to me now too and they say, "Can you speak Indian?" There are, like, over three hundred different tribes, y'know. "Can you speak Indian?" That's like saying, "Hey, can you speak Caucasian?"

[*laughter*]

But that's the name they gave us. Indians. Indians is a name Christopher Columbus gave us, which is incorrect. He named us Indians because he thought he was in India. Sure glad he wasn't looking for Turkey.

[*laughter*]

Would change a lot of things. Columbus discovered America. They taught me that when I was a kid. Columbus discovered Indians. That was my education . . . I went to Custer Memorial Junior High.

[*laughter and applause*]

They taught me a lot of things I couldn't relate to. Like the Pilgrims. They weren't my forefathers. Pilgrims came to this land four hundred years ago as illegal aliens. We used to call them whitebacks.

[*laughter*]

They started unloading the boats, building houses. First thing we asked them, "You guys gonna stay the night?" Doesn't that just burn you up when people come over and they never leave?

[*laughter*]

Good crowd. . . . I just have a dream, and that's that someday I will get into the movies, right? And then I will win an Academy Award—and then I'll refuse it because of the mistreatment of Marlon Brando.

[*laughter and applause*]

Mitzi Shore beamed with pride. "I was sitting right next to Mitzi, and it meant so much to Charlie that she was there," says Argus Hamilton. "We were right in the front row. It was his first time on national television, and he just *destroyed*. We were all so happy for him, and he cried afterward. Mitzi was so proud of him."

More than fifteen million viewers watched Charlie Hill's stand-up debut, and he was suddenly in demand. He was asked to play white comedy clubs, mainstream talk shows, Indigenous fundraisers, and Native gatherings. "It was almost like talking two different languages when you'd play to each crowd," said Hill. "I learned how to do it in both worlds."

From there Charlie Hill appeared on *The Mike Douglas Show*, sharing the panel with actor Elliott Gould. Charlie's brother Norbert Jr. was in Boulder, Colorado, adjusting the rabbit ears on his twenty-eight-inch television set, trying to improve the reception. Mike Douglas kidded with the comedian, "Charlie, I bet when you were a kid you played a lot of cowboys and Indians." The program's producer, Roger Ailes, was caught off guard by Hill's response. "It has never been cowboys and Indians," he replied. "That's a myth. It has always been *government* and Indians. When I was a child, my father took me by the hand and said, 'Charlie, my boy, someday . . . none of this will be yours.' No, we never played cowboys and Indians. But we did play Nazis and Jews. The rules are the same."

Hill appeared on *The Mike Douglas Show* and *The Merv Griffin Show* several times. The daytime talk show circuit was like a farm league for those working their way up to *The Tonight Show*, and Hill found himself sharing panels with Anthony Quinn, Mel Tormé, Buddy Rich, William Shatner, Julia Child, Gavin MacLeod, Dr. Joyce Brothers, Eartha Kitt, Mickey Rooney, and Milton Berle. TV critic Jack O'Brian wrote, "Charlie Hill, the Indian comic with Merv Griffin, was a most original clown with bitingly fresh, cheerfully impudent material about an essentially solemn condition: the plight of the Indian over the centuries of broken treaties, bigotry, rejection, suffering, and worse."

Three years after arriving in Hollywood, he had firmly established himself. The tours with Buffy Sainte-Marie, the nights at the Comedy Store, the honky-tonks in the San Fernando Valley—all of it led up to his big moment. Jim McCawley might have rejected Williams and Ree, but he worked with Charlie Hill to perfect his debut as the first Native American comedian in *Tonight Show* history.

Charlie showed up on the soundstage wearing a silk western shirt, blue jeans, and a large white belt buckle. He paced nervously in the greenroom and exchanged pleasantries with the musical guest, Mel Tillis. Hill had come a long way. In a few minutes, Johnny Carson would be introducing him. It was a monumental moment not only for Charlie Hill but for Native Americans everywhere.

"We used to be from New York. . . . We had a little real estate problem." The audience loved it, and Johnny Carson could be heard cackling off-camera. Hill tugged at his collar and muttered in a Rodney Dangerfield voice, "I tell ya—Indians get no respect." He went into Henny Youngblood: "Take my land—please." When Hill finished, Carson flashed an okay sign, chuckling, "Take my land—*please*. We'll be [*laughing*] . . . we'll be right back." When Charlie returned to the greenroom, he found a bouquet of roses and a card: "You did great, kid. Love, Robin Williams."

"After Charlie appeared on Johnny Carson, Indians felt proud," says Norbert Hill Jr. "They stood a little taller. There was this feeling: 'He's one of us.'" A newspaper back home wrote, "There he was, right there on *The Tonight Show*, saying he was an Oneida Indian from Wisconsin, and knocking 'em dead as a stand-up comic. He is Charlie Hill, indeed from Oneida, Wisc., where his father, Norbert, is vice chairman of the Oneida tribe. 'I'd like to see a team named, say, the Kansas City Caucasians,' he said in his appearance recently on the Carson show. 'They could have a white [mascot] in center field dressed in a leisure suit dancing around a mobile home.'"

The triumphant performance led to other high-profile jobs. He landed a guest shot on *The Bionic Woman*, the popular spin-off of *The Six Million Dollar Man*, in which Lindsay Wagner played a robotic crime fighter. It was campy family fare with a strong female role model, marketed to kids in the form of lunch boxes, board games, and bedsheets. Hill played a doctor who, after being murdered by mobsters, returns as a ghost to have sex with the Bionic Woman. The interracial, interdimensional love scenes were groundbreaking, according to the program's star. Lindsay Wagner says, "*The Bionic Woman* was a breakthrough for women on television even though it was basically a kids' show. It was a whole time of change. We were intentionally doing stories about things we wanted to see accepted and embraced in the culture. The fact that Charlie's character was dating the Bionic Woman in this episode was a *huge* thing. That just did not happen on television. The star of a show never did any interracial dating."

Hill invited his Comedy Store cronies to visit him on the Universal lot. Argus Hamilton, Allan Stephan, Mike Binder, and Ollie Joe Prater all took full advantage of the free food provided by craft services. "It was a kick hanging with him there," says Hamilton. "But we didn't have a lot of time with Charlie on the set. He was in Lindsay Wagner's trailer—*a lot.*"

Wagner was one of the biggest television stars in the country at the time, and it was Hill who hipped her to the differences between Native nations. He convinced her to join him at a powwow in Colorado. "She had her own plane, and they flew up to Boulder," recalls Norbert Jr. "I picked them up at the airport and we went out to eat, but some dorky kid recognized her and she got mobbed. The next night we went to the powwow and word spread that she was there, and we had to *run* back to our car. It was hard to go anywhere, but she was delightful."

"I learned a lot and became very active in Native American issues as a result of our relationship," says Wagner. "He really educated me in a much clearer way. When we met, the Sun Dance, the religious ceremony, had *just* been legalized. It was against the law for a hundred years. That was shocking to me. I had no idea."

From afar it looked like romance, but Wagner says network executives frowned on anything beyond friendship. "At that time my career was going at lightning speed. I didn't get to do a heck of a lot of anything outside of my work. We were interested in each other and it could have possibly turned into dating, but it was an awkward time. There was pressure from certain parties that this might not be a good idea."

IN THE LATE 1970s, one of the most popular comedies on television was *Barney Miller*. One of Charlie Hill's best friends was Max Gail, the white actor who portrayed Detective Stan "Wojo" Wojciehowicz on the sitcom. Gail had worked as a musician before entering the acting field. "I was dating a woman who was best friends with Buffy Sainte-Marie," says Gail. "She hired me to open for her at the Indian Center in Oakland in front of three hundred people. I didn't even know there was an Indian Center in Oakland. I didn't know there were three hundred Indians in Oakland. I didn't know anything about this world. I had just been cast on *Barney Miller*."

Gail had been playing classical piano in upscale hotel lounges. His muscular frame looked incongruous as it burst through his tuxedo, but it was a look that served him well as an actor. "I was working in San Francisco, playing music in a piano bar, when I started taking acting lessons," he says. "I saw in the paper they were looking for understudies for a new production of *One Flew Over the Cuckoo's Nest*. I ended up understudying as the Chief. A few days in, the guy who was playing the Chief got into a shoving match with one of the actors, and suddenly I had the part. I realized that Ken Kesey, the guy who wrote it, only had a superficial concept of Indians, so I started reading things like *Bury My Heart at Wounded Knee* by Dee Brown to give myself a better understanding."

After a spell playing menacing hoodlums on TV shows like *Cannon* and *Ironside*, Gail joined the cast of *Barney Miller*, playing a ne'er-do-well police officer alongside Hal Linden, Ron Glass, and Jack Soo. By the time his girlfriend dragged him to his first powwow, his face was on the cover of *TV Guide*.

Attendees squinted in disbelief as the *Barney Miller* star wandered the grounds. Buffy Sainte-Marie introduced him to her friends. "I climbed into the back of Buffy's camper and found Charlie Hill lying there catching some sun," says Gail. "Charlie and I had a lot in common. We both grew up in Detroit, we were the same age, and we connected immediately." Sainte-Marie also introduced him to AIM leader Dennis Banks and the Sisseton Wahpeton Dakota singer Floyd Westerman, sometimes referred to as "the Indian Johnny Cash." Gail says, "Floyd took me to Vine Deloria Jr.'s house. I didn't even know who he was, but after that I got some of his books like *Custer Died for Your Sins* and read them. It opened up a whole new world to me."

The actor used his newfound celebrity to bring attention to various Native causes. He was an unlikely ally, bantering with Abe Vigoda in Hollywood one day, marching in protests with Dennis Banks the next. His sitcom contemporaries thought he was bonkers. "I'd tell people at *Barney Miller* about this stuff and I'd get one of two reactions—'Wow, that's so cool,' or 'Jeez, Max is losing it.' A lot of people didn't understand."

The careers of Max Gail and Charlie Hill were at an all-time high. Between appearances on *Don Kirshner's Rock Concert* and *Make Me Laugh*, Hill was performing at fundraisers that supported Leonard Peltier's legal defense. An enforcer and bodyguard for Dennis Banks, Peltier was accused of widespread criminal activity throughout the 1970s, including several murders. Aware that he was being sought by the FBI, Peltier went underground and eluded authorities until 1975. That summer he was present during a gun battle at Pine Ridge in which two FBI agents were killed. Charged with double homicide using an AR-15, his supporters were convinced he was being railroaded. Peltier became the latest symbol of the age-old battle between the federal government and Native peoples, but David Treuer, the Ojibwe author of *The Heartbeat of Wounded Knee*, says it amounted to the deification of a violent misogynist: "Those who see him as a hero . . . [say he] had been targeted for his politics, even though . . . he hadn't done anything much more political than accompanying Banks . . . and whatever reasons the cops had for arresting him were probably very real. The only thing clear . . . was that Peltier was dangerous."

Charlie Hill stood in a packed federal court building in downtown Los Angeles during a Peltier solidarity event. Scanning the crowd, Hill caught the eye of a Navajo woman named Lenora Hatathlie. "That's how my mom and dad met," says Charlie's daughter Nasbah Hill. "They noticed each other through the crowd and began the courtship. My mom was an activist. She came from Arizona with a big group of people to the Peltier event in Los Angeles. My dad liked my mom because she was traditional, she knew about ceremonial life, and she spoke her language. He had never met a woman who had come from that background. He came from Oneida, but a lot of our culture was lost. There were no ceremonies going on in Oneida. The language only returned much later through the hard work of the community. So when he met my mom and discovered that she knew her culture, her language, her cultural ways—he was very attracted to that."

For their first date, Hill invited her to his small Venice Beach apartment, where he warmed a clump of canned clam chowder and told her about Richard Pryor, Mike Douglas, and *The Tonight Show*. She wasn't impressed with his credits or the clam chowder, but when he spoke about the need for proper Native American representation on television, her ears perked up. Their relationship flourished over the next several months, and soon they were married.

Some of their happiness was dashed when, after eight hours of deliberation, an all-white jury convicted Leonard Peltier of double homicide. He was sentenced to two consecutive life terms.

Initially held in the Marion maximum-security prison in Illinois, Peltier was transferred to the Lompoc Federal Correctional Institution in California, where rumor had it that a fellow prisoner had been hired to kill him. Hearing about the plan and fearing for his life, Peltier staged a successful prison break.

The FBI immediately descended on Peltier's friends and supporters as part of a frantic manhunt. A wire story from the Associated Press reported: "Max Gail who plays Detective Wojciehowicz on ABC-TV's *Barney Miller* show barred three FBI agents from searching for Peltier in a home used by Indian defense committee members near Lompoc on Saturday because they had no warrant."

"I learned about the Peltier story from people I knew and

trusted," says Max Gail. "I believed he had been falsely convicted. I went with Buffy and Charlie to a powwow near Lompoc. I went to see Peltier to tell him that maybe I could be of some help, as I was on TV and had a certain amount of visibility. We got up there and they told us, 'Leonard isn't feeling well and can't come out.' So instead we went over to his defense committee headquarters, which was nearby. Somebody from the defense committee gathered us all around and said, 'Listen. We want you to know—Leonard is making a bid for his freedom tonight.' And then it came over the news. Leonard Peltier had escaped. We sent the women and children down to my place in Los Angeles in a van, and I stayed with the defense committee all through the night, listening for updates. In the morning, in the kitchen, we decided that if anybody came to question us, we would not answer the door. Just as we were agreeing to this, two people walked by our kitchen window and made eye contact with me. They were FBI agents. I said, 'Shit, I just made eye contact with them.' Everybody went into the living room, and I answered the door. They said, 'We're with the FBI. Leonard Peltier has escaped. Is he here?' I said, 'No.' They said, 'Would you tell us if he was?' I said, 'Well, fortunately I don't have to make that decision—because he's not.' They went quiet, and then one of them squinted. He said, 'Hey . . . aren't you from *Barney Miller*?' "

Three days later Peltier was found hiding out on a farm in Santa Maria, California. An additional seven years was added to his double life sentence. His case helped forge a bond among Floyd Westerman, Buffy Sainte-Marie, Max Gail, Dennis Banks, and Charlie Hill. Westerman and Banks had been through the grist mill of residential-school abuse. It wasn't something they spoke about much, but they had a mutual understanding. "There were psychological scars, physical beatings, sexual abuse," lamented Charlie Hill. "Some people were so beaten down that they never wanted to talk about it."

Chippewa actress Kateri Walker was renting a guesthouse on Westerman's property in Los Angeles when she was introduced to

Charlie Hill and welcomed into their circle. "Floyd and Dennis were taken away from their families when they were five years old and sent to the same boarding school," says Walker. "I had also been in a residential school, so they understood me when I talked about it. Most people don't understand what we went through. They took our land, our homes, our children. They put the kids in these genocidal boarding schools where they beat the Indianness out of you. My grandfather was raped by one of the priests. When he grew up, he went on to hurt his wife and his kids. It gets passed on. Our elders taught us that our hair is where our memories are stored—so we grew our hair. The first day of boarding school—they cut all of your hair off. They removed your identity and gave you a name like Billy or Sue and told us our grandparents were dead. We were stolen from our families. I was nine years old, holding on to my mother, I didn't want to leave her. I got in trouble from the nuns for holding on to my mother too long. I took a little piece of fur from her coat and I got in trouble for it. The nun said to me, 'We don't hang on to our mommies here.' I thought I would never see her again. They woke me up at five a.m. every morning for six weeks and they made me skin the dead animals that white people had left on the back porch. They figured we would eat anything because we were Indians. At my boarding school, we weren't allowed to have emotions. You couldn't laugh, you couldn't cry, you couldn't whisper. If you did, you were beaten. They used to sprinkle flour on the floor of the school because they said the devil could see up from hell and was trying to steal our souls. I would lie awake all night waiting for the devil to come. We were told we were dirty heathens, nobody wanted us, and nobody would ever love us. When you get raped by a priest or abused by nuns and then get thrown into America, where you're treated like a Hollywood stereotype—people expect us to assimilate and lead normal lives, but most of us were traumatized as children. We are a traumatized people. Floyd Westerman and Dennis Banks and Charlie Hill took me in. They understood. They could relate.

Jackie Keliiaa Thinks, "Holy Shit, This Is *Amazing*."

Jackie Keliiaa was born in Hayward, California, twenty miles from San Francisco, the youngest of four girls. The Paiute-Washoe stand-up did her earliest gigs at the Brainwash Café and Laundromat in San Francisco, an amateur venue that birthed contemporary comedians like Ali Wong and Al Madrigal. Conscious of her lineage growing up, Keliiaa listened intently to her grandparents as they spoke in Paiute and Washo. "They attended Stewart Indian School in Carson City, Nevada," she says. "My grandpa got a job at the naval air station after World War II and moved his family out to California. All of their friends and family were Native. There was a huge Native population out here because of urban relocation." Under that program, Native Americans were bused from rural reservations to urban areas, provided with dilapidated apartments for a maximum of six months, and told to find a job. As with termination, it was the brainchild of Dillon S. Myer, the man behind the Japanese American concentration camps during World War II.

"A lot of Native people were sent to the Bay Area, where they had no family," says Keliiaa. "My grandpa Marvin would drive up and down the coast, encouraging these men to join in Indian baseball tournaments. That's how the Indian leagues got started in the East Bay. And it's the area where I was born. . . .

"I attended Cal [UC Berkeley], where I was part of the Inter-Tribal Student Council. We put on massive events with over two thousand attendees. I got involved with powwows and tutored students at the American Indian Child Resource Center. The university held a comedy night, and Charlie Hill was the headliner. I thought, 'Holy shit, this is *amazing*.' It was transformative. I always loved comedy, but here I understood a second meaning to all of his jokes and I fell in love with his performance. I knew then that it was something I wanted to do."

Someone Calls the Cops on the 1491s

The effect the 1491s are having as a sketch troupe today is not unlike the effect Charlie Hill had in the late 1970s. Theirs is a comic voice otherwise absent in popular media. Much of their material operates on two levels. A YouTube sketch like "The Indian Store" can rack up six hundred thousand views by appealing to a wide audience with its broad antics while at the same time retaining references and characters recognized by Natives alone. "That video is about that non-Native idea of what 'Native art' is supposed to be," says Migizi Pensoneau. "You see all these buffaloes-floating-in-the-clouds-type paintings because they sell. Well, now there's a pushback against those kinds of things, a pushback against the marketplace of what white people want to buy from us. And the 1491s make fun of that."

The 1491s create content to first and foremost please a Native audience. Crossover interest is a welcome, albeit unnecessary, by-product. "The popularity of 'The Indian Store' was a little confusing to us," Pensoneau continues. "It was very broad and a bit obvious. It's still a funny video, but it's like if you put out an album, and that's the big hit. 'Why do people keep wanting to hear *that* song?' It strikes a chord. But our mission was to just make Native people laugh. That's all we started out to do. The fact that other people started paying attention and liking it, that was great, but we would be just fine on some rez making a bunch of kids laugh rather than making a bunch of liberal white people laugh. If it's a full Native audience, they get it on a different level. Not better or worse, just different.

"Around 2012 we really started going hard with performances around the country. My girlfriend was going through law school and she saw us get stiffed at a gig, so she started coming with us as our manager. We needed someone watching our back, and she structured our asking rate and all of that stuff."

They wrote comedy that addressed mascot controversies, racist Halloween costumes, and the over-the-top personalities of powwow emcees they encountered. They simply followed their own instincts, trusting that what the five of them found funny, others would as well. It led to an invite from one of the most popular comedy programs in the country—*The Daily Show with Jon Stewart.*

The segment opened with a clip of Dan Snyder, the owner of Washington's NFL franchise, defending the use of a racial slur: "The name of our team is the name of our team. And it represents honor, it represents pride, it represents respect." From the Dupont Circle Hotel in Washington, D.C., comedian Jason Jones interviewed three of the 1491s—Bobby Wilson, Thomas Ryan RedCorn, and Migizi Pensoneau—alongside artist Gregg Deal, journalist Simon Moya-Smith, and lawyers Tara Houska and Amanda Blackhorse. Pensoneau wore a shirt advertising the Cleveland Caucasians. Wilson wore a shirt with Chief Wahoo, the Cleveland Indians mascot, as a skeletal image based on the Misfits band logo. In typical *Daily Show* fashion, Jason Jones played a dense journalist, playing devil's advocate:

> GREGG DEAL: The most popular mascots in the country are Indians and animals.
>
> JASON JONES: Right. 'Cause we all love animals—and we all love Indians.

THOMAS RYAN REDCORN: We're not mascots.

MIGIZI PENSONEAU: It [Redskins] is a dictionary-defined racial slur.

JASON JONES: Okay, but that's according to what?

MIGIZI PENSONEAU: The dictionary.

In a separate room, Jones filmed an interview with four non-Natives draped in football regalia, defending the name of their favorite team.

FOOTBALL FAN #1: If the Redskins' name is changed and I have children one day—what will I pass on to them?

FOOTBALL FAN #2: I think sometimes the conversation that's happening right now—is that we need to be sitting down talking to the people that actually are offended.

With that, the door opened and a production assistant ushered the 1491s into the room. The confrontation turned heated, and one of the football fans burst into tears. "This goes way beyond mocking," she said later. "Poking fun is one thing, but that's not what happened. . . . I didn't consent to that. I am going to be defamed." Two days later she phoned the police to lodge a complaint: "Native Americans accused me of things that were so wrong. I felt in danger."

"To commit genocide, you have to dehumanize people so much," says Sterlin Harjo. "That's how there's still 'the Redskins.' Because we were so dehumanized. And we're only now slowly crawling out of that space and being treated as humans. It's so insane that it's only now happening. Even with friendly liberals that love us—they love us too much. They feel an ownership over us because we were so dehumanized in the past. They feel like they can speak for us and know exactly how we feel and how we should act."

The media descended on the 1491s to talk about the segment,

posing the inevitable question, "Aren't there more important issues to worry about than the name of a football team?" Thomas Ryan RedCorn had to field the question constantly. "The media will only contact Indians when there's a problem with their football," he points out. "They ask us, 'Aren't there bigger issues than the name of a football team?' Well, we know the answer. Of course there are. But the *Washington Post* doesn't ever phone us to talk about contaminated water."

Charlie Hill and the Swimming Number with Joe Namath

"If they switch all the mascots—even something that simple would be a slight metaphysical shift," said Charlie Hill. "But the teams don't let it go because there's all this money involved. They always put money over humanity."

Charlie Hill's visibility was at an all-time high in 1980 when he was hired for a new NBC variety series called *The Big Show*. It featured an eccentric collection of comedy stars including Graham Chapman, Steve Allen, and Andy Kaufman. Variety shows had dominated television in the 1970s. Everyone from Howard Cosell to Sha Na Na had hosted their own program, and the genre became something of a joke with kitschy titles like *The Ken Berry "Wow" Show*, *Tom Smothers' Organic Prime Time Space Ride*, and *Don Knotts' Nice, Clean, Decent, Wholesome Hour*. But by the 1980–81 season when Hill joined *The Big Show*, they were out of favor. Against all industry advice, NBC sank several million dollars into two new variety shows. One of them was *Pink Lady and Jeff*, starring Comedy Store comedian Jeff Altman with a Japanese singing duo delivering their lines in phonetic English. The other program was *The Big Show*, a gaudy, expensive, overambitious production with swimming pools, ice rinks, and dancing girls.

"*The Big Show* was two hours, prime time, every week," says

Steve Binder, director of the series. "We shot it on these huge stages at Sunset Gower Studios. We removed a wall and created a gigantic space—eighty feet high, two stages wide—an ice rink on one end, a roller rink on the other, a swimming pool in the middle with a huge theatrical stage and dancing water. This was all at the same time, all on one set. We used Olympic skaters and swimmers and a trapeze artist who swung over the swimming pool. We did this every single week. Remember the swimming number with Joe Namath?"

Namath was just one of many celebrity guests with whom Charlie Hill shared the stage. Others included Loni Anderson, Victor Borge, Sid Caesar, Imogene Coca, Barbara Eden, Jamie Farr, Tony Randall, Don Rickles, Steve Lawrence, Shirley MacLaine, Gene Kelly, Dean Martin, and Hervé Villechaize. The recurring company of players consisted of one veteran—Monty Python's Graham Chapman—and a roster of new talent including Edie McClurg, Joe Baker, Paul Grimm, Pamela Myers, Owen Sullivan, Mimi Kennedy, Gallagher, and Charlie Hill. Steve Allen explained that Andy Kaufman was dropped from the repertory because "the only thing he was willing to do was wrestle a woman."

"I loved that Charlie Hill was part of our repertory," says Binder. "I had never seen an Indian comedian." Producer Nick Vanoff gave Hill permission to remove anything he considered stereotypical or off base, and he chimed in regularly, fighting for respectful representation. "They had an army sketch and [Don] Rickles was in it," recalled Hill. "They wanted me to come out of the shower wearing a loincloth. I said, 'You know, my old man was in the service during the war. Let me wear a uniform and be a regular guy in this and change the jokes around.' They let me do that."

When the program was profiled in the press, it was Hill who got the ink. "Ever see a funny Indian on the movie screen?" asked television columnist Charles Witbeck in Ohio's *Mansfield News Journal*. "Such a concept never occurred to Hollywood writers. They see Indians as the bad guys, stoics with paint on their faces. That historically distorted image is being corrected on NBC's *The Big Show* of all places, when Oneida Indian comic Charlie Hill steps out on Tuesday nights and gets laughs with his monologues." Viewers used to white people playing Native Americans on TV were confused. A woman from Indianapolis wrote to her local *TV Guide*: "I've seen comedian Charlie Hill on 'The Big Show' and I was wondering if he really is an Indian—or is that just an act?"

The series featured short sketches and blackout gags in the tradition of *Laugh-In*. Hill was seated at a news desk in one scene, wearing a suit, clutching a pile of papers. Referencing a famous newsman of the era, he spoke into the camera: "Good evening, I'm Roger Mudd." At that, the ceiling opened and a torrent of mud poured down on his head. After the director yelled cut, Steve Allen walked over and pointed at Charlie's mud-soaked suit: "Hey, Charlie—looks like you got some of your land back."

To be treated as an equal by Steve Allen and Don Rickles was tremendously gratifying for Hill. "Part of this whole thing was I got to meet all the comedians. Don Rickles said, 'Where you from?' I said, 'Wisconsin.' He said, 'Who are your people?' I said, 'We're the Oneidas.' Then he looks around the room and says to everyone, 'I'm talking to the Indian like I'm the wagon master!' That killed me."

In a sketch titled "The Indian Press Conference," he played himself as he fielded questions from a White House–style press pool:

REPORTER #1: Mr. Hill . . . your people have followed the buffalo for hundreds of years. What has it taught them?
HILL: To be very careful where they step.
REPORTER #2: How do you like our city?
HILL: Fine, how do you like our country?

Scheduled against hit shows on the other networks—*Hawaii Five-O*, *Three's Company*, and *Taxi*—the program was a ratings failure. It left the air after a mere eleven episodes—canceled on the same day as *Pink Lady and Jeff*. Altman and Hill both returned to the Comedy Store. Altman was dejected, but Hill cheered him up. "There was nobody better to be around than Charlie," says Altman. "When you arrived at the Comedy Store and when you left the Comedy Store, Charlie was always there, and he made you *want* to be there. You'd come offstage and he'd be quoting lines from your act. He had the greatest laugh, and it made you feel so great when you heard it. Charlie just had a way of endearing himself to you. We hung out at the back of the Comedy Store all night long."

It was an ideal time for comedians. Comedy clubs were a new business craze. Stand-up scenes had sprung up in Boston, Philadelphia, Cleveland, Atlanta, Miami, and Houston. Armed with major television credits and five years of experience, Hill headlined new comedy clubs in Milwaukee, Minneapolis, Tucson, and Honolulu. He performed at Chuckles with Elayne Boosler and Crackers with Dave Coulier. When he arrived in Denver to play the Comedy Works, his opening act was a local housewife named Roseanne Barr. He was at the top of his game. And without even realizing it, he was influencing a whole new generation of Native American kids who suddenly saw comedy as a possibility.

Larry Omaha Investigates a Foul-Mouthed Parrot

"The first time I ever walked onto the Comedy Store property, I noticed this comic in the parking lot talking to the other comedians," says Yaqui-Zapotec stand-up Larry Omaha. "I thought to myself, 'Wow! That's Charlie Hill.' He had just been on Johnny Carson's *Tonight Show*. He wasn't just the top Native comic but one of the top comics at the Comedy Store during that period. He had a lot of heat. As I was walking into the club, he just happened to turn and look in my direction—and he *knew*. He called me over, offered me a hit of his weed, and asked me what tribe I was from. From that point on it was like we had known each other forever. He started giving out my name and helped me get a lot of bookings. Without his help, I would have floundered a lot longer."

Unlike his benefactor, Larry Omaha had never dreamed of being a comedian. On the contrary, when he was young he wanted nothing more than to be incarcerated. "The guys I looked up to when I was a kid were gang members. Most of them went to prison, and I remember thinking it would be cool if I got sent to prison too. I was very unhappy. I grew up in Omaha, Nebraska, the youngest of six children. Both of my parents worked in a slaughterhouse, and I figured I'd end up there too. My dad was Zapotec and my mom was Yaqui, but I didn't connect to those roots until I was older."

He didn't identify with his Native background growing up, but that didn't stop racists from targeting him. "One time I went with my friend to his girlfriend's house. He was Native and she was Caucasian. Her uncle walked in, saw us, grabbed a rifle, and started shooting. I took off running, and the bullets whizzed right past my head."

As he entered adulthood, Omaha moved aimlessly from one working-class job to another. "I drove taxis, painted houses, welded—I was just searching for something," he recalls. "I met some social worker types when I was twenty, and they got me to enroll in the University of Nebraska. I became the complete opposite of what I had been up to that point. Everything I did from that moment on was in the name of positive change. I went to law school and became a civil rights investigator. People came to us if they felt discriminated against in employment or housing, and then I would go out and question people, gather that information, and make the assessment." One of his assignments concerned a discriminatory eviction. It was the type of thing he'd soon be talking about onstage. "A guy told us he'd been evicted from his apartment for speaking Spanish. We agreed to take his case. During my investigation, I learned that he was evicted because he had a parrot that yelled Spanish profanity all night long."

Omaha considered turning the more absurd experiences into comedy material, but there were no outlets in Nebraska at the time. "I started looking for places to perform in 1977. There weren't any comedy clubs yet, so I just emceed fundraisers. I had no act. I just made fun of people in the audience. Then in 1979, an actual one-night-a-week comedy room opened called Oliver's Back Alley. It was a long room, a lounge with a large stage. It held about a hundred twenty-five people. I did it every Sunday night for a year—and was getting laughs." Initially he relied on gimmicks. "I tried to learn guitar so I could do song parodies, but I couldn't figure out how to play it, not even close. So I decided I was going to be one of those juggling comedians. There was a trick where you juggle an apple, an egg, and an odd object, and you take bites from the apple. At the end of the bit, instead of the apple, you smash the egg in your mouth and get the laugh. I mastered it at home, but when I attempted it onstage—the lights blinded me. I couldn't see *anything*. I thought, 'Okay, fuck this shit.'"

He modeled his style on one of the most influential stand-ups of his generation, *Tonight Show* regular Robert Klein. He worked hard on observational material and wordplay. When he had enough of an act, he packed his bags, quit his job, and fled to Hollywood on June 22, 1980. "I packed up the car and drove to Los Angeles with my wife and two kids. I took a day job as a painter, worked in the early mornings, slept all afternoon, and then hit the open mics every night," he recalls. Omaha's first stop was the Comedy Store. "There was a long line of comics hoping to go up. I got in line at six p.m. and they told me I would be the third open-mic'er. I thought, 'Wow, great.' Little did I know, the regulars would drop in whenever to do their sets. By the time I went on, it was two-thirty in the morning and there were six drunks left in the audience. The whole experience was *horrible*. Nobody laughed. I couldn't get myself to go back onstage for weeks, but I finally shook it off. It took me a year to get noticed by Mitzi Shore, but she finally started giving me spots at one a.m. The whole thing was exciting for me—and I was on track." Omaha's contemporaries included Arsenio Hall, Andrew "Dice" Clay, and Garry Shandling. "We were always working the club together," says Omaha. "Several months later, I had a pretty good set, and as I walked offstage, I heard this voice: 'Hey, man, you're a real funny dude. Real funny dude.' It was Richard Pryor."

Omaha entered comedy at the right time. A couple of years earlier, he couldn't find a single comedy room. Now, with twenty minutes of material under his belt, Omaha could travel clear across the country playing a different comedy club in each town. The 1980s comedy boom was in full swing. From the Comedy Haven in Palm

Springs to Coconuts in Miami Beach, the Punchline in Atlanta to the Laff Stop in Houston, he lined up hundreds of gigs. "After years of looking for places like these, suddenly they were opening up all over the country. It was really unbelievable. A full house every night. There was a magazine being published called *Just for Laughs*, and it had listings for every comedy room in the country. I'd flip through it, call the places I wanted to perform, and send a VHS recording of my act. I planned my first tour that way and did the road for four months straight. I had a Nissan Sentra with three hundred thirty-five thousand miles on it, and I was making real money."

Terry Ree Becomes the First (and Last) Native American Comedian on *Hee Haw*

As the comedy boom accelerated, the hundreds of hotel lounges along the Silver Circle lost their luster, and Las Vegas showed arthritic signs of age. Venues that had once been the epitome of Rat Pack cool were now considered square. Tastes had changed. Elko, Sparks, and Reno, clinging to a 1940s style of comedy, had somehow survived in the early 1970s—but now that Richard Pryor, Eddie Murphy, and *Saturday Night Live* were mainstream, the old-fashioned rim-shot comedians were personae non gratae. The main attraction in Nevada was no longer show biz but brothels. The young people stopped coming, and the state became a show-biz graveyard. The region was drowning in bad news. A gambler attempted to blow up Harvey's Resort Hotel on Lake Tahoe with a thousand pounds of dynamite. An unhinged motorist intentionally mowed down twenty-nine people in front of the Club Cal Neva. Riots broke out in the streets on New Year's Day after racists in Reno attacked Middle Eastern residents, blaming them for the Iran hostage situation. Las Vegas was corporatized and downsized, and the days of Mob rule gave way to Reaganomics. And then an unlikely savior came along to single-handedly resurrect the Silver Circle.

The Jim Halsey Company started as a broker for country music acts in the late 1950s. It was a modest agency until 1968 when it lucked out, serving as the talent pipeline for a new TV show called *Hee Haw*. The success of the cornball variety show turned hillbilly comedians mainstream—and it made Jim Halsey a potent force. The agency started booking its television clients around Nevada, where the venues were desperate for a fresh injection. In the 1980s, Las Vegas became known as a country music destination, and tourists flew in from around the country to see Halsey clients like Roy Clark at the Aladdin, Mel Tillis at the Sahara, Lee Greenwood at the MGM Grand, and Lynn Anderson at the Frontier.

The agency also represented the Oak Ridge Boys, one of the most successful country vocal groups of the era. When their opening act at one engagement remained onstage for an hour instead of their contracted twenty minutes, the Oak Ridge Boys were furious. They fired their opener and needed a replacement in a hurry.

The comedy team of Williams and Ree happened to be working for scraps in a nearby lounge. Hired as emergency pinch hitters, they did exactly twenty minutes. Their well-worn banter was new to the country music tourists, and they went over big. The Oak Ridge Boys phoned the Jim Halsey agency and asked that Williams and Ree be added to the bill permanently.

For the next year the duo played the massive showrooms of Las Vegas and Lake Tahoe. When the Oak Ridge Boys completed their residency, the Halsey agency sent Williams and Ree on the road with the rest of their roster. For the next several years they opened for Roy Clark, Kenny Rogers, Tammy Wynette, and Merle Haggard, and their income skyrocketed. Earning as much as $10,000 per gig, Williams and Ree proclaimed themselves "the highest-paid unknown comedy act."

The connection couldn't have come at a better time. The Jim Halsey Company had been hired to supply talent for a new cable channel called The Nashville Network. TNN debuted on March 7, 1983, presenting a round-the-clock showcase of country music, new and old. Williams and Ree capitalized on the opportunity and moved to Tennessee.

TNN's flagship program was *Nashville Now*, hosted by the cantankerous disc jockey Ralph Emery. It had a late-night talk show format, but the smug emcee was no Johnny Carson. "Ralph Emery would ask questions and never listen to your answer," says Terry Ree. "We wanted to do bits, but he didn't want that. One day he said, 'I wish you guys would get your own show so you'd stay the hell off of mine.' So we did. It was a cooking show with Florence Henderson."

The *Brady Bunch* matriarch prepared meals with a country music celebrity every Sunday on *Country Kitchen*. Halfway through each episode Williams and Ree appeared in aprons, throwing eggs and spilling olive oil. It was an unlikely trajectory for a Lakota comedian, but Terry Ree was making incredible money and having a great time. "We did the show with Florence Henderson for eight years. It was strictly a money gig, but we got paid more in five days than we would ever make on the road."

Hee Haw, the long-running variety program, became one of TNN's main attractions. The hayseed comedy had been through several iterations, from its original network run in the late 1960s to syndication in the 1970s to its revitalized form on TNN. Veteran country comedians Minnie Pearl and Grandpa Jones were still around when Williams and Ree joined the cast. "TNN put us on *Hee Haw* for two seasons," says Ree. "They wanted us to write our own material but wouldn't pay us as writers. Bruce and I [had always] improvised onstage, and our material evolved. We didn't know how to do it any other way, so we said, 'Get your writers to put something together and we'll do it.' Well, they wrote us the unfunniest shit, but we did it." In a pathetic attempt at relevancy, *Hee Haw* replaced its old cornfield backdrop with a shopping mall in the belief it would attract teenage viewers. "*Hee Haw* was still a good show to be on," says Ree, "but it was a dead horse, and they were flogging it."

The material made them cringe, but it was worth it to Ree just to work alongside show-biz legends. George Lindsey, best known as Goober on *The Andy Griffith Show*, was a regular cast member. "They only had this one large communal dressing room for the men, so we'd be hanging out in there with Grandpa Jones and George Lindsey and the others," says Ree. "George Lindsey took off all of his clothes in order to change into his Goober outfit, and he never wore underwear. He had *huge* testicles. He'd put his balls between his legs and then poke one out and walk over to Grandpa Jones shouting, 'Look, Grandpa, I'm a girl, I'm a girl.'"

The actual pay they received for the program was small, but the mass exposure they received helped raise their price on the road. "*Hee Haw* had enormous coverage," says Ree. "[The show itself] didn't pay particularly well, but it meant we could tour all over. We did two hundred twenty dates a year, earning seventy-five hundred dollars, sometimes ten thousand, per booking." Their act was essentially the same as it had been in the beginning. They retained the ethnic insults no matter the venue, no matter the year. However, while their act seldom changed, attitudes about ethnic humor did. Williams and Ree had always been considered innocuous, but society started to do laps around them. Ethnic jokes were out, and what was once considered family-friendly was about to become controversial—so controversial, in fact, that they would be bombarded with death threats.

Ryan McMahon Has a Life-Changing
Experience in Winnipeg (of All Places)

"I've had many, many death threats," says Ojibwe stand-up Ryan McMahon. "I taped a comedy special for CBC [the Canadian Broadcasting Corporation], and some guy threatened to shoot up the theater because he said it was 'Indian propaganda.' I was born in a community called Couchiching First Nation. I was raised in the border town of Fort Frances [Ontario], a small pulp and paper mill town beside our First Nation. My mom is Ojibwe, and both her parents were Ojibwe. My dad's mother was Ojibwe and his father was Irish. My parents used to travel on the weekends, and my aunt would babysit me. I was at her house when Eddie Murphy's *Delirious* came on TV. I remember looking around and seeing all the adults laughing. That sent me on the trajectory. I got into the Centre for Indigenous Theatre in Toronto in 1999. Herbie Barnes was an Anishinaabe teacher at the school and one of the original Theatresports [improv comedy] guys. He formed a Native improv troupe with us called Other People's Kids. It was my first taste of comedy. We were probably the first Native improv troupe in the world. Around that time I got into the Second City program. It was surreal for a poor kid from the reserve to be in the halls and see the pictures of John Candy, Mike Myers, and all of these comedy legends. For me, as a Native person, it felt special to be accepted into that world."

And then he witnessed a stand-up performance in 2005 that changed everything. "I saw Charlie Hill perform at the Winnipeg Comedy Festival. He was so political, so unapologetically Indigenous. He destroyed the room for thirty minutes, and it changed my life. I had never considered stand-up comedy. I found my hero. I decided right then: I want to do that."

Charlie Hill Isn't Offered Anything but Crap

When Charlie Hill lined up with the other comedians outside the Comedy Store for the first time, it was hard to tell who among them would emerge triumphant and who would fall by the wayside. Some thought the cleverly crafted jokes of Ed Bluestone would make him a household name, while others dismissed the affable stand-up Michael Keaton. The comic with the most clout was Jimmie Walker, who, thanks to his sitcom *Good Times*, could throw an occasional bone to less fortunate comics like David Letterman. But by the mid-1980s, nobody knew Ed Bluestone, Michael Keaton was a major movie star, and David Letterman was throwing the occasional bone to Jimmie Walker.

Letterman was aware of his good fortune, and he frequently booked old Comedy Store friends to keep them afloat. Gary Mule Deer, Tom Dreesen, Johnny Dark, John Witherspoon, Jeff Altman—none of them had star power, but they all appeared on *Late Night with David Letterman* with regularity. Letterman was loyal—something for which Charlie Hill would always be grateful.

"My next guest is a comedian who will be appearing December twenty-first at the state penitentiary in Stillwater, Minnesota," Letterman told his television audience. "There may still be a few seats available. Please welcome—Charlie Hill." Hill sauntered across the stage, grabbed the microphone, and threw the mic stand to the ground. He went into a mix of new and old material:

"My name is Charlie Hill—I'm an Oneida Indian. We're originally from here in New York. Now we're from Wisconsin. Had a little real estate problem. . . . The thing I didn't like about school was the history books. Y'know, I always thought they were one-sided. . . . History books called us vanishing Americans. But we're still around. When was the last time you saw a Pilgrim?"

After his final joke, Hill saluted the crowd with a clenched fist and sat down on the panel. "Okay, Charlie, tell me about this," said Letterman. "December twenty-first at the state penitentiary in Stillwater. Is that . . . What is that like . . . working in a prison?"

"It's a captive audience."

Late Night with David Letterman was arguably the most innovative show on network television, and it showcased important new comedians like Bobcat Goldthwait, Gilbert Gottfried, Emo Philips, and Sam Kinison. At the same time, cable TV was propelling the 1980s comedy boom. Williams and Ree were making a killing on TNN while their contemporaries told jokes in front of brick-wall backdrops on Showtime, MTV, and HBO.

Mitzi Shore felt the time was right for America's first all-comedy cable channel. She had a huge roster of talent at the Comedy Store. She just needed the right investors and the proper shows. Out of her own pocket, she financed a series of pilots and filmed a series of speculative promos featuring Charlie Hill for something she was calling The Comedy Channel. "She's putting finishing touches on an ambitious and risky labor of love," reported *Variety*. "A compilation of eight tv 'minisitcoms' featuring 60 standup comedians from her nightclub."

Among the "minisitcoms" was *Private Dicks*, a show about two comedians who quit show biz and set up shop in Chinatown as private detectives; *Spy in the Kitchen*, concerning an Italian chef who is secretly a Soviet secret agent; and *Here Today, Gone Tomorrow*, about "a funky black funeral parlor run by two inept undertakers."

"They used a restaurant that Mitzi leased across the street as a studio," says Argus Hamilton. "Ted Lange from *The Love Boat* directed the pilots. She hired Dick Shawn [best known as Hitler in *The Producers*] to be supervising writer and producer . . . and they held a big industry screening in the [Comedy Store's] Main Room in December of 1986." It might have succeeded had the format been straight stand-up, but very few of the comedians involved had any acting experience. Shore was overambitious, and the profitability of the comedy boom was clouding her judgment. "The success of the stand-up comedy boom led Mitzi a bridge too far," says Hamilton. "It was hubris. Nobody knew what they were doing. She made sure the *whole town* attended this fiasco—and it was a huge bomb. The debacle made her a failure in the eyes of her peers at the networks. . . . All in all she probably lost four hundred thousand dollars."

She wasn't about to give up while the comedy boom was still flying high. In the mid-1980s, she invested time and money to open the Comedy Store at the Dunes Hotel in Las Vegas. The 535-seat theater was originally built in 1955 as a performance space for the classic film star Maurice Chevalier. "The Dunes was the place that really made Mitzi wealthy," says comedian Allan Stephan. "It was an old showroom with booths and long tables, and it made ridiculous money. She'd use five of us comics, each doing a different amount of time, and it was *fun*. Everything was free—the food, the booze, the rooms. We really had the run of the Dunes . . . well, until Roseanne got thrown out for [bashing] Kip Addotta's head into the bar."

Rotations of five comedians swapped out every couple of weeks. Charlie Hill was usually on the bill with the hard-drinking, good ol' boy comic Ollie Joe Prater, and the two became close friends. Hill was a political radical and pothead. Prater was a loud redneck and cokehead. They were an unlikely pair, but they forged a bond typical of the stand-up brotherhood. After years of hard drinking and hard drugs, Prater died in 1991. Hill would call Argus Hamilton every year on the anniversary of his death: "Did you hear the news? Ollie Joe Prater has gone another whole year without drink or drugs."

During the early 1990s Hill was doing stand-up on television programs like *The Arsenio Hall Show, Comic Strip Live, Stand-up Spotlight,* and A&E's *An Evening at the Improv.* At first glance it indicated the healthy state of the comedy industry, but in reality it was oversaturation. Comedy clubs saw a dip in attendance for the first time in years. Larry Omaha noticed the slump right away: "From 1985 to 1990 my calendar was booked up nine months in advance. All of a sudden in 1991, I only had bookings for three weeks. That's when I realized there was a big problem. There were too many rooms, not enough talent, and hundreds of clubs closing down. People stopped coming."

The Comedy Store lost its contract with the Dunes Hotel after the Vegas bosses complained about profane material. "Mitzi scheduled a young comedians show for a week at the Dunes," says Argus Hamilton. "The lineup was Pauly Shore, Tommy Davidson, Muhammad Ali's daughter May May, and Chris Rock. The Dunes had a lot of walkouts who thought these kids were impertinent and dirty." The Comedy Store was bounced from the venue, and Charlie Hill lost his regular gig. It was terrible timing. There wasn't any work to replace it.

The comedy boom collapsed around him and his income all but disappeared. He and his wife, Lenora, were raising four kids— Nizhoni, Nanabah, Nabahe, and Nasbah—splitting their time between Charlie's home in Venice Beach and Lenora's house in Coal Mine Mesa in the Navajo Nation. "I lived with my dad in Los Angeles, and then my mom wanted us to move back to the reservation," says Nasbah. "They had this long-distance marriage because he had to be in Los Angeles for his career. My mom wanted us to have more of a connection to our culture and learn our language. My mom, as a child, was removed from her family and taken to an Indian boarding school. It was very traumatic for her, so whenever she was away from home, it kind of reminded her of that. She wanted to be back home, and she wanted us to have a connection to our culture and learn our language, which is why my siblings and I all have Navajo names. My mom lived in Coal Mine Mesa, about thirty miles from Tuba City, Arizona. It's a house in the middle of the desert. The nearest neighbor was ten miles away. My dad would visit us for a couple months at a time, but my dad wasn't about that rez life. That was hard for my dad, but it was just as hard for my mom to stay in Los Angeles."

"He loved his family dearly," says Allan Stephan. "And they had a tough life sometimes. Sometimes he was here in Los Angeles, and a lot of the time his wife was on the reservation. He had to support four kids. I don't know how he survived."

"My dad went to work just to provide for us and gave us everything we wanted," says Nasbah. "If we wanted something, my dad would never say no. Sometimes he didn't have the money to get it for us and he'd say not right now, but he would make a deal with us. He loved being a dad."

Charlie had the chance to subsidize his stand-up engagements with occasional acting gigs, but most were stereotypical roles. He was broke, but turned down nearly every offer he received out of pride. His daughter recalls, "He had the chance to play a very large part in a major movie, but he said he wouldn't be able to live with himself. It would have been a lot of money, but he said, 'No way, I'll never sell out my people.' He didn't want that to be part of his legacy." Hill's integrity remained, but his income did not. Friend and fellow actor Kateri Walker says, "They weren't offering him anything but crap. There was a period there where he just didn't work at all."

The 1491s Reluctantly Agree to Do a Shakespeare Festival

Ever since their appearance on *The Daily Show*, the 1491s have grown in popularity. Their video "Blasphemy" addressed the thoughts some Natives might have but would never dare say out loud. It was another tremendous hit. With each new video, they've become a little more popular. They are embraced, respected, and admired. Part of it is the result of hard work, but more than that—they have the knack.

"We get so much respect from community members from all over Indian Country," says Sterlin Harjo. "It's a beautiful thing."

The distinguishing characteristics of the 1491s are as pronounced as those of Groucho, Chico, and Harpo, as contrasted as those of Larry, Curly, and Moe. Dallas Goldtooth has a devilish and commanding star quality. Migizi Pensoneau is the quiet wit. Bobby Wilson has an elastic physicality. Thomas Ryan RedCorn is a master of deadpan. And the filmmaker responsible for their aesthetic, Sterlin Harjo, is the glue that holds it all together. Like any great sketch troupe, when their five distinctive personalities are fused, it sets off a chemical reaction. The result is an undeniable comedic harmony.

"Everybody sort of brings a different humor to it, but we don't have a straight man," says Pensoneau. "We'd have to hire somebody from outside to be the Zeppo or the Kitty Carlisle. Bobby has got an incredible gift for physical comedy with his giant eyes and expressive face. He's a natural and gifted performer on stage and screen. Sterlin is this incredible storyteller. Ryan and Dallas have a similar sense of humor, but one is from the South and the other is from the North. So we all bring a different power to the table."

Rhiana Yazzie, the artistic director of the New Native Theatre in Minneapolis, is a big fan. For years she's been pushing the 1491s to do an epic sketch comedy performance in the guise of a full-length play, but until now she hasn't had the resources to fly them to Minnesota. She has just convinced the Oregon Shakespeare Festival to foot the bill for a coproduction. She has asked Wilson to phone the rest of the 1491s to let them know. "The Oregon Shakespeare Festival is really interested in having us do a long-form piece," Wilson tells them. "They produce shows that often end up on Broadway and win Tony Awards." After a long pause, one of the 1491s breaks the silence: "Bobby, what the fuck are you talking about? We're not going to do Shakespeare in the Park."

While the Oregon Shakespeare Festival has been in operation since 1935, the Bard has taken a back seat in recent decades. Today it is one of the leading theater festivals in North America, with Broadway luminaries descending to help nascent productions before potential Broadway runs. The 1491s were receiving one of the most prestigious offers in the American theater, even if they didn't realize it at the time.

"We were all really skeptical," says Pensoneau. "We wanted to do a TV show or a feature, so when this play came along everybody was kind of like, 'Nah.' We weren't really sure what they were offering or who they were. It wasn't our world. But they flew down to Tulsa to watch us."

"It was perfect because we always sell out in Oklahoma," says Wilson. "There's a lot of Indians there, and we usually kill. They met with us afterward and talked about what this show might look like." The OSF will cover all of the production costs, providing union carpenters, painters, costumers, set designers, choreographers—and is assigning an Obie-winning director named Eric Ting to implement their vision. All the 1491s have to do is write the production—and get paid.

The 1491s see it as a potential way to counteract the plays about Native Americans that dwell on the bleakest, most depressing topics. "Almost all [of it is] about alcoholism, poverty, all that stuff," says Thomas Ryan RedCorn. "There's no question there are very real and dire circumstances in many tribal communities, but the 1491s want to showcase the upside generally ignored by media."

"People don't know the rhythm and the humor that Natives have," says Sterlin Harjo. "It's like watching the British [version of The] Office for the first time. The first episode, you're kind of taken aback, but once you get the rhythm of that, it becomes one of the funniest things you've ever seen. . . . Indian humor is so unique. It has not been captured well—ever. But a lot of it is about the pauses in between, where the punch line isn't as funny as the silence."

For a sketch troupe with no professional experience, it's a daunting task, and they're uncertain that they'll be able to pull it off. The Oregon Shakespeare Festival is staking its reputation on their success, investing hundreds of thousands of dollars to design the show. It's a huge risk for everyone involved, but also a huge opportunity to overthrow racist myths. "Native communities always say that humor is a big part of our culture, but you wouldn't know that from mainstream media," says Wilson. "They have these preconceptions about what that means. I hate when people are like, 'What do Indians find funny?' I'm like, *Huh? Oh yes, I think it's really funny when turtle interacts with eagle.*"

Sierra Ornelas Sells Sitcoms Like It's the Santa Fe Indian Market

Sierra Teller Ornelas has just hired Bobby Wilson to write on her new television sitcom. "I saw *Between Two Knees* and I trust he can be a staff writer," says Ornelas. Having worked on popular sitcoms like *Happy Endings* on ABC, *Superstore* on NBC, and *Brooklyn Nine-Nine* on Fox, she is arguably the most successful Native comedy writer in the industry. "As someone who was given a shot when I probably wasn't really ready," she says, "I am very open to meeting with people who aren't fully formed writers."

Born in Phoenix and raised in Tucson, Ornelas was taught the art of weaving at an early age. It's a family tradition, passed down for at least six generations. "I was just raised to believe that you should learn to weave. My family always told me that even if you don't weave as a job you should learn so that you could pass it down to your family."

Her mother is a master of the loom, sometimes spending as much as four years on one project, and winning several international awards in the process. "I'm a sixth-generation Navajo tapestry weaver," says Ornelas. "So for the first ten years of my life we sort of lived rug to rug through her artwork."

As a child, Ornelas learned how to hustle at the Santa Fe Indian Market and the Heard Fair in Phoenix. When she moved to Hollywood, she quickly secured writing jobs during sitcom "staffing season" and credits her childhood experience as the reason. "My mom [would do] two shows a year—the Heard Fair in Phoenix and the Santa Fe Indian Market. I sold Native jewelry. I would make beadwork all summer and then . . . in one weekend I would try to make as much money as I could. I *hustled*. I was like, 'Hi, I'm Sierra and I'm only five and I made all this jewelry here. Would you like to try this on?' And so, weirdly, staffing season is like Indian Market. You are just on your grind, trying to make people remember you, and remember your booth number. There's a lot of similarities in terms of how I was raised and how I have to find a job out here. My mom's whole thing was, 'Make sure people know you. Put your shine on.' She was very much about that."

While her mother worked on art, Ornelas and her brother watched comedy in the living room. "Weaving is very sedentary, so my mom would say, 'Okay, go to Blockbuster and rent six movies.' And then we would just watch them in succession while she wove. My dad had always wanted to be a stand-up comic, that was like his dream, so he raised us on Richard Pryor and George Carlin and Steve Martin, [Johnny] Carson, and *Saturday Night Live* . . . and I just adored it."

While majoring in film at the University of Arizona, she joined a sketch troupe called Comedy Corner, producing their weekly campus show. Upon graduation she accepted an internship with the Smithsonian. "I was a programmer at the National Museum of the American Indian and we programmed a lot of film and television," she says. "I learned about filmmakers from the 1910s, like James Young Deer, and I learned what was going on in Canada and New Zealand with the infrastructure they had." Whenever the museum hosted Native filmmakers, Ornelas was envious of their careers. "I would get to meet these filmmakers when they would come to town [and] they'd be like, 'I'm going to Berlin, I'm going here, I'm going there,' and I'd just be so jealous. I really wanted to write for television, and there [were] programs for Native writers [in] New Mexico. So I wrote a really bad *30 Rock* to get in, and then I applied to a bunch of programs. I quit my job and left my boyfriend, put all my shit in storage, and I came out to Los Angeles. It was super scary, but it was also like there was no other choice for me."

She reached out to other Natives in Hollywood for support and advice. "I got to Los Angeles and there were people like Migizi Pensoneau, who was writing, and Sterlin Harjo, who was making movies. And when I became more established, I saw that Lucas [Brown Eyes] got into the ABC writing program and I reached out to him. I just cold-called him to try and pay it forward. I was like, 'Hey, we should talk.' I wanted to offer the same heads-up I was given. It's a sort of underground support network."

Her first sitcom gig was at ABC. "My first job in television was *Happy Endings*. There were three other women writing on that show, which was rare at the time, and it was an incredibly supportive and funny room. Everyone on that show became showrunners and went on to do great stuff. From there I went on to a bunch of other shows including *Brooklyn-Nine Nine,* then landed on *Superstore* for three seasons."

Michael Schur, the creator of *Parks and Recreation* and *Brooklyn Nine-Nine,* has championed her work. Together they are developing a series for NBC called *Rutherford Falls.* "It's all about the town of Rutherford Falls . . . adjacent to a Native reservation," says Ornelas. "The town is sort of turned upside down when there's talk of moving a statue that commemorates the founder of the town, this guy Lawrence Rutherford. And the last Rutherford in the town is this guy Nathan, played by Ed Helms, and he just loses his mind over it."

Now in a position to hire her own staff, Ornelas is actively helping other Native comedians get into the industry. "I've been in writers' rooms where I was the only brown person or only brown woman in the room. And I knew that if I had my own show, I didn't want that. I wanted there to be multiple types of people. Mike Schur said, 'How many writers do you want on the show?' I said, 'Maybe ten.' He said, 'Well, half should be Native.' I was really excited because the old diversity programs had created this culture of 'I'm the only one and I have to look out for myself rather than help other people.' It was kind of weird for a while. But this new generation I'm a part of doesn't want to do it that way. We're all kind of helping each other."

Among those writing on *Rutherford Falls* with Schur, Ornelas, and Wilson are Tazbah Chavez, Jana Schmieding, and Tai Leclaire. Together they comprise the largest number of Native comedy writers ever assembled for an American television show. "When there's no other person who has any shared experiences with you—it's that much harder to bring your full self to a space," said Ornelas. "[So it] has been a truly wild experience to come to work every day and have no qualms about my jokes and . . . having people understand them. Being able to be myself is truly a revolutionary feeling."

Vincent Craig Performs on the Back of a Flatbed Truck

"Most Native comics will tell you that our communities are chock-full of comedians that haven't tried to do it professionally," says Ojibwe comic Jim Ruel. "There are all kinds of funny Natives—but they stick within the community."

Thomas Ryan RedCorn of the 1491s agrees: "The American narrative dictates that Indians are supposed to be sad. It's not really true, and it's not indicative of the community experience itself."

First Nations comedian Vance Banzo of the Canadian television comedy *TallBoyz* says, "There aren't very many news articles about how twenty-five Ojibwe people just laughed and couldn't stop laughing in a community hall, but we can always laugh and find comfort."

RedCorn and Banzo are among a new generation of comedians who have emerged during the modern comedy boom. Approximately one hundred Indigenous stand-up, sketch, and improv performers have entered the field. It is a phenomenon new to many Native communities, despite being a core cultural practice for ages. "The sacred clown is an element that runs deep in most tribal cultures," says Kiowa-Apache comic Adrianne Chalepah. "From coast to coast, north to south, you can find a tribal clown in almost every region. It is deeply ingrained. The tribal clowns are ancient, their dances are ancient. These clowns point out the backwardness of society."

Anishinaabe stand-up Ryan McMahon concurs: "In Ojibwe communities, it's *Nanabozho*. In Cree communities, it's *Wesakay-chak*. In Lakota communities, it's the *heyoka*. These are the comic figures that are part of our cosmology. They're in our languages— dating back millennia."

Humor as a coping mechanism may be something of a cliché, but if there's a circumstance where it applies, Chalepah says, it is here. "It can feel sometimes like our communities are in a constant state of mourning, like there aren't enough tears to cry about every single tragedy. Being able to laugh is important. Native humor is part of why we survived. It's allowing yourself to feel a little bit of joy in a moment that might otherwise break you."

As the stand-up comedy boom ended in the early 1990s, comedians were panicking all over. But in Native communities there remained a whole school of performers who continued to make audiences laugh unaffected, as they'd never bothered with comedy clubs in the first place. Most played large gatherings and powwows around the country. "The thing non-Natives don't understand about powwows," says Chalepah, "is they're really not that deep. They're our Coachella—minus the appropriation."

The origins of these celebrations date back to the late 1800s, when the federal governments of Canada and the United States banned religious ceremonies. Powwows were a way for Native communities to clandestinely keep their songs and dances alive in the face of oppressive laws. Most events had a powwow emcee. They were not unlike stand-up comics.

"Powwow emcees, for hundreds of years, have hosted our cultural events," says Ryan McMahon. "Like a lot of our cultural practitioners, they are often funny."

"For some of the people who have successfully moved from Indigenous communities to stand-up, they're coming out of that space," explains Thomas Ryan RedCorn. "Those are the spaces where people are cutting their teeth and learning to talk in public. There's a certain amount of theater at play with your powwow emcee. He's up there with a rough outline of what's supposed to happen, but also filling the gaps and providing jokes. There's also an element of teasing or roasting. There are powwow emcees who roast people and have achieved a certain level of success with it. A lot of the Native comics I have talked to have started doing that onstage. Normally teasing is something you might do in private, but not publicly—but now it has bled into that space."

The comedian Jonny Roberts was introduced to the concept as a child: "Going to powwows when I was growing up, you'd hear the local emcees roasting the people in the crowd. It was about bringing people together and ensuring everyone was having a good time. The BS-ing of the powwow emcees was a definite influence on me."

Jim Ruel recalls, "I often saw powwow emcees telling jokes. A lot of times I was like, 'Wow, this guy is actually doing material.' I was always surprised that more of them didn't try stand-up, but they were old-school."

Among the old school was Sammy Tone-Kei White, a man who emceed more powwows than anyone else of his generation. A profile in *Indian Country Today* said, "For anyone who's ever attended a powwow within the United States, Canada, or Mexico, chances are that Sammy 'Tone-Kei' White of the Kiowa Nation served as a master of ceremonies." Tim Giago, the Oglala Lakota journalist, marveled at White's "repertoire of jokes that he can rattle off all day and night without break." White did hundreds of shows over the course of five decades, retiring only when his health started to fail at the age of eighty-four. "It's my life," he said. "It's a wonderful feeling to have someone call and tell you they need you. 'Could you be the master of ceremonies?' That's quite a feather in your cap. I keep going as long as I'm needed."

The 1491s lampooned the subculture with a series of recurring sketches. "A Day in the Life of a Powwow Emcee" portrayed a world rife with loud, vainglorious, overweight, middle-aged men, high on bravado and lacking in self-awareness. The vivid characterizations are among their most popular sketches. "We're taking the stage persona of the powwow emcee and then placing them into an everyday situation," explains Thomas Ryan RedCorn. "That's the comedy of 'A Day in the Life of a Powwow Emcee.' Does the powwow emcee act the same way when they're at home with their family as they do when they're onstage with that crazy energy, shouting and roasting? So that's the idea of it—and then when you get a whole group of powwow emcees together in one place at one time, are they just shouting all the time?"

In real life the 1491s have great affection and respect for the role of the powwow emcee, and RedCorn underscores their importance. "They're completely underappreciated as comedians. Technically, they're doing stand-up. If there's thirty or forty minutes to kill, they'll fill the time between roasting people or talking about insider things. It's very localized, but very fast and very smart. It might not be accessible to anybody outside of that room, but they can be ruthlessly funny."

Bridging the gap between powwow emcees and stand-up comics, Charlie Hill referred to the world of Native-centric comedians as the "private stash." He said the purpose of the "private stash" comedian was "to make people laugh, but only those who are Indians or people who live in our world."

A Navajo humorist named Vincent Craig fell into that category. He could sell out two-thousand-seat theaters all around the Four Corners region—Nevada, Utah, Colorado, and New Mexico—while non-Natives had never heard of him. The *Navajo Times* called him "one of the most beloved public figures in the Navajo Nation."

Vincent Craig logged hundreds of hours of stage time in the 1980s and '90s, playing outdoor picnics and concert halls, large powwows, small saloons, even flatbed trucks parked in open fields. Having never once set foot in a comedy club, he was a Navajo comedian doing Navajo comedy for a Navajo crowd.

In 1991, at a huge show at Lake Powell, Arizona, his vast stage experience was evident. At the end of his two-hour set, patrons stomped their feet, shouted his name, and demanded more. Not a single person made a move to leave. He returned to the stage and took requests—prolonging the show for another three hours. By the time attendees finally spilled into the parking lot, it was four in the morning and daylight could be seen on the horizon. A journalist who stayed for the duration asked one of his fans what it was about Craig that they found so appealing. He explained, "If you grew up on the rez, you understand his humor exactly."

Vincent Craig's family lived a short distance from the Puerco River along the Arizona–New Mexico state line. His father was Bob E. Craig, a decorated Navajo code talker who fought with the Fifth Marine Division at Iwo Jima in World War II. They were driving down the highway in July of 1979 when they heard the news on the car radio. The largest radioactive calamity in American history had occurred just a few miles from their home.

The United Nuclear Corporation had spilled ninety-three million gallons of solid radioactive waste—one thousand tons—into the Puerco River. A liquid more corrosive than battery acid poured into the local streams after a dam burst, destroying entire ecosystems. The company failed to inform the citizens of Church Rock when it washed up onshore. In order to minimize negative press coverage, the governor of New Mexico refused to declare it a federal disaster area. It became known as the Church Rock uranium mill spill, and it was the largest nuclear disaster on earth prior to Chernobyl.

Vincent Craig was thirty-five years old, working as a White Mountain Apache tribal police officer at the time. He knew the area well, having driven up and down the highway in his police car a thousand times. Reacting to the devastation, Craig created a comic strip for the *Navajo Times* called *Muttonman*. It concerned a superhero who gained his powers "after eating mutton stew from a sheep that had drunk from the Puerco." Readers were charmed by the crudely drawn Muttonman ("More powerful than the Bureau of Indian Affairs!") and the local jokes resonated with the readership.

Craig interpreted the positive feedback as sign. He told the *Santa Fe New Mexican*, "The themes I work with are culturally exclusive. Things that Navajos recognize by observation and are usually kept to ourselves." Picking up an old guitar, Craig wrote a series of novelty tunes from a Navajo point of view and invested $200 to manufacture three hundred cassettes. He rented a table at the Navajo Nation Fair and played the songs next to a display of tapes with hand-drawn covers. He ended up selling all three hundred copies in thirty minutes.

Throughout the 1980s, Vincent Craig drove from powwow to powwow, eventually selling more than twenty thousand copies of the homemade recording from the trunk of his car. The tapes were currency, passing through hundreds of hands across the Four Corners area. No rez car was complete without a Vincent Craig album in the tape deck.

He composed hundreds of novelty songs but is best remembered for the regional hit "Rita," the story of a rez kid who steals a candy bar. To non-Native ears it is meaningless. The song utilized a Navajo accent, and the familiar cadence brought laughs of recognition.

Isiah Yazzie, a Navajo improv comedian now in his early twenties, saw Craig perform in New Mexico while in elementary school. "I saw him at the Farmington Civic Center way back in the day. I bought the cassette tape with 'Rita,' the song about the candy bar. I had it memorized when I was a kid. I have fond memories of being in the back of my uncle's truck as a Vincent Craig tape was playing and we were holding our stomachs laughing and laughing. He was *very* big in the Navajo community."

DREW LACAPA WAS speeding down the highway in the early 1980s when he was stopped by the tribal police. He recognized the man issuing the citation. Lacapa exclaimed, "Vincent Craig! Man, I was thinking of trying comedy!" Craig shrugged with indifference, handed him the speeding ticket, and said, "Then do it."

Born in Whiteriver, Arizona, the son of a White Mountain Apache carpenter, Drew Lacapa and his five brothers helped their father herd cattle in the summer and build houses in the winter. In the evenings he was hypnotized by television comedy, never missing an episode of *The Carol Burnett Show* or *The Red Skelton Hour*. By the time he enrolled in Arizona State University, the 1980s comedy boom was under way, and Lacapa fell in love with Paul Rodriguez, Whoopi Goldberg, and Jerry Seinfeld. When his university booked a Native American comedian named Charlie Hill, Lacapa was surprised. He loved comedy but had never heard of the Native comedian.

One of Lacapa's classmates lobbied on his behalf and talked the school into having Lacapa open the show. It was his first time on-stage, and he was nervous. He closed his eyes so he wouldn't have to see the audience and confessed his hatred for the sacred sweat lodge ceremony because it gave him body image issues. Surrounded by shirtless, muscular Natives in the sauna-like heat, he begged the Creator for mercy—and better abs.

The routine killed, and Lacapa had found his calling. "Just like everybody else on the reservation, I've gone through that angry phase [where you] just want to go someplace and hurt somebody, but I've found a good release—and this is it."

Monologues about sweat lodges went over big with Native

crowds and led to a lot of community bookings. Lacapa became a "private stash" comedian.

THE NAVAJO COMEDY team of James Junes and Ernie Tsosie is another duo that Charlie Hill referred to as "private stash." They can pack a two-thousand-seat auditorium in Arizona but have never attempted a non-Native venue. "I've always been intimidated," says Tsosie, who got his start as Vincent Craig's opening act. "The only reason I even tried stand-up comedy was because it was a Native event and they were looking for comics. If it hadn't been a Native event, I would have been too scared. I never had the courage to go to Phoenix or Albuquerque to do open mics. I guess I still carry that fear."

Ernie Tsosie has a rotund figure and a kind face. A working actor, he's been a beneficiary of the New Mexico film boom as Hollywood film companies poured into the state to take advantage of tax credits. Now with two appearances on *Better Call Saul* under his belt, Tsosie reflects on how far he's come.

"I'd open for Vincent Craig at Native community events where they'd have multiple entertainers throughout the day. He was the big name at the end of the night wherever he performed. I learned how to make people laugh at these grassroots events where everything is working against you. No proper stage, no proper sound. We did an outdoor show on the back of a flatbed trailer, and they had me speaking into a podium with a mic attached to it. You had to make it work in those moments. And I used his audience as leverage to get my own thing going."

Tsosie grew up in the Navajo Nation in the late 1970s, the son of a schoolteacher and a construction worker. "The family wasn't stable. My dad was a drinker, and I spent a lot of time with my grandmother, and my mom made sure I graduated high school and went to college. I was watching stand-up comedy when it was kicking into high gear. I recorded every stand-up and had all of these

VHS tapes of random comics like Brian Regan doing their thing. I went to Tucson and got my training, three years of college-level stage work, and went on to professional theater. I got hired for a Native exercise video called *RezRobics*. It featured Drew Lacapa, the Apache comedian, and I told him, 'I've been thinking about trying stand-up.' He didn't really care one way or the other. I saw this real small ad in the *Navajo Times* that said they were seeking Native comedians for a competition. I called and signed up, but I had so little confidence that I used a fake name: Concho Roman. I didn't know anything about stand-up comedy. I memorized a set like I was learning a play. I was an actor playing a stand-up comedian. One of the other comics was this guy James Junes, who I'd never met. We shared a dressing room. I was pacing, and he was sitting in a corner dressed in traditional Navajo attire. I went on third, and I killed. James went on last, and he killed too. His act switched back and forth from English to Navajo."

Tsosie started getting small gigs, and it took a year until his act was passable. "I was getting little jobs at random Native events, small community gatherings and conferences," he recalls. "I was thrown to the wolves, and it was pretty rough. There was never any proper performance setup, so eventually I bought my own equipment and brought it with me. I was working solo for a year when I got booked at a youth event in Tuba City. It turned out James Junes was on the same show. They were behind schedule and wanted to condense the show. They asked us to go on together to speed things up. We said, 'Um, no, that's not how stand-up comedy works.' They begged, 'Please, guys, come on, we're way behind time.' Reluctantly we agreed. James did a bit from his act, and then I did a bit from mine. It flew by, and we got a standing ovation! We got offstage and said, 'What was *that*?' We stayed up until two in the morning talking about it. 'That was amazing, man. Let's team up.' So that's how we got started as a comedy team—and within two years James and Ernie took off."

They performed half in English, half in Navajo, and Charlie Hill found their dynamic compelling: "Most comedy teams, when they're on, there's a friction where they argue back and forth, and that's the source of the comedy. But these guys—they don't do that. They're real courteous to each other. . . . I don't think they did it intentionally, it's just an expression of who they are. . . . What they do is real, real Navajo."

The persona of James Junes was that of a Navajo in touch with his language and history, while Ernie played the English-speaking friend oblivious to his own culture. "In grade school I got teased for not being Navajo enough," says Tsosie. "James got teased for being *too* Navajo. So there is this weird balance there—and that's the dynamic we play off of."

They've been together now for a decade, and Tsosie goes out of his way to mentor the new generation of Native comics. "When I started, there were three Native comedians," says Tsosie. "Now almost every tribe has a comedian. Vincent Craig was really generous in sharing his stage and helping me when I started out. I told myself that if I ever got in a position to do so, I would be generous like Vincent. I will share my stage with any Native comedian that is coming up behind me."

Isiah Yazzie Does Improv for an Empty Room in Shiprock, New Mexico

"I saw James and Ernie perform when I was just a kid, and their comedy was *so* relatable," says the young Navajo comic Isiah Yazzie. "It was the funniest thing I had seen up to that point. To see it right in front of my eyes—a pair of Navajo comedians—it was as important to me as a legend like Richard Pryor would be for someone else. That was my first exposure to live comedy. I fell in love with it. I wanted to make a career of it.

"I was born and raised in Gallup, a border town off the Navajo reservation. I grew up with that rez lifestyle, helping my grandma butcher sheep to make *ach'íí* and things like that. I took the improv classes at Second City [in Chicago] and then came back to Gallup. I wanted to do improv, but it didn't exist anywhere around here. I messaged James and Ernie and told them I wanted to try stand-up. They let me open for them in Gallup. From there I started emceeing events—the Navajo Nation Fair, the Miss Navajo Nation Pageant, the Fire Rock Casino, the Northern Edge Casino, the Black Mesa Casino—I did them all. And then I tried to start an improv night with Ernie, but improv was new on the reservation. No one understood what we were doing. We were doing shows in a small restaurant in Shiprock. We called it Rez City Improv. Nobody showed up. . . .

"I'd book comedians to join us, and it'd take them two hours to drive in from Albuquerque just for fifteen dollars. So that was kind of tough. Whenever James and Ernie were booked at a casino, Ernie would bring me up at the end to do a quick five-minute improv set to plug Rez City Improv. We did improv shows in Window Rock, Farmington, Tohatchi. We taught improv at the Six Directions Indigenous School and small Navajo chapter houses. We were building it up. It took a long time, but now we're doing it all over the place."

Howie Miller Does Impressions.
Do You Guys Like Impressions?

Standing before a white tourist crowd in Niagara Falls, the Cree comedian Howie Miller is destroying a comedy club audience with the most common impressions in the business—Arnold Schwarzenegger, Sean Connery, Christopher Walken. Miller concedes they are the same voices done by nearly every impressionist in the world, but twenty years ago, when he was first starting out, they served as his entrée into the business. On the surface, the voices seem innocuous—but as Miller explains, he mastered these impressions for a specific reason.

"I do this just so I can be treated as an equal," says Miller. "Where I grew up, I was the only Native kid for miles around. I was trying so hard to be the same because there was a sense of being different. I latched on to the comedians that became something else. Jerry Lewis. Rich Little. Robin Williams. They became somebody else—and on a subconscious level, that's what I wanted to do."

Born on the Paul Band First Nation in northern Alberta, Miller was placed in an Edmonton foster home as a young child. "I was in rough shape. They found me malnourished in a hotel room. Apparently I had been there for two days by myself. I was six months old. My foster mother told me that my birth mother loved me, but she just couldn't control her issues. They fostered a number of children, including me and my two older brothers. My foster family had me for years, but at any point I could have been taken back and put on a reservation fifty miles west of Edmonton, a place that I didn't know anything about. So the first ten years of my life was *fear*. Every three months [child services] would come and check on us. I was eight when my older sister said, 'If they try to take you, then you and I are running away.' I was terrified. Growing up, I was very fearful of Natives. I feared my own culture. I heard only negative things. I internalized it to feel bad about myself. Eventually this all led to a need to shine—and that feeling came at an early age. I was a chubby Native kid, and they were so far removed from my experience, but I couldn't stop watching Monty Python. I just couldn't get enough of them. Monty Python—I filled myself up with that."

Miller fathered his first child at the age of seventeen, and it circumvented any comedy ambitions he might have had. "I suddenly had the responsibilities of a thirty-year-old adult. By the time I was twenty-four, I had four young boys. For seven years I did every job you can think of—washing cars, computer engraving, fighting forest fires—anything to make ends meet." At the end of his workday, Miller met with friends for drinks. "We were regulars at a pub where a guy sang pub tunes, and we'd sing along," he recalls. "At the time there was a comedian-impressionist named André-Philippe Gagnon who had been on *The Tonight Show* singing 'We Are the World,' and he did an impression of every famous singer in that song. I could do about half of those same voices. I started going up at the pub and singing songs as different people. The pub singer would say, 'Should we get Howie up here?' and all the regulars would cheer. People kept coming up to me: 'Are you a stand-up comedian?' There was a comedy club in town, so I signed up for their Wednesday-night amateur night and did all the most common impressions that everybody does. I did Sylvester Stallone working at a McDonald's drive-thru, and Sean Connery working as his manager. Jack Nicholson as a customer, and Jim Ignatowski [Christopher Lloyd] from *Taxi* was the janitor. It was just this little thing and it felt really good and I was asked to return. I downplayed being Native because I didn't want to be niche. I wanted to talk about things in my own way, but not have this Native thing on my back. But then I thought, 'Well, maybe I should ease into this.' As it worked out, it was better financially to market myself as a Native comedian. It opened doors for me beyond comedy clubs, because I was the only Native comedian doing impressions."

Miller started playing road gigs in little working-class towns in the late 1990s. Bigoted hecklers were common. "During my first year of stand-up, I was booked in Grande Prairie, Alberta. They were right in the front row and started saying something along the lines of 'your drunk squaw mother.' Like a real professional, I jumped off the stage and got into a fistfight." After paying his dues with barroom brawls, Miller made his way to the most important comedy festival in the world—Just For Laughs in Montreal. "Just For Laughs furthered my dream," Miller says. "It opened my eyes to what I was doing, that I have a voice, that I'm here."

The Beef with Don Burnstick

Don Burnstick has never played Just For Laughs. He has never even played a comedy club. And yet he might just be the most prolific of all Native comedians. Burnstick has traveled to hundreds of reservations, doing stand-up under trying conditions. The ongoing fallout of colonization—poverty, disease, suicide, intergenerational trauma—is apparent in each community he plays. For any comedian playing the reservation circuit, it's a good idea to have a sense of what's happening in each community before you start cracking jokes.

"You need to know what a community is going through when you show up, because you don't want to make things worse," says Adrianne Chalepah. "We did a show in a community where someone committed suicide two hours before the show. And there had just been another suicide the night before. This was a tiny, tiny community with two suicides in twelve hours—and then we were going to do stand-up comedy. It's heavy stuff. But we did the show, and they laughed so hard—it was like the community needed it."

Comedians love to swap war stories about their toughest gigs, but walking directly into a crisis situation is a lot more intense than being heckled by a bachelorette party at Giggles Comedy Club. For twenty-five years, Don Burnstick has performed almost exclusively on reservations, bringing stand-up to thousands of people who would otherwise never see a live comedian. "Unfortunately, the

214

issues—addiction, suicide, poverty—are across the board in Indian communities," says the Cree comic. "Our people are going through crisis, so if I can get these people laughing and healing—that's my focus."

When he started in the 1990s, Burnstick was emulating Eddie Murphy, roaming the stage with a cocky swagger, wearing a black leather jacket, a bristle mustache, and a Cheshire cat grin. Whereas other observational comics joked about the differences between men and women, Burnstick made a name for himself deconstructing the differences between the Ojibwe and the Cree. Some of the gigs were incredibly remote, like the Weagamow First Nation, 850 miles north of Toronto. The performing conditions were seldom ideal, but playing two hundred dates a year for more than two decades gave him the confidence to handle even the most impossible situations.

Born on the Alexander First Nation northwest of Edmonton, Alberta, in 1963, Burnstick was deeply affected by the federal government's child separation policies and the literal torture administered in residential schools. "I was very small and too young to go to school, and it was weird because all of the kids were *gone*," he says. "From the time they were five until the age of seventeen, you had to send your kids to these places. Whether you wanted to or not—it was the *law*. The boarding schools were run by the churches to assimilate the Native kids, teach them English, teach them the Bible, teach them a completely different belief system. It was really a tough scene. My family were Cree speakers. When my brothers returned from boarding school, they no longer spoke Cree. They had had long black hair, but now their hair was all short. They had been my loving, caring family—but when they came back, it wasn't that way no more. There was a big gap in the community. The parents were in so much pain because their children were taken away—and that's when the drinking started. When the kids came back from the boarding schools—there were a lot of secrets. All of my siblings were brutalized. They were starved. That's what these places were like.

When they got back home, it led to a lot of ugliness—a lot of drinking, a lot of violence, with everyone inflicting pain on each other. I ended up in foster care. I became a bully with my mouth, acting out, and eventually fell into addiction. I drank so much I almost froze in the streets. It took a long time to reevaluate my life. I was sitting in a rehab center, trying to get to the source of what made me drink like that. A lot of it was learned behavior and a lot of it was my pain, the rage I had inside. I had to purge my pain, purge my rage, and really explore the other side of who I was. I looked everywhere—Jehovah's Witnesses, Baha'i Faith, all this kind of stuff. The last place I looked was my own culture. I connected with my people and learned the ways of the pipe and the sweat and the Sun Dance. Once I engaged in those things—that's when I was able to calm down, get centered, get focused. I got over my addictions and learned to heal."

By the mid-1980s, Burnstick was lecturing on sobriety, touring schools with an antidrug campaign. "Young people wouldn't listen to me unless I put humor into my talks," he says. "Through that I got a reputation for being funny. Back then nobody would ever have thought of a Native comedian. I started volunteering at gatherings. Gatherings would have singers and cultural performers, but they never had comedians. I didn't have a set. I just went up there and did it. My stuff was not very real—I was too nervous. But over the years it evolved. I started getting booked for events as word of mouth spread. Now, all these years later, I really focus on the craft. Most of my audience is Native. Every now and then white people straggle in, but most of my shows are for Indian people."

Unknown to white comedy fans, he became a household name on reservations. "When I started, I just wanted to be a Native comedian who traveled to our communities, performed, and then ate some mutton and fry bread. My intent was to just go around and meet people and entertain them, but it evolved into this thing of its own. Now I'm kind of the guy."

When he started in the business, Burnstick had something of a monopoly. But as new comics entered the picture, tensions mounted. Ojibwe comic Craig Lauzon says, "There's a young Cree comedian named Chad Anderson, a really funny guy. He saw Don Burnstick on TV as a kid, and that's what inspired him to do comedy. When he started getting gigs, Don attacked him . . . told him he wasn't a real Native and all of this stuff. And this happens whenever comics open for Don on the road. As they get more and more adulation, he starts cutting them down. Don Burnstick has done a lot of good in terms of traveling to every single tiny community in North America, and he goes places where only thirty or forty people live and does comedy for them—and that's fantastic. But there's another side to him. He's a bastard when he interacts with other comics."

"Other comedians hate me," Burnstick admits. "Most of my work is in remote communities. I'm walking in the villages, talking to the kids, going to the schools, meeting with the elders. It's not just going onstage. But a lot of these other comedians can't do that. It's too hard for them—so I get bashed."

But fellow Cree stand-up Howie Miller insists that the real reason Burnstick gets bashed is that he's guilty of stand-up's greatest sin: "He stole material, and I really have a problem with that. He literally just took Jeff Foxworthy punch lines and treated them like his own."

Ryan McMahon explains, "Don Burnstick stole Jeff Foxworthy's material and changed one thing. He did all of Jeff Foxworthy's jokes and then switched 'You might be a redneck' to 'You might be a redskin.'"

"It is wrong on multiple levels," says Lauzon. "People started calling him out on it. Everyone told him to stop stealing. Then he started to go onstage and say, 'You know Jeff Foxworthy, who does that 'You might be a redneck' routine? Well, I've changed it up a little bit.' And then he just does it!"

If you attended one of Burnstick's shows in the late 1990s, you could purchase a cassette, a compact disc, or a VHS tape of his self-produced stand-up special *You Might Be a Redskin*. The racial slur didn't sit well with his colleagues. Dené comedian Dakota Ray Hebert says, "White comics can just go onstage and do jokes without thinking about it, but we have to be cognizant of what we're saying. Don Burnstick is almost giving white people the okay to call us 'redskins,' and that's not good."

Burnstick acknowledged the controversy, dropped the routine, replaced it with a new catchphrase, and denied any wrongdoing. "Yeah, people said I was doing Foxworthy . . . It was brought to my attention that 'redskin' was a racist word in the States, so I phased it out. My humor evolved. Now I say 'cuzzin' instead. All my merchandise is 'cuzzin' stuff. I even copyrighted 'cuzzin' because there is a lot of plagiarism going on in the comedy circuits. My manager took care of it. I don't know if you know this, but it's happening right now in the Indian circuit. Native comedians are stealing each other's stuff."

A producer named Lara Rae booked Burnstick for an all-Indigenous comedy special on CBC Television called *Welcome to Turtle Island*. Rae worked hard to persuade the TV executives in Toronto that the idea was worthwhile. The white gatekeepers were skeptical, uncertain anyone would care. But with Charlie Hill signing on as emcee, the event achieved a level of legitimacy. There was a spirit of camaraderie backstage and a feeling that the taping was a unique moment in history. However, some of the goodwill was dashed when backstage jealousies flared. Howie Miller was scheduled to close the show, but the veteran Don Burnstick insisted that he should be the headliner since he had the most experience. "I was sitting in the makeup chair when the producer came in," recalls Miller. "He said, 'Don Burnstick is having a fit. He demands to close the show or else he's walking.' My first thought was, 'Well, great, if he leaves, I'll get to do more time.' " Ryan McMahon says the two comics started shouting: "They wanted to fucking kill each other.

Don Burnstick and Howie Miller had to be separated in the makeup room."

Rather than spoil the evening, Miller conferred with the executive producer and buckled to Burnstick's demand. "We let Burnstick close," says Miller. "I decided, 'No, that's fine. I don't care. I'm bigger than this.' So a few weeks later the producer called and said, 'I think you'll like how it turned out.' They edited the show so that I was closing."

Charlie Hill's presence made the comics feel like something special was happening. "He was so loving and supportive throughout the whole thing," says Miller. "He'd get this excitement in his eyes. He just had this great big heart pumping full of life and positivity."

Despite the drama, Craig Lauzon remembers it as one of the most meaningful events of his career. "I made lifelong friends that week. The best moment for me was walking offstage and Charlie Hill was standing right there in the wings and he said, 'That was fucking funny, kid.' It was a moment I'll never forget, because he was my hero."

Lauzon performed a character piece about a Native wrestler having a crisis of conscience over his use of stereotypes. "I started thinking about what it was these Native wrestlers were doing and how that might affect them in different ways," he explains. "I started doing this character in comedy clubs, and it developed into the piece I did on *Welcome to Turtle Island*." The performance was something of a revelation for a handful of future comedians who saw it on television in 2005.

"The first Native person I ever saw on TV was Craig Lauzon doing his sketch about an Indigenous wrestler," says Dakota Ray Hebert. "I was *glued* to the TV. I was so excited! There's a Native person on the screen doing comedy! I thought, 'Wow, maybe *I* could do that.'" Vance Banzo of the Fishing Lake First Nation had a similar experience. "I grew up watching *SNL*. I loved comedy. And then CBC aired this First Nations showcase. I saw some of my own people doing comedy for the first time, and that lit a spark in me to go for it. It was meaningful because it wasn't a white person making a joke about a Native person. To see a Native person on TV—it just had deeper meaning. I had never seen that before."

Lara Rae, the executive producer, said, "It was the young comics who moved it forward so that the mainstream crowd could see the difference between edgy comedy and demeaning pandering. Don Burnstick had his day, but that day is over, in my opinion."

Marc Yaffee Is Weirded Out by His Own Mother

"Charlie Hill liked encouraging other people, but he wasn't encouraging to me," says Don Burnstick. "I really admired him, but he was standoffish. I'm not sure why."

Charlie Hill was desperate for more television exposure. The heat he had enjoyed in the late 1970s had long since cooled. Hollywood wasn't exactly pining for middle-aged Native comedians with graying hair. While other minorities made inroads in the new millennium, television shut out Native Americans, as it had always done. "Charlie and I talked for years about getting something on TV," says Larry Omaha. "We weren't getting any exposure. And then one day, out of the blue, I got a phone call from Paul Rodriguez's manager, Scott Montoya. He said, 'I'm producing comedy specials for Showtime. I was thinking we'd produce one devoted to Native American stand-up.'"

Long before diversity became a show-biz trend, Montoya packaged stand-up specials for specific demographics—*The Original Latin Kings of Comedy*, *Pacific Rim Comedy*, *The Latin Divas of Comedy*, and *Pride: The Gay and Lesbian Comedy Slam*. The quality of the specials varied wildly, but many of them featured future stars. "I pitched the idea of a Native comedy special pretty hard, but the concept wasn't well received," says Montoya. "Showtime always wanted *names*. The executive told me Charlie Hill wasn't a name and that there just weren't enough well-known Native American comedians to justify a special. I argued that maybe the comics aren't famous, but some of them *will be*—because I had used Russell Peters and Tiffany Haddish before anybody knew who they were. Finally they came around."

After recruiting Howie Miller from Canada, Omaha and Hill sought out other comedians for the taping. They discovered that a new group of stand-up comics was touring as a collective called the Pow Wow Comedy Jam. Three of them were fresh to the scene—Jim Ruel, Vaughn Eaglebear, and JR Redwater—and one, Marc Yaffee, was an experienced veteran. Yaffee founded the Pow Wow Comedy Jam in an attempt to carve out something for himself after years of thankless road gigs.

"I was born in East Los Angeles in 1961 and raised by my adoptive parents," says Yaffee. "I always knew I was adopted because I was really tall and my dad was this little bald Jewish guy. My mom was this little, tiny Mexican lady. I loved Flip Wilson and *Sanford and Son* and the Norman Lear shows. In the fourth grade we were doing papier-mâché and I made Archie Bunker's house. I was always into comedy."

At the age of twenty-six, he received a FedEx delivery with a nine-page, handwritten letter from his biological mother. "She had been looking for me for years. She included some pictures and explained that my father was Navajo and that my grandfather came from the Four Corners area. She came to meet me a couple months later, and we hit it off. Man, it was so weird to stare at someone with the same physical traits. She tried to put me in contact with my real dad, but he evidently had a lot of history with substance abuse and prison and there was a lot of dysfunction. And then my grandfather ended up dating my dad's ex-wife or some weirdness, so I had to let it go."

Learning about his lineage altered his life perspective—and it fed his early attempts at stand-up. When he saw live comedy for the first time in 1984, he was living in northern California looking to escape a dead-end job at the DMV. "I went to see a show at Cal State. There was a terrible turnout, maybe twenty students in the crowd. They introduced the comedian. It was Sam Kinison. He blew me away. It planted the seed for me that maybe I should be doing stand-up. I developed an act where I talked about my Native heritage." Yaffee worked the road for years, and he made mental notes each time he bumped into another Native comic. At a comedy club in Spokane, Washington, he met a Colville-Lakota comedian named Vaughn Eaglebear, who had a joke-writing style reminiscent of Mitch Hedberg:

"I was at an ATM machine and it said, 'Would you like to make your transaction in English or Spanish?' I picked Spanish. 'Cause a hundred dollars in America, that's, like, a thousand dollars down in Mexico. . . . I was in a restaurant the other day and a waitress came up to me: 'Do your people still eat the buffalo?' I said, 'No, just the wings.' I donated some blood a couple weeks ago. One of the nurses asked me if I was a full-blooded Indian. I said, 'Not anymore.' This lady said to me, 'What's your name?' I said, 'Vaughn Eaglebear.' She said, 'Gee, you don't hear a name like that every day.' I said, 'Yeah I do.' "

Shortly thereafter, Yaffee was booked in a Milwaukee comedy club where he saw a young Native comic working the crowd. "We got a lotta white people here," said Jim Ruel, looking out at the audience. "That's fine. I hope you guys enjoy the show . . . and the land . . . and the guilt. You guys didn't even know we told jokes, did you? Well, we joke together all the time. We just don't do it around you. We don't want you to steal our jokes."

Ruel was a science prodigy well on the way to making that his career when he saw Charlie Hill do stand-up for the first time. "My mom is from the Bay Mills Reservation in Michigan, and she had a pretty hard life," he says. "I loved comedy because it made her laugh. I was attending a conference of the American Indian Science and Engineering Society. They hired Charlie Hill to be the entertainment. I had heard about Williams and Ree, but I had never heard of Charlie Hill. Well, he *destroyed*. I thought, 'Wow—that is something I want to do.'"

He went to Los Angeles in the early 2000s to participate in an NBC diversity program. While hanging out in front of a comedy club on Melrose Avenue, he bumped into a new Native comedian named JR Redwater.

Redwater had just arrived from Standing Rock on a Greyhound bus. Born in Fort Yates, North Dakota, Redwater spent his early years on the reservation. His family moved off-rez once his parents enrolled in university, and Redwater was thrown into a white environment for the first time. He found his surroundings disorienting: "I was in the second grade, going to this white school, [and] everybody laughed at me because I talk slow. Everyone was telling me, 'You're funny!' But it was because of how I *sound*. I always sound like I'm drunk, but I'm *not*. I'm just high."

Ruel invited Redwater to join Yaffee and Eaglebear, and the four of them started to tour as the Pow Wow Comedy Jam. Their concept was based on the Original Kings of Comedy and the Blue Collar Comedy Tour, showcases of all-Black and all-southern comedians, respectively. An all-Native comedy show was such a novelty that they managed to pack massive venues without any previous experience. "Early on we did a show in Albuquerque," recalls Ruel. "It was during the Gathering of Nations—one of the biggest powwows in the country. The place sold out—eighteen hundred people."

"It was remarkable," says Yaffee. "People were super excited because they'd never had an all-Native comedy show before. We got booked at large tribal gatherings and did shows for the National

Congress of American Indians. I thought, 'Oh, we've got something here.' We rode the wave—and then things deteriorated."

Instant success created swelled heads. They became competitive and started to bicker with each other over who was most responsible for their success. "There was the issue of who was contributing the most or who was contributing the least," says Ruel. "We did not get along."

What started as an inspiring venture descended into a clash of egos. "We were eating at Tony Roma's and a fight broke out," says Yaffee. "Vaughn and JR were pushing and shoving, and we ended up missing a plane. Everything disintegrated." And then, in the middle of all the chaos, just as they decided to break up, they got a phone call from Charlie Hill about America's first ever all-Native stand-up special, *The American Indian Comedy Slam.*

Yaffee, Redwater, Eaglebear, and Ruel suppressed their mutual hostility and flew to Los Angeles to join Miller, Omaha, and Hill onstage at the El Rey Theatre. Hill emceed and acted as a backstage mentor, cheerleader, and elder statesman. He emphasized how important the evening would be for Native Americans everywhere.

The Showtime special aired on December 31, 2009. It barely made a blip in the popular press, but it was embraced in Native communities and boosted the profiles of its participants. In the three years that followed, Larry Omaha was booked "on every reservation you could name." Vaughn Eaglebear said the special "opened so many doors and performing opportunities—it was nothing less than amazing." It circulated on DVD and was commonly sold at sidewalk street markets. Executive producer Scott Montoya was amazed to learn how many people owned a copy: "Every Native American I meet tells me, 'Oh, yeah, I've got the DVD!' And I go, 'Really? Well, we never made one.' Bootlegs were everywhere."

Danny Littlejohn, a Ho-Chunk stand-up and regular at the Comedy Underground in Seattle, was inspired by the group. "I saw this show with an all-Native lineup—Jim Ruel, JR Redwater, Marc Yaffee, Vaughn Eaglebear—and I went, 'Holy shit! Natives can do comedy? I'm going to try this!' Now, all these years later, I'm opening for Marc Yaffee at the Ho-Chunk Nation casino." An explosion of new Native comedians entered the scene. Jim Ruel concludes, "I think the influence we had . . . may have been quite a bit."

Jonny Roberts Quits His Job

As the sun rises on a Thursday morning, Jonny Roberts is wrangling the eight young children who dictate his daily life. At the end of a winding dirt road in the Red Lake Nation, Roberts prepares breakfast like a worker in an army mess hall. During his tenure as a social worker, his family has expanded. Beyond his two biological teenagers and two adult children, he and his wife have opened their home to two five-year-olds, one four-year-old, three three-year-olds, and two two-year-olds. Rather than watch newborns languish in the limbo of Minnesota's child protection bureaucracy, the Roberts family took on the responsibility of raising these kids themselves.

"There's a lot going on in our home with all of the foster kids," he says. "We've adopted six of them and are in the process of adopting the last two. The 'foster' is no longer part of our vocabulary. They're just our kids. They've known us since birth. My wife and I are like prison guards, making laps around the house, making sure they're not getting into something they shouldn't. I can't really sit down and watch a television show the whole way through. It's impossible."

When he was a kid, Roberts watched TV all the time. He found himself enamored with the 1980s stand-up comedy boom. "Eddie Murphy was the big one. Hearing one person getting that kind of response from a big crowd—people understanding where he was coming from—that got my interest. My real dad wasn't around, so it was my uncle Joe and my grandpa Shorty who were the positive male influences. They *loved* comedy, and they had a lot of VHS tapes. And they were always joking at the most inappropriate times, at funerals and things like that. I must have been six years old when my school brought in a ventriloquist named Buddy Big Mountain. I was amazed at the effect he had on this huge crowd. But growing up around here, there wasn't any opportunity to see live comedy. I went to Bemidji State University and took mass communications, but couldn't put off work any longer because I already had a young family to support. Growing up in Red Lake, you don't have friends off the reservation, so even though I never finished college, it was valuable just to meet new people. My wife was working as a social worker and she got me a job in the same office. It was one of the best things—and one of the worst things—I could have ever done. It was eye-opening to see what some of our people are going through. The mental health, the alcoholism, the drugs, the cycle—the things that happen in the darkness. I couldn't believe some of the things I was reading about. And it gets passed on. You see a lot of kids go from foster home to foster home, and we felt that we had to step up to make sure these kids had a stable environment. We've fostered thirty-one kids in the last twenty-one years. Right now we are sponsoring eight kids who wouldn't otherwise have a family life. It's tough. A lot of the kids were born with all kinds of behavioral issues. We're told they will always be like that, but hopefully we can have a positive effect by raising them as our own." It's a noble effort, and one that simply doesn't seem possible for a person with stand-up ambitions.

ROBERTS TAKES THE ramp onto Interstate 94 just after 11 p.m. He's leaving Minneapolis after a lukewarm gig at Rick Bronson's House of Comedy, a club located inside the Mall of America. "Rejection I can deal with," says Roberts. "But the alone time on the road . . . It's just the loneliness." He cues some upbeat songs on his phone to keep him alert during the long drive back. "I sing as loud as I can to keep my focus. Five hours is a long drive at night." His unlikely playlist oscillates between Frankie Valli and the Beastie Boys. He hits play as he reflects on the weekly routine. "I have a very understanding wife who believes in my comedy goals. When I do a show down in Minneapolis, I leave at noon while the kids are in day care. She picks them up by herself, showers and feeds them, and puts all eight kids to bed. After doing a show that's five or six hours away, I'll drive right back home. I return at three in the morning and wake up at six to get them ready for school. I've done that so many times—Red Lake to Minneapolis and then back."

Roberts did his first stand-up set in 2009. "There was a Native talent night where I did five or ten minutes of *pure garbage*. There were maybe two laughs—but that's all it took to spark something in me. My friend was head of marketing at the local casino. I told him, 'Hey, man, I'm ready. I did my first set. I want in.' I kept bugging him, and finally about four months later he said, 'All right, I've got you down for our first ever Native American comedy night.' They paid me two hundred bucks, and it was packed. There were eight hundred people there. You could just feel the energy, and the body heat, and the wave of laughter. I fed off that crowd. I did ten minutes, and right then I knew it was what I wanted to do full-time. But that was years ago. And I'm still trying to figure out how to get stage time."

The next morning, Roberts is setting up recording equipment in his laundry room. Even with the washer and dryer tumbling, it's the quietest room in the house, the place where, for his makeshift podcast, he muses about his gigs, his kids, and his stressful day job. He struggles with the buzz from an errant ground wire, then lays the microphone on an upside-down laundry basket and starts recording. The water running through the pipes is audible in the background, and a mysterious clicking sound partially sabotages the audio. He powers through the podcast, revealing a new development in his life. "When I first started as a social worker, I knew what I was getting into. It wasn't really something that I wanted to do, but I was in between jobs. I needed something. I applied and they hired me. But, you know, reading the files and meeting some of the clients—it got too heavy. You want to save everybody. I did see a lot of success stories and turning points, but there were still those who struggled. I still have a hard time believing some of things that happen in this day and age. Trauma gets passed on from generation to generation. Opioid addiction has been hitting everyone here too, and it's hard to see more cases being opened than closed. There was only so much I could do. It got stressful, and things got tense in the office. I was already stressed out, and then office politics added to it. I told my wife, 'I can't do this anymore,' and she said, 'Yeah, you'll feel so much better if you leave.' But a few days later I changed my mind: 'No, I have to stay. I can't let these clients down.' My wife said, 'No, Jon, you can't help anybody else if you're not able to help yourself.' It just got to be too much."

Without any backup plan, Roberts is calling it quits and walking away from his day job. From now on the focus will be comedy. "It'll be tough with all the kids," he says. "I won't have the cash flow I'm accustomed to—but we'll get there. Something will happen . . . or maybe it won't."

Netflix Summons Adrianne Chalepah to Minnesota

Tired of driving ninety minutes to the small airport in Durango, Colorado, every time she was booked for a stand-up gig, Adrianne Chalepah has moved to a new home in Albuquerque. "I had to move because of the travel," she says. "I lived in the middle of nowhere."

Chalepah is glad to be in an urban center where Native people are visible and vibrant. "Lots of people suggested I should move to Los Angeles, but I didn't want to uproot my children from their family and their culture," she says. "The flights out of Durango were very expensive. I was driving an hour and a half to get there while I was pregnant. I decided if I'm going to continue in this industry, I had to move. Albuquerque was the compromise. It has direct flights, and it's close to all the Native culture."

She has been touring of late with two other women—Teresa Choyguha and Deanna MAD. Together they call themselves the Ladies of Native Comedy. It's an attempt to widen the field. "Before I started, I hadn't heard of any Native women doing stand-up. I wanted to collaborate to reflect these different voices."

Chalepah found her first recruit back in Durango. "I was hosting a comedy workshop at Fort Lewis College—and *bombing*. I asked for volunteers, and nobody would come up. Somebody said a student named Deanna MAD was really funny, and they flagged her down in the hallway. I asked her to get up and tell a story."

MAD explains, "I'm Tonawanda Seneca. My tribe is from New York, but I grew up on three different Kumeyaay rezzes in Southern California: Viejas, Manzanita, and Pala. I did some acting when I was really young and had an agent for, like, three seconds. I was taking cultural research management at Fort Lewis College. I was one of those really idealistic Native kids who was like, 'I'm gonna get my degree and then help the people and protect our sites and our objects and our history.' I was so into it that I was sure it would be my life. Adrianne was doing this workshop, and she was kind of struggling. Some friends called me over to get up and tell a story. Afterward she asked me if I had ever considered doing stand-up comedy, but at the time I was a serious academic. She said if I was ever interested, she'd have me open for her. I eventually took her up on it, and everyone was surprised that I didn't suck. She found another woman, Teresa Choyguha, and the three of us performed together for the first time at the Gathering of Nations in Albuquerque. There were a ton of people at that powwow. It was nerve-racking—and I bombed. I remember getting offstage and feeling really stupid, but we had a taste of what it might be like as a group. It gave us a lot of exposure and a lot of momentum. It invigorated us. From there we started touring, doing community-based stuff, and we were contacted by different tribes to do events. We went to Florida and Washington and Minnesota, mostly these really small 'Native Comedy Night' things, all over Indian Country."

The Ladies of Native Comedy was strictly a DIY operation. "It was hard starting out because we didn't have the resources," says Chalepah. "Trying to do comedy on a dirt floor in the middle of the desert—trying to stay in the range of a car's headlights—we really bombed. No tour manager, no greenroom, you don't have anything."

But after three years together, the Ladies of Native Comedy are about to receive their first national exposure. Larry Charles, the longtime producer of *Seinfeld* and the director of *Borat*, is filming a Netflix series called *Larry Charles' Dangerous World of Comedy*. He's traveling the world, profiling comedians doing stand-up in difficult and unlikely circumstances. For an episode about race, he's set up an interview at a Minnesota reservation with Tonia Jo Hall. A member of the Mandan, Hidatsa, and Arikara Nation, Hall is known for her broad character comedy. She has requested that the Ladies of Native Comedy be included in the segment, and while the production is open to the idea, they've stopped short of footing the bill. Chalepah and MAD will have to convince a Minnesota casino two hours away to cover their travel expenses. In exchange, they'll put on a show. "I see it as an opportunity to be seen by more than just our own community," says Chalepah. "It's a chance for people to just see us for who we are."

"There's very little visibility when it comes to Native people, and we are very rarely given the space to talk for ourselves," adds MAD. "It's nerve-racking because you know these opportunities are few and far between. And because you're part of a group that's so poorly represented, you end up becoming the face and the voice of the whole group. Some people will see it and say, 'Oh, so *that's* what Native people think,' just because you said one fucking thing. So it's panic-inducing—and I'm worried about coming across a certain way. It's called the *Dangerous World of Comedy*, but we had a hard time figuring out what's 'dangerous' about us."

When the episode aired, their interview cut to Adrianne Chalepah joking onstage: "My husband and I had a traditional Native American wedding . . . we waited five years and had two kids first." Moments later the camera cuts to slow tracking shots of a dilapidated reservation. The Ladies of Native Comedy don't live on this reservation, although that seems to be the implication. "We have to take what we can get," says MAD, "but I wasn't a fan of how it was framed."

"I don't like being viewed as at-risk," says Chalepah. "Even

Elaine Miles Assumes She Was the First Woman to Do It

"I think I was the first Native woman to do it," says Elaine Miles. "I mean, I hadn't seen any. I hadn't even seen any Native men do stand-up other than Charlie Hill. I am enrolled in the Umatilla Confederated Tribes in eastern Oregon, right outside the town of Pendleton. There are three tribes on that reservation: Cayuse, Umatilla, and Walla Walla. I'm enrolled Cayuse on my mother's side. My father's side was Nez Perce. My parents moved to Seattle and that's where I went to school, but we returned to the rez every weekend to stay with my grandparents. My parents were very traditional and taught me traditional ways. People told me I was great at making people laugh, and I thought, 'I want to be like Charlie Hill,' but I didn't think they'd let some Indian girl do this. I had never seen it on TV or anything, and Natives are always at the bottom of the list anyway. There's never even been a TV show."

In May 1990, Miles and her mother were driving to a powwow in Canada when their lives were suddenly altered. Her mother had been renting a room to a young woman who suggested the elder Miles to a CBS casting director.

"My mom and I powwowed. We traveled around. I was dancing at powwows, and I would win and my mom would win. We'd call my dad: 'We won—so we're headed to the next powwow. We'll see you in a couple weeks.' So we were headed up to Canada, and on our way we stopped in downtown Seattle for this casting call. There were all these Indian women dressed to the nines with the hair up and the jewelry. I sat there waiting for my mother to finish, and I kept looking at my watch because I didn't want to be late for the powwow. They had a pop machine in the waiting room and I put a quarter in and it wouldn't work. I was hitting it, kicking it, banging it, and my mom was *glaring* at me and told me to sit down. I was like, 'It ate my quarter!' The guy behind the desk got up to help me and asked, 'Are you here for the audition?' I said, 'No, I'm here with my mom.' He said, 'Would you think about auditioning?' I said, 'No, I don't want to be involved.' The producers came out, and the casting agent kept looking at me and asked, 'Do you have long hair? Can you take your bun out? Would you read for the part?' My mom said, 'Just do it—and then we can leave for the powwow.' I went in and the producer said, 'Oh my God, she's perfect.' This was on a Friday. I got a callback on Monday. They cast me as Marilyn Whirl-wind, and I started filming my first episode of *Northern Exposure* that Wednesday—and my whole life changed."

Miles appeared in all 110 episodes of the award-winning CBS series, and it led to a chance encounter with her idol. "I was doing *Northern Exposure* and got booked at a conference for the National Congress of American Indians as their celebrity guest. Charlie Hill was booked to do stand-up. I was honored to meet him, because he was the only Native comedian on TV at the time and he was writing for *Roseanne*. He was praising me: 'Your little brown face is seen by millions of people every single week!' I said, 'Yeah, but *you* are the inspiration.' He was just the coolest guy."

She transitioned from *Northern Exposure* to the big screen in 1998, appearing in the indie film *Smoke Signals*, which was play-ing film festivals around the country. It led to a gig costarring in a movie with comedian George Lopez. "I was hired to do a movie with George in New Mexico. We would sit around and tease each other, and George said, 'You're crazy, girl. You need to do stand-up.' He took me to one of his shows and had me take the stage for a few minutes. It went really well, and afterward George said, 'You didn't write anything?' I said, 'No, I just played off the people.' He said, 'You're so good at it. You need to keep doing this.' So that was kind of cool, to actually have George Lopez start me in comedy. Once I started doing it, my management booked me on shows throughout the Southwest. They loved me down there. It was raw humor that played off the crowd, nothing family-friendly. I started doing Indian casinos throughout New Mexico and all over California. I would do Native comedy nights in Seattle with JR Redwater and Jim Ruel, and I'd do the comedy club in Seattle when George came to town. I played hundreds of communities. But then at the height of my career, my mother got very sick. I stepped away from acting and I kind of quit stand-up so that I could take care of her around the clock. But anyway, yeah. I guess you could say I was the first."

Dallas Goldtooth Rides His Bicycle through Standing Rock and Sterlin Harjo Mocks the Hippies

Dallas Goldtooth of the 1491s worked as a logistics coordinator during a watershed moment for modern Native America. Standing Rock was both a protest and a gathering that inadvertently became a metaphor for the age-old fight between Native interests and industrial greed. Private mercenaries, militarized police, and a heavily armed national guard squared off against thousands of unarmed Native peoples who opposed the building of a pipeline across Native land. Energy Transfer Partners, a company owned by the controversial Texas billionaire Kelcy Warren, planned to build the Dakota Access Pipeline through Bismarck, North Dakota. But when white residents of the town objected, the pipeline was rerouted through the Standing Rock Reservation. Natives objected in the same manner as those in Bismarck, but this time the concerns were ignored. Standing Rock resident Bobbi Jean Three Legs said, "It pretty much just makes us feel like, 'Oh, it's just Indians, y'know.' We're humans too. We're *human beings*."

Marginalization was a federal policy in both Canada and the United States for 150 years. The purpose has always been to get people out of the way so that industry could exploit natural resources and claim them as their own. The Declaration of Independence refers to "Indian savages" three times, while the document itself failed to apply to Native peoples. (Charlie Hill joked, "You'd think they would at least change it to 'Native American savages.'")

In Canada, it was against the law for Native peoples to form a political organization, so as to limit their ability to fight back. Until 1951, Canada defined a "person" as any individual "other than an Indian."

The interests of corporations were always considered paramount. As of this writing, 25 percent of First Nations reserves in Canada have no drinkable water. Eighty communities are currently under long-term water-boil advisory, some of which have been in effect since the 1960s. In nearly every case, the water supply was contaminated by private industry extracting resources at any cost. Likewise, in the United States, 40 percent of the Navajo Nation lives without water after reckless mining interests poisoned the groundwater with uranium by-products.

Canada and the United States both justified their jurisdiction over Native lands by invoking the Doctrine of Discovery. Originally devised in the fifteenth century, it had the blessing of the pope and served as the basis upon which Holland, England, France, Portugal, and Spain colonized foreign lands. It stated that if a Christian explorer found a country without Christians—even if it was already inhabited by millions of people—ownership of the land automatically reverted to the host country of the Christian explorer.

Canada still invokes the Doctrine of Discovery as a legal defense whenever industrial resource projects are challenged in court by Native nations. When the United Nations Declaration on the Rights of Indigenous Peoples (UNDRIP) was ratified by the international community in 2007, it deemed the Doctrine of Discovery illegitimate and a violation of international law. It compared it to the codes that had once justified slavery on legal grounds. Canada, Australia, New Zealand, and the United States were the only countries that refused to ratify UNDRIP. Canada held out for several years until government lobbyists secured an amendment—Article 46—stating that they would support UNDRIP so long as they would not have to honor it. At the core of every pipeline dispute today is the contested Doctrine of Discovery and the debate over who actually holds title to the land.

In early 2016, the Indigenous Environmental Network, an activist group founded by Dallas Goldtooth's father, established a "water protectors' camp" in the path of the pipeline. The act of civil disobedience halted further construction. Over the next several months, Native nations from around the world lent their support to the campaign. Thousands of people traveled to Standing Rock, setting up tents and refusing to move, in an act of defiance. It became one of the largest displays of nonviolent, direct action in a generation.

Riding a bicycle through the camp, Dallas Goldtooth made the rounds to ensure that everyone was doing okay. He coordinated media requests, kept tabs on encroaching police mobilizations, and live-streamed updates to the world at large. "I am helping to handle logistics . . . tell people where to be . . . but the content is all of these amazing people," he said. "All of these folks that are on the front lines . . . who are fighting this battle . . . they are the reason why we are here. My job is to help coordinate that effort to make sure it comes off as smoothly as possible. . . . We want to see the decision toward 'no' for the approval of the pipeline—that is the projected outcome. Our hope is that we do a good enough job here to convince all of those involved in the decision-making process to open their eyes and see the reality that this is not a good thing for the United States. . . . It is not a good thing for Native people. We want to send the message that this is not something that we want."

Standing Rock was just the latest stage in a movement opposed to extreme methods of energy extraction—from hilltop mining to fracked gas. Many countries around the world have banned such practices, considering them too dangerous, too destructive, and a menace to public safety. But in North America the oil and gas industry has given lofty promises to Native communities about jobs and economic development. Their assurances haven't been particularly convincing in the wake of massive environmental disasters, often the result of criminal negligence. An offshore oil rig operated by BP in the Gulf of Mexico exploded and sank in 2010. It was the greatest marine disaster in American history. Eleven workers were immediately killed, and a hydrant of oil gushed continuously into the ocean for weeks. "It was the harrowing combination of the oil giant's complete lack of preparedness for a blowout at those depths, as it scrambled for failed fix after failed fix, and the cluelessness of the government regulators and responders," wrote author Naomi Klein. "The investigation and lawsuits that followed revealed that a desire to save money had played an important role in creating the conditions for the accident."

Ten days after the BP gusher was plugged, one of the biggest onshore oil spills in U.S. history occurred when an Enbridge pipeline carrying diluted bitumen from the Alberta tar sands burst in Michigan, destroying the Kalamazoo River. The cleanup process took more than five years, but much of the damage was irreversible.

Canada's Imperial Oil spent $13 billion in 2010 developing an open-pit mine in the Alberta tar sands three times the size of New York City. Its massive craters can be seen from outer space. The expansion of offshore drilling and fracking have meant a massive increase in pipeline and railway traffic. Increased traffic means more accidents. Oil spills jumped 17 percent between 2010 and 2012, with an average of sixteen new oil spills every day. Oil shipments by train increased 4,000 percent between 2008 and 2013, and there were more railway oil spills in 2013 than in the previous forty years combined.

Meanwhile, the companies responsible for the accidents were spending $400,000 every single day to lobby members of the U.S. Congress. Think tanks like the American Enterprise Institute received more than $87 million from the top oil and gas producers to create effective spin and disinformation strategies to discredit Native opponents and their allies. It was with all of this in mind that the massive objection to the Dakota Access Pipeline erupted.

The Standing Rock Sioux Tribe did not feel the pipeline was worth the risk. "I have a baby," said Bobbi Jean Three Legs. "She is the reason why I kind of started with my efforts against all this. . . . Every morning she wakes up and she asks me and her dad for a drink of water. It's just that simple, you know? What am I going to do if I can't give her water or bathe her or feed her?"

Adrianne Chalepah drove to Standing Rock. "I couldn't just stand by. I have family members and friends who live there. We were constantly trying to get news from the source because the mainstream coverage was prejudiced in favor of the oil companies. I went up there to see things for myself. There was so much love and solidarity. It was really powerful."

Donations of clothing came in from around the country to help the camp survive as the cold winter months approached. "I drove the whole Tulsa donation van up there by myself, and I was ready to go to *war*," says Sterlin Harjo of the 1491s. "I went there to fight because I saw all the shit going down. But then I got there and it was just beautiful and funny and fun." There was a tremendous feeling of community spirit. Dallas Goldtooth says, "At its peak, we had nine to ten thousand people staying in the camp and surrounding camp areas. We became the tenth-largest city in North Dakota."

Amy Goodman was one of the first non-Native journalists to cover the event. Her camera crew captured images of attack dogs lunging at unarmed protesters as they were pepper-sprayed by armed militias. CNN, the *New York Times*, CBS, and the *Washington Post* ran with Goodman's footage, and the optics swayed public opinion against Energy Transfer Partners. In response, North Dakota officials drafted new laws that would classify the protesting of any pipeline as a terrorist act. And they issued a warrant for Goodman's arrest, accusing her of inciting a riot.

"A lot of folks saw it on social media and a lot of people experienced it on the ground," says Goldtooth. "You're standing shoulder to shoulder with your brothers and sisters in a peaceful manner, unarmed, and you're facing off against tanks and sniper rifles and twenty-four-hour helicopter surveillance."

Bobby Wilson says Standing Rock was a galvanizing moment that changed public perceptions about Native Americans. "It helped non-Native people, a lot of white folks, really understand the reality that a lot of our communities face. It helped a lot of people understand the greater fight here."

At the entrance to the camp, flags sent in from Native nations around the world were erected in a show of solidarity. Harjo quickly returned to Oklahoma to grab his film equipment so that he could capture the unique experience. "I went back up to Standing Rock and made a short film where I followed Dallas around," he says. "I brought Bobby Wilson along to do sound, and we had such a good time. It was so beautiful. [Comedian] Tito Ybarra was there and he had a camp and we just stayed up at night telling jokes. There was a community of all these different tribes, and you'd hear songs everywhere. It was a serious situation, but also *funny*. There were so many people cracking jokes on each other. When white people first showed up at the camp, they were all bright-eyed and bushy-tailed. They weren't worn down and fucking miserable yet. This group of college students showed up one day and they were so excited: 'Where do we go, man?' And we were the first people they bumped into. So we were like, 'Well, there are a lot of things you have to do first. We have to run you through the *tests*. Everyone who comes through here has to first pass the tests.' We had them stand on one leg for a while and then we had them assume the lotus position and then we made them jump—and they totally fell for it."

Bobby Wilson slept only three hours a night, not wanting to be absent from the action for too long. "I was super tired—but my mind was on *fire*," he recalls. "It was an amazing experience. . . . You've got hundreds of tribal nations coming together. . . . You think about the historic context . . . many of these tribal nations had never interacted with each other. . . . They have these traditions, and these ways that have been passed down, and they're all coming together in this one place for a common goal to support each other. And they're sharing those ways with each other. . . . And there are tribes that have *hated* each other for centuries—and they're just chilling. They [kept] emphasizing in Standing Rock that this is a movement of prayer. They're trying to do this in a ceremonial way . . . involving all of the Dakota Nation, the Oceti Sakowin, we call it. By bringing in all these different factions of our Nations into one place to have a unified leadership . . . It was a hundred and eighty years since the last time they did that."

There were also a lot of non-Native outsiders present who were well-meaning but clueless. They were easy targets for teasing. "So many hippies showed up," says Harjo. "By the second time I went up there, it looked like Burning Man. They were overrunning the place for a bit. So we decided to do this video where we'd give them all Indian names. I traveled around the camp telling everyone to spread the word. And probably a good sixty people showed up to receive their Indian name. [*laughs*] Bobby and all these people dressed up in what was supposed to be Native regalia, but it was just homemade stuff that we threw together from donations and blankets or whatever. We went around, giving everyone in the circle an Indian name. By the very end people started to catch on that this was fake because it was *so* ridiculous. But one woman got mad that we had tricked her. She went and told security, and they had to come over and talk to us, but they all knew who we were. They said, 'She is *really* upset.' We told her, 'Listen, you wanted to be here at this camp with us, right? Well, this is Indian shit. We tease each other. We're having fun within this stressful situation.'"

After months of relentless pressure, President Barack Obama ordered construction of the pipeline stopped. It was a major victory for those present—one that the oil industry wasn't keen to see happen again. Upon the election of President Trump, new laws were enacted to criminalize the protesting of any infrastructure project, and the concept of "ecoterrorism" was enshrined in law. Kelcy Warren, the CEO of Energy Transfer Partners, had contributed more than $100,000 to Donald Trump's presidential campaign.

Regardless of the result, Standing Rock brought Native issues into the mainstream. "It was so powerful," says Adrianne Chalepah. "For Native people, it really helped us see that we still have a voice. Sometimes being a Native person in America—it feels like you're screaming at the top of your lungs for someone to acknowledge that you exist. You are absolutely invisible in your own country. Standing Rock changed that."

"I got my first phone calls to work in TV after Standing Rock," says Harjo. "People in the film industry were suddenly open to the possibilities that are out there. All of a sudden they were paying attention.

"Nobody gave a fuck before Standing Rock, even though we still did it and were making people laugh for years. Nobody was into Indian stuff. Nobody wanted Native shit. We are slowly rehumanizing ourselves. We're entering a really amazing period. It is the rehumanization of Native peoples in every field. And it is spectacular to watch it happen. As far as perceptions in media go—there's before Standing Rock, and there's after Standing Rock."

Those Friendly Canadians Send Death Threats to Williams and Ree

Very few comedians can sustain a career for five straight decades, let alone somebody who has never achieved fame. And yet, from the Phil-Town Truck Stop to the Holiday Inn, The Nashville Network to the casino circuit, Williams and Ree have endured. Ironically, their lack of mainstream success is probably the key to their longevity. Because of their relative obscurity, they manage to get away with material that would be a career killer for anyone else.

Williams and Ree are preparing for a show at the SaskTel Centre in Saskatoon, Saskatchewan, a city of 270,000 where 10 percent of the population is Native. The show is sold out. All thirteen thousand seats are filled, and another thousand patrons are crammed into an area that is standing-room-only. The event is a memorial for members of a teenage hockey team, the Humboldt Broncos, killed in a bus accident last week.

It's the second juvenile tragedy to grip the region in recent history. Last year a young Cree man named Colten Boushie was shot dead by a white farmer for trespassing on his property. When the farmer was acquitted of any wrongdoing by an all-white jury, analogies were made to the Trayvon Martin shooting in the United States. Racism has always simmered beneath the surface of Canadian society, albeit seldom acknowledged. Canadians have prided themselves on being less racist than their neighbors to the south, but after the death of Colten Boushie, racist vitriol overwhelmed the body politic, and racial tensions were at an all-time high. Williams and Ree were oblivious to this atmosphere when they rolled into town.

"We had very little sleep Thursday night," Ree told a reporter later. "[We] drove to the Seattle airport early morning [and] flew to Saskatoon and got off the plane at five o'clock. We went to the venue at seven o'clock. The show started and we did what we do."

The evening opened with a statement from a local country music group called the Hunter Brothers. "The families are dealing with such heartache, so if there is any type of uplifting we can do, we love to be a part of that," they told the crowd. "I imagine there will be lots of emotion going through this building tonight. Hopefully, there will be some laughs, some singing, some clapping, but there's also going to be some tears shed." With that, an announcer intoned, "Please welcome your hosts for the evening—Williams and Ree— the Indian and the White Guy."

As they took to the stage with essentially the same shtick they'd been doing since the 1970s, few of those present were aware of their dense history. Through five decades of roughshod roadhouses, motor-inn hecklers, Elko, Reno, Tahoe, and *Hee Haw*, Williams and Ree have refused to change with the times. "We have always done the ethnic thing," explains Ree. "That is our forte. We call ourselves 'The Indian and the White Guy,' but in Canada they don't like that. Up there the term is First Nations. I tell them, 'Well, I grew up Indian and I *am* an Indian.' It's not my fault that Columbus got lost. I'm an Indian and I'm proud to be an Indian." They've had their fair share of press over the years, most of it regional coverage plugging appearances at state fairs and outdoor festivals. But the morning after the performance in Saskatoon, they're on the front page of every major newspaper in the country.

"An American comedy duo is apologizing for a joke they made at a tribute concert for the Humboldt Broncos hockey team that was described as racist and inappropriate by some concertgoers," reported the Canadian Press. "Bruce Williams and Terry Ree, who refer to themselves as 'The Indian and the White Guy,' emceed the concert in Saskatoon on Friday. At one point, Williams sang a song to Ree which included the line 'shake it for the Indian with STDs.' Some members of the audience took to social media to express their outrage, with several saying they left the venue. Williams and Ree . . . said they failed to consider the emotional nature of the event, which was billed as a tribute to remember the sixteen people who died in the April 6 bus crash."

Cree activist Sylvia McAdam Saysewahum, the founder of the Idle No More movement, was mystified by their material and the reaction it received: "Is the crowd laughing because the jokes are being told by an Indigenous performer, which sort of gives them permission to laugh? Or maybe they're all familiar with their routine and I'm the only one who has never heard them before? Even if their comedy was impeccable, it's still kind of a weird choice to emcee an event like this."

Talk radio fielded phone calls about the incident the following afternoon. Some demanded an apology, while others attacked the duo's critics for being "too sensitive." Local radio host Drew Dalby said, "After seeing the outrage [and] counter-outrage about Williams and Ree, I decided to look them up. Putting aside the whole race thing—man, that is some corny shit. It's some real *Hee Haw* variety hour cheese that people are going to bat for here."

Much of the controversy was divided across racial and generational lines. Older white people were generally unfazed by Williams and Ree. Younger people, Native and non-Native alike, hated their guts. Dakota Ray Hebert had been familiar with Williams and Ree since childhood. "They hosted a country music festival every year here, and I remember my dad being like, 'They're so funny! They're so funny!'" she says. "He bought their DVDs. I watched them and thought, 'No! I *hate* this!' One of their songs was called 'Rudolph the Red-Nosed Indian.' I thought, 'Jesus, they're not even subtle about it.' I didn't know they were still around until I heard about the incident at the memorial, and I thought, 'Are you *kidding*?' They could have hired *any* local comic. To hire Williams and Ree for an event about a tragedy makes no sense at all."

Just by virtue of having been around so long, Williams and Ree were a controversial act. Show-business trends had shifted, demographics had changed, societal tastes evolved. After fifty years of making crowds laugh in relative obscurity, they were discovered by a much wider audience—which loathed them. They were trashed online nonstop, to such an extent that they had to deactivate their accounts. "Hundreds [and] hundreds of hate mail," said Ree. "Death threats . . . I mean vulgarity . . . I'm telling you, it was crass."

Williams and Ree were accused of stoking hate, but Ree said it was precisely the opposite: "We were showing people how stupid it is to be racist and to hate, [while the response] certainly did invoke hate. You know, hundreds of people who have never seen us and have no idea what we do sent hate mail, and we lost a job. They canceled us at a Regina casino [that] we played every other year since the casino started. . . . I just want anybody who thinks we are [promoting] hate [to] come see the show. I can count on one hand the complaints we had up until this one. And every single one of those complaints came from a drunk white dude."

Ralphie May Starts a Fight and Then Changes His Mind

Instantaneous complaints have replaced the old-fashioned bad review. Adrianne Chalepah was thrown off-balance when she was subjected to a hostile Internet mob during her seventh year of stand-up. "I wasn't prepared for the backlash," she says. "Or the death threats."

Chalepah was a fan of Ralphie May, the comedian who came to prominence during the first season of the NBC reality series *Last Comic Standing*. She never anticipated that she'd end up in the middle of a very public feud with him. "I was a Ralphie May fan and had been familiar with his work for years," says Chalepah. "My husband bought a CD by a Native hip-hop group called Savage Family, and it had a track called 'Raise Up.' It opens with a sample from Ralphie's act. When I heard it, I was really disappointed. But as a Ralphie May fan, I just sat on those feelings for a couple of years. I didn't feel any need to talk about it. I just let it go."

The sample in question featured Ralphie May complaining that *Dances with Wolves* had beaten out *Goodfellas* for Best Picture at the Academy Awards. May shouts indignantly, "Fuck a bunch of Indians! I am sick of hearing about it. Are we supposed to boo-hoo over goddamn Indians? That shit was a hundred twenty years ago. Fucking get over it! Nobody fucking a hundred fifty years ago is making you drink now. Fucking dry up, you fucking bunch of alcoholics—and go get a real fucking job. Cut that fucking hair! Bon Jovi cut his, you should cut yours. This shit is *done*, son. It's done! Fuck you, bunch of Indians! Fuck the Indians! I'm sorry! I'm sorry they as a group never made it to the Bronze Age. I'm sorry they never invented the wheel. I'm sorry, boo-hoo-hoo-hoo-hoo. Boo-fucking-hoo. Fuck the Indians."

In the weeks before the audio surfaced, Ralphie May's smiling face could be seen flanking highway billboards for the River Spirit Casino in Tulsa, the FireKeepers Casino in Battle Creek, and the Potawatomi Hotel and Casino in Milwaukee. When Jonny Roberts of Red Lake found out May was going to be doing a show at the Sanford Center in nearby Bemidji, Minnesota, he offered his services as an opening act, and was dejected that he didn't receive a response. Chalepah messaged Roberts with a link to the rant, reassuring him, "Don't worry about it, Jon. He doesn't like Indians anyway."

Chalepah recalls, "I grabbed the audio from the Savage Family CD and sent it to Jon Roberts, and then I posted it to my YouTube page. I said, 'As a comedian I don't think this is funny, but what do you guys think?' I wasn't prepared for what happened next."

The clip quickly spread through social media, with some calling on reservation casinos to cancel Ralphie May's future gigs. Meanwhile, some of his fan base went after Chalepah. Viral vitriol gave way to absolute hysteria, with the press picking up on the story. While promoting an upcoming casino gig in Michigan, May spoke to the *Superior Telegram* and gave his side of the story. "Apparently my comedy was taken out of context when I was talking about Native Americans. It was edited, over-edited, illegally used and recorded, and they left out the punch. They left out the punch line, which is—the whole reason that I'm upset with Indians is that *Dances with Wolves* beat out *Goodfellas* for the Oscar. . . . No one, if you heard it in full context, would think that it's anything. . . . I'm not a hateful person, and this was not right for someone to do."

Native comedians found themselves in a delicate position. Anish-inaabe stand-up Tito Ybarra explained, "I was really on the fence and apprehensive about going at the issue at first because I realize [comedians] make mistakes. I myself have made mistakes early in my career. . . . He's saying the punch line was edited out. I don't believe the punchline would have smoothed that over."

The topic was debated on the public radio program *Native America Calling.* An irate listener from the Pine Ridge Reservation phoned in: "I just want to say to Ralphie that his nonapology isn't acceptable, and making excuses for doing a racist, hateful diatribe against our people is not acceptable in any form. There have been comedians—Flip Wilson [and] George Carlin, to name a few—that have done comic routines about Indians that have been really funny and acceptable. Ralphie's is just based on misinformation, ignorance, and stupidity. . . . If he came out and said, 'Hey, you know, I really messed up here. I said things that were hateful, ignorant, hurtful, and I'm very sorry and I'm going to make amends in some way—I'm going to try my best to compensate for my ignorance'—then I might be able to accept his apology."

"He got all this hate mail," says Chalepah. "Well, of course he did, but what I didn't anticipate was that he would get death threats. Ralphie had a young family, and they were threatened. Sometimes when you start these conversations, you can't control where they go. It got out of hand. People were attacking him for his weight and saying *awful* things to him. And I wasn't prepared for the backlash I received either. But I wanted him to understand. . . . We don't need anyone with a national platform somehow implying we need to 'get over it.' We don't have a huge voice in mainstream media or pop culture. . . . It's like an abusive relationship, and we keep getting verbally abused and we keep taking it and taking it. And we're not taking it anymore. But it created this huge thing. Everyone was mad. I sent him a direct message, and he responded, and we went back and forth. At first he was very defensive, and I understood that, but I was trying to educate, not attack. I was simply stating, 'You might not be racist, but you're furthering a racist narrative. You have power and a voice and I do not. You should at least hear how this affects us.' "

Casino after casino canceled his scheduled shows, and May panicked. He messaged Chalepah and asked if they could talk over the phone. "We spoke right before I had to do a gig," she recalls. "He sounded tired. He told me, 'I'm not a bad guy—I'm a real person. If you get to know me, you'll know that.' And I said, 'Me too, I'm not some troll and I'm not out to get you. I'm a fan, but I think this particular bit is harmful to a population that doesn't have a voice. You're furthering a dangerous narrative that it's okay to not care about Indians because they're inferior. It's okay to hate them because they're less than human. That's dangerous, Ralphie. If you knew the suicide rates of our children and how we're just trying to give them a reason to live—you would feel ashamed of yourself. They're fed this narrative that they're invisible, that they're not important, that their ancestors went extinct—and society doesn't provide them with any future narrative.' So we talked all about this until we got on the same page. And then we considered the next step: 'How do we fix this situation now that everybody is pissed off?' He said, 'Why don't you come and do a show with me?' I said, 'I'm down. Anytime.' We needed people to see that you could have a dispute and then come together. It was up to us to calm everybody down."

For the next month, May addressed the issue whenever he had to promote a gig. "I thought I was a well-read, educated man," he said. "I know nothing. . . . I have learned so much. . . . I want to learn more. . . . I hope to be a conduit for things that we are not taught . . . and I apologize that I added to it . . . when I said, 'Get over it.' That's so absurd to think you could get over something that is still happening."

May flew Chalepah to Los Angeles to play the Hollywood Improv alongside comedians Iliza Schlesinger, Jerrod Carmichael, and Margaret Cho. All proceeds went to the Bicona Foundation, a

Charlie Hill Phones Mitzi Shore to Say Good-Bye

Reservation casinos seldom booked Native comedians. The casinos wanted to target those demographics most likely to gamble their money away. They needed acts like Rich Little, Art Garfunkel, and Engelbert Humperdinck who would appeal to older, white people. Meanwhile, veterans like Charlie Hill were shut out. "All my comedy buddies think I'm making a fortune doing those," said Hill. "I'm rarely booked."

"They hired white people because white people were the ones going to the casinos, and white people want to see other white people," says singer-songwriter Buffy Sainte-Marie. "They're not interested in seeing me or Charlie Hill. Indian casinos are mostly run by businesspeople who have nothing to do with Indians and everything to do with outside interests. Charlie was pissed that Indian casinos wouldn't hire Indian artists."

The casino phenomenon became a source of ridicule for comedians like Tito Ybarra, who joked in his act, "Saw a white man crying at the casino earlier. I went up to him and I put my arm around him. I said, 'What's the matter?' He said, 'I lost everything!' I said, 'Good. How does it feel?' "

The whole makeup of Native nations changed at the end of the 1980s when the Supreme Court ruled that state gambling laws had no jurisdiction in sovereign Native nations. Developers from Las Vegas came to remote areas like Uncasville, Connecticut; Harris, Michigan; and Morton, Minnesota, to create an infrastructure and lend their gaming expertise. It created a new economic model—and awkward relationships between outside builders and the locals. "Only ten percent of Indian tribes have [control over] casinos," claimed Charlie Hill. "Casinos are a lost opportunity. We could've had our own infrastructure to stand alone." Hill lamented the lack of Native talent booked in the showrooms. "They have money for the white performer, but when it comes to Indians, they put everybody on a budget. . . . We're being overlooked. It's a disgrace."

Navajo comic Ernie Tsosie says, "It would seem, with all these casinos, that we as Native comics would have shows lined up all over the place. But it's not like that at all. Most of the time we're just doing Native events, conferences, or schools."

There was only one Native comedy act that truly cashed in, and it wasn't Charlie Hill. "Charlie was the real deal, and some people in show business were afraid of him," says his friend and fellow comic Allan Stephan. "He wasn't considered a crossover act, whereas Williams and Ree attracted that old, white casino crowd because their act was mostly ha-ha on the Indian."

"We got in on the ground floor," says Terry Ree. "We worked the convention of the National Indian Gaming Association for free, knowing full well it was a chance to audition for all these casinos around the country. It worked. We extended our career another twenty-five years." Williams and Ree played the Agua Caliente Casino in Palm Springs; the Grand Falls Casino in Larchwood, Iowa; the Sky City Casino in Pueblo of Acoma, New Mexico; and the Avi Resort and Casino in Laughlin, Nevada, all in a row. The pay was great and their schedule was full, but Ree concedes his act is the exception. "The Indian casinos have been great for pretty much everybody in the entertainment business—except for Natives.

There's Indian talent playing powwows and Indian gatherings all around the country, but the casinos don't throw them a bone. Some of the Indian casinos are making billions of dollars with no Indian acts. These places should be showcasing Indian artists every damn week—but they don't, because the Indian casinos are run by white people. I'm beginning to sound like Charlie Hill."

CHARLIE HILL WORKED his whole life toward one solitary goal: stand-up. He achieved the dream and then some—but as the millennium turned, he felt it slipping away. Tired of waiting for good luck to strike, he phoned his old friend David Letterman and inquired about getting on his program again. "David Letterman was a friend of my dad's, and so he just called him," says Nasbah Hill. "They talked, and Letterman told him to call the booking person at a given time and they'd get him on the show. There was no manager involved; my dad just asked directly."

Booked alongside Billy Bob Thornton and Cyndi Lauper, Charlie's act went over well, even though the material was old. Hill seldom revised his act, clinging instead to the tried-and-true routines he knew would always work. "He came up with funny things when he was joking around, but he wouldn't bother to chronicle it, memorize it, and put it in his act," says comedian Argus Hamilton. "Charlie had the same problem as a lot of comics. He wasn't a disciplined worker bee. He was a *real comic*, which means he slacked off during the day."

Allan Stephan says, "At some point he lost the desire to keep pushing. When a comic gets older, it's hard to keep it up."

As comedy shifted its focus to the Internet, Hill was convinced it was just a passing fad. "He came from an era where social media wasn't the way," says Nasbah Hill. "When things changed, he didn't see the point, and it was sort of a step backward. We'd tell him he needed a promo packet of some kind, but he didn't feel it was necessary. He felt his reputation spoke for itself. We would tell him, 'This is how people do it now,' but he just felt social media was dumb. I said, 'You have so many fans out there. They want to see what you're up to.' He'd say, 'It's none of their business!' "

The special he hosted for Showtime was his proudest moment, but when it failed to lead to new opportunities, it left him deflated. "He didn't get support from the highest sharks in the business," says Buffy Sainte-Marie. "What happened to Charlie the day after? Nothing. There was no agent. They let him sit there and bloom and then fade. He never got another break."

Hill phoned Letterman a second time and booked himself for one final network television appearance. He flew to Manhattan with his daughter and showed her around the venues he used to haunt when he was young. Nasbah Hill recalls, "We walked through Greenwich Village. We went over to the La MaMa Theatre where he started his career and took some pictures. He told me stories about what it was like, and then we went to the taping. The first guest that night was Snoop Dogg. I was in the greenroom when Snoop Dogg came offstage and started talking to my dad. Snoop told him, 'You know, I'm also Indian.' My dad raised his eyebrow and was like, 'Oh yeah? What tribe are you?' Snoop said, 'I'm from the Slap-a-Ho tribe.' Later my dad said to me, 'He had probably been waiting his whole life to tell that joke to an Indian.' "

Shortly after returning to Los Angeles, Hill was plagued with health problems. He was diagnosed with type 2 diabetes, fell victim to Bell's palsy, and suffered a heart attack, which required immediate surgery. "I'm sure it was all stress-related," says Nasbah. "There was a long period where he wasn't working, and he got very depressed. The stress level was very high, and it got hard." It got to the point where he could barely afford his Venice Beach apartment. Hill could still get spots at the Comedy Store, but it wasn't like the old days. Most of his contemporaries were either millionaires like Letterman,

Leno, and Michael Keaton, or they had retired altogether. "He loved California, but he was running out of money," says Nasbah. "He suggested we go to Oneida for the summer since we had a family house on the reservation."

Shortly after arriving in Wisconsin, Hill visited a doctor. They ran some tests and returned with a dire diagnosis. Hill had terminal lymphoma. The doctor surmised that he had one year left to live. "We planned to come only for the summer," says Nasbah. "But we ended up staying. I think, basically, he came home to die."

His energy depleted rapidly. He sat in bed, thumbing through his address book, placing phone calls to old friends. "I talked to him on the phone a few times," says Lindsay Wagner. "There are people in life that, once you know them, it never changes. You don't see them for years and years, and when you do see each other—it's like you've never been apart. Charlie was like that. In my heart, he was family."

Argus Hamilton arranged a special phone call between Charlie and his old benefactor, the proprietor of the Comedy Store, Mitzi Shore. He says, "By the time Charlie was on his deathbed, Mitzi Shore had been living with dementia and Parkinson's for years. She had been virtually incommunicado, couldn't talk, just sat around watching TV. I made a phone call. I said, 'Charlie, I've got Mitzi on the line. I know you'd like to tell her you love her before you go to the next world.' Charlie said, 'Thank you,' and I handed the phone to Mitzi. She listened for about forty-five seconds, and I swear to God, she broke up and said, 'Charlie, I love you so much. I have always believed in you. I love you.' I couldn't believe it. It was the first time she spoke a complete sentence in eight years."

Hill's wife of thirty-three years and their four children received an outpouring of love from Natives continent-wide. He had inspired scores of future performers. His vast influence was only now becoming evident. "He was the first genuinely First Nations person I ever saw on TV, and he wasn't pretending to be anything else," explains Ojibwe comedian Craig Lauzon. "To see Charlie Hill up there proudly saying he was Oneida and making jokes from that point of view? I started running around singing his 'One little, two little, three little whiteys' all the time. It was the funniest thing I had ever heard, because anytime someone found out I was Native, they'd start singing, 'One little, two little, three little Indians.' And then here comes a guy, Charlie Hill, making fun of that. Charlie Hill was coming from *our* perspective. It blew me away."

Hill always listened passively to praise, proud yet humble, dismissing it as hyperbole. "He never called attention to himself," says comedian Jeff Altman. "When you were around him, he always wanted to talk about *you*. He never called attention to the fact he was the first Native American stand-up."

Charlie Hill passed away peacefully on December 30, 2013. Nasbah Hill says, "Right before he died, he said he didn't care what happened at the funeral, so long as he received a standing ovation. My mom is a traditional Navajo woman and she made all the arrangements. The funeral was in Oneida, and then there was a reception at the local hotel." A video retrospective of choice footage was projected that evening at the Oneida Hotel. When it was finished, friends and family applauded. Nasbah says, "And he got his standing ovation."

Jeff Altman was on *The Late Show with David Letterman* the next night, sitting beside the host as he addressed the camera from his desk. "I want to make sure we take a second here to mention our friend Charlie Hill," said Letterman. "A guy that we knew from way, way back in the seventies. Never heard anybody say a bad thing about Charlie Hill." Altman nodded: "Absolutely. Absolutely."

"Throughout history there are these transitional people who are responsible for transitional moments," says Sterlin Harjo. "It may not have led to financial stability for him, but when Charlie Hill went on national television and simply spoke like a human being—it was a *huge* moment. There's no telling how many minds he changed because of that appearance. He changed the public perception about what a Native person *is*. Without Charlie Hill appearing on *The Richard Pryor Show* . . . without Charlie Hill appearing on David Letterman . . . without Charlie Hill going onstage at the Comedy Store . . . we wouldn't be here right now."

The 1491s Get a Standing Ovation
in a Small Oregon Town

The 1491s are in Ashland, Oregon, preparing the sketch comedy epic they have been working on for a year and a half. Tonight is the opening performance of *Between Two Knees*. The title is at the same time a dick joke, a hat tip to the Zach Galifianakis web series *Between Two Ferns*, and a description of the subject matter. *Between Two Knees* tells the story of Native America from the Wounded Knee Massacre of 1890 to the armed standoff between the FBI and AIM at Wounded Knee in 1973.

Ashland sits fourteen miles north of the California border. Oregon is generally considered the domain of microbrews, fixie bikes, and hipster beards, but once you get to the state's southernmost reaches you're more likely to hear a pickup truck blaring Ted Nugent than a smart car blasting *All Things Considered*. The farmers and cowboys, many now operating as rural Lyft drivers, are vocal in their resentment of having a bunch of liberal actors in the region. This is, after all, a part of the world where militias engage in backwoods training.

Ashland is essentially a bourgeois roadside attraction. Most of the local businesses reference the world's most famous playwright. From the Shakespeare Hair Salon to the Midsummer's Dream Bed and Breakfast, it is teeming with out-of-town actors, writers, and directors, many straight from the Broadway stage. The Shakespeare Festival has defined this town since 1935.

The 1491s have prepared a show that is largely about the lasting effects of settler-colonialism, something that is key to the history of Ashland itself. In the center of town, Lithia Park has a creek winding through its middle. Walking trails along the waterway are pockmarked with commemorative plaques crediting the green space to the Ladies Chautauqua Club, a turn-of-the-century women's auxiliary. *Chautauqua* is a reference to the Methodist speaking circuit of the 1800s, which presented educational lectures about patriotism and religious duty. Students from Native American boarding schools were forced to tour the Chautauqua circuit as Native "success stories."

Down the street from the park is the Thomas Theatre, where Bobby Wilson is holding court with a crowd of fans clutching their tickets in anticipation. Wilson is wearing a black baseball jacket with a beaded design that he created himself. It depicts Chief Wahoo, the Cleveland baseball mascot, hanging from a noose.

Migizi Pensoneau, despite his striking black dress shirt and hand-painted red necktie, fades into the background. Leaning against a wall near the box office, he watches as Wilson greets each patron with a wide, disarming smile, carrying on multiple conversations at the same time. "Bobby is good at this type of thing," says Pensoneau. "He's in his element. He can talk to absolutely anyone. I can't talk to any of these people." This is in essence the formula that makes the 1491s click: distinctive personalities, contradictory and complementary, the ingredients of any great comedy team.

Inside the theater, festival ushers are distributing photocopied fact sheets with a map showing the approximate locations of all the Native Nations that made up Oregon in the mid-1800s: the Burns Paiute Tribe; the Confederated Tribes of the Grande Ronde; the Confederated Tribes of Siletz Indians; the Confederated Tribes of the Umatilla Indian Reservation; the Confederated Tribes of Warm

Springs; the Confederated Tribes of Coos, Lower Umpqua, and Siu-slaw Indians; the Cow Creek Band of Umpqua Tribe of Indians; the Coquille Indian Tribe; and the Klamath Tribes. Music pipes through the lobby, showcasing a playlist of old pop songs with stereotyped themes: "Kaw-Liga" by Hank Williams, "Ten Little Indians" by the Beach Boys, "Half-Breed" by Cher, "Rosie the Redskin" by Midge Williams, and "I'm an Indian Too" from the musical *Annie Get Your Gun*. The songs follow patrons into the bathroom, where "Pocahontas" by Johnny Cash, "Apache" by Link Wray, and "Your Squaw Is on the Warpath" by Loretta Lynn echo off the porcelain.

The sellout crowd fills the U-shaped auditorium while an announcement plays over the loudspeaker. It is the voice of Bobby Wilson: "Please—no cell phones or photography. They will steal part of our soul."

For two hours the sketch comedy opus tackles brutal topics while the crowd laughs uproariously throughout. The 1491s have managed to take the least amusing subject matter imaginable and turn it into a relentless joke-driven narrative, from residential boarding schools to full-scale military slaughter. Menominee actor Justin Gauthier is the *Between Two Knees* interlocutor, a detached character named Larry who guides the story from the corner of the stage. His character was created for the specific purpose of defusing audience apprehension about genocide jokes. Sterlin Harjo explains, "What we realized early on is that we have to give non-Natives permission to laugh, because they have been trained to either think of us as dying or needing help. So with the narrator, we built it in. We used him to let the audience in on the joke."

Gauthier opens the show addressing the audience directly: "We're gonna talk about war, genocide, PTSD, and molestation. So it's okay to laugh." With a sweeping gesture of his arm, the curtain parts and a flashy game-show set is revealed. A multicolored wheel with blinking lights illuminates the stage. Gauthier shouts, "Okay, let's play a game! Welcome, friends and relatives, to . . . Wheel of Indian

Massacres!" The wheel spins past several options—the Yontocket Massacre, the Horseshoe Bend Massacre, the Sand Creek Massacre, eventually landing on the Sacramento River Massacre. "Oh, this is a good one," says Gauthier. "Y'all know about the Sacramento River Massacre, right? Happened down by Redding, California? They killed two hundred people? Yeah? No? Okay, okay, let's spin again." Sandwiched amid the list of massacres is an option labeled "Aunty's Choice." It's an in-joke for film fans, a hat tip to the "bust a deal, face the wheel" sequence in the 1985 fantasy film *Mad Max Beyond Thunderdome.*

The wheel slows down and lands on yet another sordid moment in American history. "Oh, Nasomah Massacre," says Gauthier. "I'm sure you heard about this one, right? Over by Randolph, Oregon? Whole families slaughtered? No? Yontocket Massacre? What about Horseshoe Bend? Sand Creek? Indian Island?" Gauthier reassures the silent audience, telling them not to worry, he'll find a massacre "we can all agree on." This time it lands on Wounded Knee, and an applause sign flashes. The actors take to the stage for the first scene of the play, set in 1890, among a pile of bodies.

Bobby Wilson says, "Indians—we think about these massacres all the time, so we really wanted to do a play that at least starts out with an Indian massacre." But rather than a depressing harangue, the 1491s have structured these horrible lessons of American history and designed them to emulate the Mel Brooks film *History of the World, Part I.* Absurd jokes propel the story, and the heavy influence of comedy films like *Airplane!* and *The Naked Gun* is apparent.

The story follows the lead character, Isaiah, as his life intersects with key moments in twentieth-century Native America. As a newborn he is rescued in the aftermath of Wounded Knee and sent to a nightmarish residential boarding school, where he meets Irma, his future wife. Their romance leads to a wedding presided over by a vacant new-age hippie played by Rachel Crowl.

"The scene was based on my actual wedding," says Sterlin Harjo.

"We were in Lake Tahoe, and my buddy picked this woman to marry us who listed 'Native American Prayer Ceremony' as one of her specialties. During the ceremony she directed it all toward me because my wife was non-Native. She didn't even mention a specific tribe, which is always a clue that this type of thing is *bullshit*. She said, 'This is a Native American prayer . . . ,' and then talked about 'the raven,' and 'the eagle,' and 'the wind,' or whatever. She was so happy she finally had a Native to connect with because she had probably done this prayer for five thousand white people. So I wrote this scene in *Between Two Knees* that made fun of that new-age liberal thing, where they want to connect with us so badly but always approach it the wrong way."

The OSF gave the 1491s free rein to ridicule whatever they wanted, regardless of how much it might upset festivalgoers. However, there was one exception. Thomas Ryan RedCorn says, "There was only one time that they told me a joke went too far. There was a line in there somewhere about a character doing things that upset their parents: 'You know, I was just doing white people's stuff like going to the farmer's market and attending plays at the Oregon Shakespeare Festival.' They made us take that out."

Six nights a week *Between Two Knees* played to sold-out crowds. For the majority, it was the first comedy they had ever seen from a Native American perspective. Theater critic Patrick Thomas of the website Talkin' Broadway wrote, "They have found a way to get a nearly all-white audience to laugh along as they remind them of the horrors their ancestors committed against native people and celebrate the concept of a sort of virtual reverse genocide, closing with a sing-along of 'so long, white people.' Playing with decades of racial stereotyping, it's subversive, sarcastic . . . and disturbing."

Although the play was universally praised by theater critics, some veteran patrons of the Oregon Shakespeare Festival walked out in anger. Bobby Wilson says, "Somebody came up to the usher and said, 'I've been coming here fifteen years, and this is the worst play I've seen! This is the last time I'm ever coming to the Oregon Shakespeare Festival!' Others wrote these long letters saying we had done a terrible thing, that we shouldn't be telling jokes about Indian tragedies, and then they would cite another Indian play that they had seen and say, 'Now, *that* was a good one.' The OSF has a page on their website where the audience can rate the play, and all of our ratings were either one star or five stars, with nothing in between. Either people really enjoyed it or they fucking hated it. And we ate that up."

If the show was jarring to some, that was the intent. "We were so happy that we were hitting the right nerve," says Migizi Pensoneau. "If we received middling notices, then that would have meant we didn't accomplish what we set out to do. We were so pleased that it was either five stars or zero stars. At the very beginning of the show, we tell the audience, 'You're going to be confronted with the source of your social power. But don't worry—after this you'll still own everything.' We're basically saying, 'Yeah, you might not be bad guys, but you profited *because* of bad guys.' That still gets people pretty irked. Nobody likes hearing that what they love and what they believe in is built on the oppression of someone else."

"It can be really difficult to look back at those things like the Wounded Knee Massacre," says Wilson. "It's a fucking terrible thing that happened. Boarding schools—it's super dark. It's some of the darkest stuff that exists on the planet. But if you take somebody like Mel Brooks—what I admire so much about him . . . Mel Brooks took some of the darkest times of his people's history and found a way to make his people laugh through that dark history. . . . [In] Mel Brooks's *History of the World* . . . there's a song about the Spanish Inquisition, and it goes through some of the *worst* things that ever happened to Jewish people . . . they made a musical out of it! It's insane and really brilliant and really beautiful. I would love it if we had something like that—that Indians can look at and laugh at. But it's harder for us because we still live in America—and that's exactly where all of the worst things that have ever happened to Indians *is*. . . . But I think a lot of what Native comedians have to offer is really beautiful. . . . I'm not saying we're saving the world or anything like that, but it's just a solid contribution."

"This was our best attempt to subvert the narrative of what it means to be a Native person in the world right now," explains Dallas Goldtooth. "We went into this with an intention to challenge how we see ourselves [as] Native people, how white folks see us, how the outside world sees us in general. I'm pretty happy with the accomplishment here. . . . We need to allow ourselves the freedom to laugh."

Jonny Roberts Is Stunned to See the Literal Writing on the Wall

Jonny Roberts is rifling through his notes, waiting to go onstage at the Laugh Factory in Hollywood. From the wings he watches a Lakota comedian named Will Spottedbear. It's the rarest of nights in a comedy club—every act on the show is Native American.

Spottedbear mostly performs at Courtney's Comedy Club in Fargo, North Dakota. Until this show came along, he didn't even know there were any other Native comedians. "Most Native comics don't start in comedy clubs, so I didn't really run into anyone," he says. "And then I got invited to come do this all-Native stand-up showcase. I'm meeting all these Native comedians—JR Redwater, Ernie Tsosie, Jim Ruel, Jonny Roberts—this is a defining moment for me."

After their respective sets, the comics soak up the atmosphere of the Sunset Strip. Jonny Roberts can hardly believe that he's here. "I used to watch a TV show in the early 1990s that was done from the Laugh Factory," he says. "It featured all the hardworking comedians who never reached superstardom—comics like Dennis Wolfberg and John Caponera—to see their pictures on the wall tonight, it feels like something special."

Together they walk a few blocks up the street to the Comedy Store, where they've been granted some stage time in the upstairs

Belly Room. Roberts is still in awe: "Here I am coming from the Red Lake Nation, a reservation where there's no stand-up. To come from Red Lake and get to do a set at the Comedy Store—this is *amazing*."

At the end of the night, the excitement remains, and the comedians are too full of adrenaline, too wired to go home. They stroll through the back hallway, posing for photos with one another and stopping to admire the outdated head shots of Garry Shandling, Arsenio Hall, Roseanne Barr, and David Letterman. As the show spills out of the Main Room, Roberts heads in the direction of the parking lot.

"We were all walking out at the end of the night," he says. "And just as we turned the corner where they have all the signatures of the comedians painted on the wall—we saw his name. All of us came from nowhere or grew up on rezzes. And there was the name of the guy who started it all for us Native comedians: Charlie Hill. It was magical."

Acknowledgments

A special thank-you to all those who helped along the way: Brian Bahe, Joy Barr, Roseanne Barr, Steve Binder, Elizabeth Breeden, Lucas Brown Eyes, Don Burnstick, Sara Bynoe, Adrianne Chalepah, Joey Clift, Jackie Curtiss, Howie Echo-Hawk, Graham Elwood, Wayne Federman, Max Gail, Freya Giles, Sophie Glidden-Lyon, Dallas Goldtooth, Mary Jane Gorshenin, Daniel Greenberg, Argus Hamilton, Sterlin Harjo, Dakota Ray Hebert, Laura Hernandez, Nasbah Hill, Norbert Hill Jr., Jay Johnston, Jackie Keliiaa, Jessica Kelley, Don Kelly, La MaMa Theatre, Craig Lauzon, Jocelyn Littlechief, Danny Littlejohn, Sean Manning, Merrill Markoe, Scott McGee, Ryan McMahon, Heidi Meier, Elaine Miles, Howie Miller, Larry Omaha, Oregon Shakespeare Festival, Sierra Ornelas, Zaim Paine, Migizi Pensoneau, Ruth Pierich, Sara Pocock, Sara Radovanovitch, Kristen Rattray, Thomas Ryan RedCorn, Terry Ree, Jon Roberts, Buffy Sainte-Marie, Julie Seabaugh, Mark Skwarok, Will Spottedbear, Bobbi Stamm, Allan Stephan, Ernie Tsosie, James Urbaniak, Lindsay Wagner, Kateri Walker, Bobby Wilson, Marc Yaffee, Isiah Yazzie, Christa Zagnas, the project's consultant Jessica Elm, and a special thanks to Tzipora Baitch.

A Note About the Notes

Several hundred archival newspapers were used in the research. The overwhelming majority published before the 1980s used racial slurs right in the headline. For this reason, a decision was made to excise those titles from the endnotes, although the date and name of each newspaper remains.

Notes

2   *"They've tried comedy shows at the casino here"*: Interview with Author.

2   *"A survey by the"*: *Washington Post*, March 25, 2005.

3   *"It's an advanced age for sure"*: *Jonny R.* podcast, Episode 14, January 2, 2018.

4   *"These wild"*: Laura Browder, *Slippery Characters: Ethnic Impersonators and American Identities* (Chapel Hill, NC: University of North Carolina Press, 2000), 57.

5   *"an Indian Princess and Child rescued"*: Christine Bold, "Fellows Find: Seeing 'the Indian' in Vaudeville," *Ransom Center Magazine*, November 3, 2016, https://sites.utexas.edu/ransomcentermagazine/2016/11/03/fellows-find-seeing -the-indian-in-vaudeville/.

5   *"If this were permitted"*: Thomas Henry Tibbles, *The Ponca Chiefs: An Account of the Trial of Standing Bear* (Lincoln, NE: University of Nebraska Press, 1972), 48.

5   *"peaceful Indian to come and go"*: L. G. Moses, *Wild West Shows and the Images of American Indians* (Albuquerque, NM: University of New Mexico Press, 1999), 294.

5   *"passed during and after the Civil War"*: Vine Deloria Jr., *Custer Died for Your Sins: An Indian Manifesto* (New York, NY: Avon Books, Sixth Printing, September 1971), 15.

6   *"There was nothing scientific"*: Edited by Kathleen Ratteree and Norbert Hill, *The Great Vanishing Act* (Golden, CO: Fulcrum Publishing, 2017), 130.

6   *"When the school is on the reserve"*: Official Reports of the Debates of the House of Commons, Volume 2; Volume 14, 1883.

6   *"Funded by the federal government"*: Bob Joseph, *21 Things You May Not Know About the Indian Act* (Port Coquitlam, BC: Indigenous Relations Press, 2018), 65.

6   *"When students spoke"*: *The Fifth Estate*, CBC Television, March 3, 2019.

7   *"Indian boys and girls"*: Joseph, *21 Things*, 59.

7   *"forgetting all the kindness"*: Joseph, *21 Things*, 64–65.

7   *"Buffalo Bill Cody presented"*: Deanne Stillman, *Blood Brothers: The Story of the Strange Friendship Between Sitting Bull and Buffalo Bill* (New York, NY: Simon & Schuster, 2017), 61.

7   *"So, too, by his own account"*: Stillman, *Blood Brothers*, 33.

NOTES

7   *"the most important commercial vehicle"*: Christine Bold, *The Frontier Club* (New York, NY: Oxford University Press, 2013), 163.

7   *"Buffalo Bill's slogan"*: Philip J. Deloria, *Indians in Unexpected Places* (Lawrence, KS: University Press of Kansas, 2004), 58.

8   *"The late 1880s"*: Deloria, *Indians in Unexpected Places*, 69.

8   *"The Office of Indian Affairs"*: L. G. Moses, *Wild West Shows and the Images of American Indians* (Albuquerque, NM: University of New Mexico Press, 1999), 66; Ralph and Natasha Friar, *The Only Good Indian . . . The Hollywood Gospel* (New York, NY: Drama Book Specialists, 1973), 56; Linda Scarangella McNenly, *Native Performers in Wild West Shows* (Norman: University of Oklahoma Press, 2012), 39.

8   *"Indians must conform"*: L. G. Moses, *Wild West Shows and the Images of American Indians*, 74.

9   *"Suddenly it became much harder"*: McNenly, *Native Performers in Wild West Shows*, 59.

9   *"It was as if"*: Rich Hall's Inventing the Indian, BBC Television, October 28, 2012.

9   *"About thirty Native Americans"*: Browder, *Slippery Characters*, 59.

9   *"All the Indians in Buffalo Bill's show"*: Browder, *Slippery Characters*, 58.

9   *"mistreatment of seventy-five Indians"*: McNenly, *Native Performers in Wild West Shows*, 44, 59.

9   *"A new policy was implemented"*: Moses, *Wild West Shows and the Images of American Indians*, 33.

10 *"After the captives were shackled"*: Roxanne Dunbar-Ortiz, *An Indigenous Peoples' History of the United States* (Boston, Beacon Press, 2014), 151.

10 *"What benefit has the Indian derived"*: Moses, *Wild West Shows and the Images of American Indians*, 101.

11 *"insisted that the filming take place"*: Deloria, *Indians in Unexpected Places*, 53.

11 *"Parking a mobile stage in a town of yokels"*: "Rolling Thunder Kiowa Indian Ointment," National Museum of American History, Smithsonian, https://americanhistory.si.edu/collections/search/object/nmah_209853; "On the Phenomenon of the Indian Medicine Show," Travalanche, November 19, 2013, https://travsd.wordpress.com/2013/11/19/on-the-phenomenon-of-the-indian-medicine-show/.

12 *"Irish and blackface comedy"*: Browder, *Slippery Characters*, 71.

12 *"The allotment policy sought to divide"*: Deloria, *Indians in Unexpected Places*, 150.

13 *"amazed, amused, and puzzled"*: Edited by Daniel F. Littlefield Jr. and Carol A. Petty Hunter, *The Fus Fixico Letters*, 37.

13 *"Well, so Big Man at Washington"*: Littlefield Jr., Petty Hunter, *The Fus Fixico Letters*, 87.

13 *"The dialect was immediately"*: Littlefield Jr., Petty Hunter, *The Fus Fixico Letters*, 1.

13 *"wanted him [Posey] to take his humor on the stage"*: Daniel F. Littlefield Jr., *Alex Posey: Creek Poet, Journalist and Humorist* (Lincoln, NE: University of Nebraska Press, 1997), 184.

14 *"But before the scheduled gig could occur"*: Littlefield Jr., *Alex Posey*, 5.

15 *"I wrote these commentaries"*: Interview with Author.

16 *"I was friends with his cousin"*: Interview with Author.

17 *"Laughter and joy is very much a part of Native culture"*: Indianz.com, March 23, 2011.

17 *"Dallas and I, ever since we were little kids"*: "Red Man Laughing—The 1491s Interview," https://www.redmanlaughing.com/listen/2013/10/red-man-laughing-the-1491s-interview, October 14, 2013.

17 *"My family is 'traditional'"*: *The Extraordinary Negroes*, with guest Dallas Goldtooth, January 29, 2018.

17 *"We had just watched one of those bad APTN shows"*: Interview with Author.

18 *"When you grow up in these"*: *The Cuts* podcast, IndianandCowboy.ca, October 21, 2017.

19 *"That's where I first met Ryan"*: "Red Man Laughing," October 14, 2013.

19 *"The two lived near"*: *The Cuts* podcast, IndianandCowboy.ca, October 21, 2017.

19 *"Basically the idea of the video"*: Interview with Author.

20 *"We couldn't quit laughing"*: *The Cuts* podcast, IndianandCowboy.ca, October 21, 2017; *Willamette Week*, April 18, 2016.

21 *"I was teaching a weeklong poetry"*: *The Cuts* podcast, IndianandCowboy.ca, October 21, 2017.

21 *"This propaganda of a"*: "1491s Play with Themselves," Tedx Talks, August 7, 2013.

22 *"Vaudeville theaters presented"*: Chief Poolaw Eugene H. Jones, *Native Americans as Shown on the Stage* (Metuchen, NJ: Scarecrow Press, Inc., 1988), 121.

22 *"The most popular Native act in vaudeville"*: *Philadelphia Inquirer*, August 8, 2017.

23 *"penal institutions where little children"*: Ward Churchill, *Kill the Indian, Save the Man* (San Francisco, CA: City Lights Books, 2004), 44.

23 *"The word 'murder' is a terrible word"*: Churchill, *Kill the Indian, Save the Man*, 36.

23 *"Advent of Aboriginal mirth-makers"*: *Philadelphia Inquirer*, February 22, 1909.

23 *"gave a particularly clever impersonation"*: *Carlisle Arrow*, May 12, 1916.

24 *"Pete Red Jacket sat at a desk"*: *Leavenworth Times*, October 29, 1907.

24 *"Pete Red Jacket and His Comedy Donkey"*: *Central New Jersey Home News*, July 15, 1911.

24 *"droll little redface comedian"*: *Scranton Republican*, June 24, 1911.

24 *"Sometimes billed as the Broadway Girl and the Indian"*: *Huntington Herald*, November 22, 1916.

24 *"Originally from South Dakota"*: *Bridgeport Telegram*, May 29, 1925.

24 *"impersonations of Joe Welch"*: *Salt Lake Tribune*, December 20, 1917.

24 *"Bijou Theatre"*: *Wausau Daily Herald*, September 1, 1916.

25 *"positive riot"*: *Salt Lake Tribune*, December 20, 1917.

NOTES

25 *"the pocket edition of Fred Stone"*: P. G. Wodehouse, "Fred Stone," *Vanity Fair*, December 1917.

25 *"His celebrity status"*: *Elmira Star-Gazette*, January 6, 1923.

25 *"under the general supervision"*: *Variety*, May 13, 1921.

25 *"Indeed, he is a sort of a wonder child performer"*: *Dayton Daily News*, June 18, 1920.

25 *"The Clifford Wayne Trio . . . have gotten away"*: *Variety*, May 13, 1921.

25 *"youthful versatile entertaining comedian"*: *Variety*, September 9, 1925.

26 *"Worst-case scenario is you're booked"*: Interview with Author.

31 *"Durango is out of the way, and glad of it"*: *History La Plata: Snapshots in Time*, May 2019, Volume XXV.

31 *"The Cherokee Nation established a newspaper of its own"*: Judith Nies, *Native American History: A Chronology of the Vast Achievements of a Culture and Their Links to World Events* (New York, NY: Ballantine, 1996), 248.

31 *"The Cherokee leader"*: Yagoda, *Will Rogers: A Biography*, 4.

31 *"Andrew Jackson campaigned for president"*: Yagoda, *Will Rogers: A Biography*, 7.

32 *"The state of Georgia then sent in its own troops"*: Nies, *Native American History*, 244.

32 *"The Indian Removal Act was passed by Congress"*: Liz Sonneborn, W. David Baird, *Will Rogers* (Broomall, PA: Chelsea House Publishers, 1993), 25.

32 *"They were nicknamed the Old Settlers"*: Yagoda, *Will Rogers: A Biography*, 4.

32 *"Those who survived the Trail of Tears"*: Yagoda, *Will Rogers: A Biography*, 6.

33 *"A Cherokee woman named Mary Schrimsher"*: Amy M. Ware, *The Cherokee Kid: Will Rogers, Tribal Identity, and the Making of an American Icon* (Lawrence: University Press of Kansas, 2015), 27.

33 *"As his father had done in 1830"*: Yagoda, *Will Rogers: A Biography*, 8.

33 *"The enslaved person known as Rabb fought for the North"*: Homer Croy, *Our Will Rogers* (New York, NY: Duell, Sloan and Pearce, 1953), 14.

33 *"He was taught the ways of the rope by Dan Walker"*: Ware, *The Cherokee Kid*, 38–40.

34 *"Are we powerless to enforce"*: *Ethnohistory*, Volume 56, Number 1, Winter 2009, 9.

34 *"His situation worsened when Henry L. Dawes"*: Ware, *The Cherokee Kid*, 44.

34 *"the Dawes Act"*: Stan Steiner, *The New Indians* (New York, NY: Dell Publishing, 1968), 162–163; Yagoda, *Will Rogers: A Biography*, 34.

34 *"Will Rogers was listed on the Cherokee Authenticated"*: Edited by Arthur Frank Wertheim and Barbara Bair, *The Papers of Will Rogers, Wild West and Vaudeville, Volume 2* (Norman, OK: University of Oklahoma Press, 2000), 347–351.

36 *"But he shed not a single tear Sunday"*: *San Bernardino County Sun*, January 8, 1979.

38 *"The studios used it as a secret testing ground"*: Leonard Maltin, *Hooked on Hollywood: Discoveries from a Lifetime of Film Fandom* (Pittsburgh, PA: GoodKnight Books, paperback edition, 2018), 197.

38 *"I don't think I've ever been so nervous"*: Interview with Author.

39 *"I feel like this is a great opportunity"*: FNX Comedy Experience, FNX Television, March 9, 2018.

41 *"He was bounced from multiple schools"*: Ethnohistory, Volume 56, Number 1, Winter 2009, 10.

41 *"It was rumored that Clem Rogers hired"*: Yagoda, *Will Rogers: A Biography*, 25.

41 *"A murdered grandfather"*: Yagoda, *Will Rogers: A Biography*, 41.

41 *"A few months later, Will Rogers was walking"*: Yagoda, *Will Rogers: A Biography*, 25.

42 *"Equipped with the roping dexterity"*: Ware, *The Cherokee Kid*, 58.

42 *"I know it would be a slam"*: Betty Rogers, *Will Rogers: His Wife's Story* (New York, NY: Garden City Publishing, 1941), 19–20.

42 *"While vying for a contract"*: Variety, January 4, 1956.

43 *"Rogers commuted to each gig by train"*: Wertheim and Bair, *The Papers of Will Rogers*, 256.

43 *"Occasionally a Rogers rope trick would miss"*: Wertheim and Bair, *The Papers of Will Rogers Vol. 2*, 134.

43 *"I'm handicapped up here"*: Yagoda, *Will Rogers: A Biography*, 92.

43 *"After a year on the road"*: Wertheim and Bair, *The Papers of Will Rogers Vol. 2*, 195.

43 *"Onstage he wore a red western shirt"*: Yagoda, *Will Rogers: A Biography*, 21.

43 *"Cherokee ranching culture influenced the way"*: Ethnohistory, Volume 56, Number 1, Winter 2009, 1.

44 *"Rogers grew friendly with the Three Keatons"*: Ware, *The Cherokee Kid*, 81; Wertheim and Bair, *The Papers of Will Rogers Vol. 2*, 181.

44 *"Well, I reckon I'm about as real an American"*: Ethnohistory, Volume 56, Number 1, Winter 2009, 18.

44 *"I [have] just enough white in me"*: Rogers, *Will Rogers: His Wife's Story*, 45.

44 *"Indian Territory was absorbed"*: Ethnohistory, Volume 56, Number 1, Winter 2009, 15.

44 *"We had the greatest territory in the world"*: Ware, *The Cherokee Kid*, 212.

45 *"The ceremony was performed at my mother's"*: Rogers, *Will Rogers: His Wife's Story*, 102.

45 *"Will Rogers—the Droll Oklahoma Cowboy"*: Yagoda, *Will Rogers: A Biography*, 122–123.

46 *"A male actor's monolog in a girl show"*: Edited by Bryan B. Sterling, Frances N. Sterling, *Will Rogers: Reflections and Observations* (Waterville, NY: Thorndike Press, 1993), 32.

46 *"I guess I'm a couple [newspaper] editions ahead of you folks"*: Yagoda, *Will Rogers: A Biography*, 142.

47 *"The future Hollywood mogul"*: Yagoda, *Will Rogers: A Biography*, 160.

47 *"The films were 'rube melodramas'"*: Richard D. White Jr., *Will Rogers: A Political Life* (Lubbock, TX: Texas Tech University Press, 2011), 34.

47 *"I don't know the candidate and don't want to"*: Croy, *Our Will Rogers*, 172.

48 *"Rogers was packing a suitcase in New York"*: Croy, *Our Will Rogers*, 164.

48   *"His written output was enormous"*: Croy, *Our Will Rogers*, 173.

48   *"If we didn't have two parties, we would all settle"*: Will Rogers: Wise and Witty Sayings of a Great American Humorist (Kansas City, Missouri: Hallmark Editions, 1969), 23.

48   *"We are always saying, 'Let the law take its course'"*: Rogers, *Will Rogers: Wise and Witty Sayings*, 47.

48   *"I have a scheme for stopping war"*: Rogers, *Will Rogers: Wise and Witty Sayings*, 55.

48   *"We could never understand why Mexico wasn't just crazy"*: Rogers, *Will Rogers: Wise and Witty Sayings*, 35.

49   *"I would like to state to the readers of the New York Times"*: Croy, *Our Will Rogers*, 185.

49   *"He seemed to speak for the little man"*: Man of the Year, NBC Television, 1955.

49   *"Most of the politicians Rogers ridiculed took it in stride"*: White Jr., *Will Rogers: A Political Life*, 54; Sterling, *Will Rogers: Reflections and Observations*, 5.

49   *"After President Harding's sudden death in 1923"*: David Greenberg, "Help! Call the White House! How the 1927 Mississippi Flood Created Big Government," Slate.com, September 5, 2006; Sonneborn, Baird, *Will Rogers*, 76.

50   *"At a time when the population of the United States was 120 million"*: Sterling, *Will Rogers: Reflections and Observations*, 3.

50   *"Come on, now, Henry"*: Yagoda, *Will Rogers: A Biography*, 288.

50   *"He took the opportunity to reestablish his roots in California"*: Ware, *The Cherokee Kid*, 95–96.

50   *"Rogers referred to it as"*: Beverly Hills Historical Society, "Will Rogers Jr. speaks with the Beverly Hills Historical Society in Will Rogers Park (1988)," YouTube, April 22, 2012, https://www.youtube.com/watch?v=ceKce3W5pFk.

51   *"Rogers was fortunate that he could afford another property"*: Sterling, *Will Rogers: Reflections and Observations*, 110.

51   *"Pretty good money in an era when the average"*: Sterling, *Will Rogers: Reflections and Observations*, 19–25.

51   *"The new medium of radio was more important"*: Yagoda, *Will Rogers: A Biography*, 214.

52   *"In contrast to the stark seriousness"*: Sterling, *Will Rogers: Reflections and Observations*, 44.

52   *"irresponsible financial speculation by the wealthiest"*: Sonneborn, Baird, *Will Rogers*, 88.

52   *"to get something for nothing"*: Palladium Item, November 23, 1929; Sonneborn, Baird, *Will Rogers*, 88.

52   *"There is one rule that works in every calamity"*: Boston Globe, November 1, 1929.

52   *"You will say, what will all the bankers do?"*: Yagoda, *Will Rogers: A Biography*, 198.

52   *"People want just taxes"*: Boston Globe, November 2, 1924.

52   *"When a party can't think of anything else"*: Buffalo Times, October 26, 1924.

52   *"Frank Phillips of oil fame was out the other day"*: Yagoda, *Will Rogers: A Biography*, 289.

53   *"I think the camera has done more harm for politics"*: Sterling, *Will Rogers*, 136.

53   *"It just shows that if you can start arguing over something"*: *Miami News*, February 14, 1930.

53   *"Last year we said, 'Things can't go on like this.'"*: Croy, *Our Will Rogers*, 242.

54   *"Here I am on* The Steve Allen Show*"*: Interview with Author.

61   *"The Pilgrims were a very religious people"*: Bryan B. Sterling, *The Best of Will Rogers* (New York, NY: M. Evans & Company, 1990), 181.

61   *"It's as I told you before, the Apache Indians owned the land"*: *Richmond Palladium-Item*, March 15, 1930.

61   *"it took 400 years for the Government to build a hospital"*: Sonneborn, Baird, *Will Rogers*, 90–91.

62   *"I got no use for him or any of his methods"*: Sterling, *Will Rogers: Reflections and Observations*, 129–130.

62   *"His transformation was terrifying"*: White Jr., *Will Rogers: A Political Life*, 142.

62   *"Famed cartoonist Rube Goldberg"*: Yagoda, *Will Rogers: A Biography*, 281.

62   *"He cried when he told me about it many years later"*: Croy, *Our Will Rogers*, 60.

62   *"He was vastly reserved"*: Yagoda, *Will Rogers: A Biography*, 280.

63   *"What all of us know put together don't mean anything"*: Yagoda, *Will Rogers: A Biography*, 281–282.

63   *"As the country plunged into depression"*: Edited by Steven K. Gragert and M. Jane Johansson, *The Papers of Will Rogers Volume 5: The Final Years* (Norman, OK: University of Oklahoma Press, 2006), 111.

63   *"Will Rogers is the man talkies were invented for"*: Yagoda, *Will Rogers: A Biography*, 259.

63   *"He'd read his script and say"*: Scott Eyman, *Print the Legend: The Life and Times of John Ford* (New York, NY: Simon & Schuster, 2015), 131.

63   *"In his film* So This Is London*"*: Ware, *The Cherokee Kid*, 119.

64   *"Rogers became a huge movie star"*: Rogers, *Will Rogers: His Wife's Story*, 182; *Variety*, February 6, 1934.

64   *"Our record with the"*: White Jr., *Will Rogers: A Political Life*, 141; Yagoda, *Will Rogers: A Biography*, 308–309.

65   *"The words to the song are cowboy all right"*: *New York Daily News*, January 22, 1934.

65   *"simply using a term which was common"*: Ware, *The Cherokee Kid*, 195.

65   *"Three times during his coast-to-coast broadcast"*: Yagoda, *Will Rogers: A Biography*, 309.

66   *"Mr. Rogers . . . related that during his youth he not only lived with"*: *New York Age*, February 3, 1934.

66   *"His attitude toward blacks was as patronizing"*: Yagoda, *Will Rogers: A Biography*, 200.

66   *"Will Rogers, by using a certain insulting epithet"*: *New York Age*, February 10, 1934.

66   *"Carita Roane, superintendent of the New York State Employment Service"*: *New York Age*, January 27, 1934.

66 *"The* New York Age *took it further, recommending that its readership"*: New York Age, February 10, 1934.

67 *"I want to say this . . . I think you folks are wrong"*: Yagoda, Will Rogers: A Biography, 309.

67 *"We were just barely over the trees"*: Yagoda, Will Rogers: A Biography, 323.

68 *"As the plane chugged north"*: Sonneborn, Baird, Will Rogers, 101.

68 *"If they can just keep [Alaska] from being taken over"*: Yagoda, Will Rogers: A Biography, 327.

68 *"Was you ever driving around in a car and not knowing"*: Sonneborn, Baird, Will Rogers, 101.

68 *"They were flying out of Barrow, Alaska"*: Croy, Our Will Rogers, 303.

69 *"The name of this program is* Man of the Year*"*: Man of the Year, NBC, 1955.

70 *"I was five years old and I would listen to tapes"*: Interview with Author.

72 *"loud in their complaints"*: Deloria, Indians in Unexpected Places, 92.

72 *"The Indian's aim is true"*: Motion Picture News, July 10, 1915.

73 *"Two delegations of Anishinaabeg from Minnesota"*: Deloria, Indians in Unexpected Places, 91.

73 *"distorted Indian life"*: Deloria, Indians in Unexpected Places, 92.

73 *"Indians Protest Against Indian Pictures"*: Moving Picture World, March 18, 1911.

73 *"Dear Sirs: To the average child"*: Moving Picture News, December 16, 1911.

74 *"Dear Sir – If the directors of the moving pictures"*: Moving Picture World, November 4, 1911.

75 *"From the standpoint of a student"*: Deloria, Indians in Unexpected Places, 90.

75 *"Audiences don't know the difference"*: Deloria, Indians in Unexpected Places, 93.

75 *"Cherokee Indians have turned to eradicating the stain"*: Miami News, December 17, 1921.

75 *"A movement emerged"*: Minneapolis Star, July 11, 1928.

76 *"Film studios pled ignorance"*: Variety, May 15, 1935.

76 *"Now as many as 150 Indians can be delivered"*: Ogden Standard-Examiner, September 28, 1927.

76 *"Jim Thorpe, the famed Sac and Fox Olympian"*: Deloria, Indians in Unexpected Places, 105.

76 *"Only American Indians for American Indian Parts"*: Variety, May 15, 1935.

76 *"Murray W. Garsson, special assistant to the Secretary of Labor"*: Variety, February 14, 1933.

76 *"Thorpe's campaign merged with the War Paint Club"*: Time, June 11, 2015.

76 *"Our present membership is seventy-seven"*: Friar, The Only Good Indian, 247–248.

77 *"Hollywood's habit of casting palefaces in Indian roles"*: The Rochester Democrat and Chronicle, December 3, 1939.

77 *"Honest Injuns—The Marx Bros. are hard at work"*: Modern Screen, June 1940.

78 *"Filmmaker Raoul Walsh convinced Warner Brothers"*: Hollywood Magazine, December 1941.

78 *"Such protests were common"*: The Orangeburg Times and Democrat, August 19, 1939.

NOTES

78   *"During the filming of a Gary Cooper western"*: The Fort Myers News-Press, June 15, 1951.

78   *"Chief Thundercloud, the first actor to play Tonto"*: International News Service, December 2, 1940.

79   *"I'm an enrolled member of the Cowlitz Indian Tribe"*: Interview with Author.

81   *"I deliberately tried not to be humorous or funny"*: Arizona Daily Star, June 15, 1970.

81   *"But he did inherit his father's interest in politics"*: Ware, The Cherokee Kid, 207.

82   *"I should like it to be known that I disagree with the sentiments"*: Burlington Free Press, October 25, 1935; Chicago Tribune, February 2, 1943; Los Angeles Times, April 30, 2000.

82   *"We like him, not because of his father"*: Gazette and Daily, February 3, 1943.

82   *"As World War II raged on, Rogers resigned from Congress"*: Boston Globe, November 1, 1944; Ware, The Cherokee Kid, 208.

82   *"A mother and three daughters"*: San Antonio Light, February 7, 1947.

83   *"A lot of us are veterans—and we're beginning to wonder what we fought for"*: Los Angeles Times, February 14, 1947.

83   *"Pima war hero Ira Hayes also gave a speech"*: Press Democrat, March 6, 1947; Pittsburgh Courier, April 5, 1947; Reno Gazette-Journal, March 25, 1947; Press Democrat, March 6, 1947.

83   *"Rogers started advising the Truman administration"*: Richmond Palladium Item, December 30, 1948.

83   *"Myer was considered a good candidate"*: The Chicago Tribune, March 4, 2004.

84   *"We must proceed"*: Dunbar-Ortiz, An Indigenous Peoples' History of the United States, 174.

84   *"After World War Two we had the idea"*: Minneapolis Star Tribune, March 16, 1968.

84   *"In 1949 Rogers became a lobbyist for the Navajo Nation"*: Wilmington Daily Press Journal, February 5, 1949.

84   *"The NCAI was the leading Native American advocacy group"*: Associated Press, June 23, 1953.

84   *"Through this organization, the American Indian speaks for himself"*: Ware, The Cherokee Kid, 208.

85   *"Senators Paul Fannin and Barry Goldwater"*: The Arizona Daily Star, June 15, 1970.

85   *"Both in terms of statistics"*: The Public Papers of the Presidents of the United States, 343, https://www.google.com/books/edition/Public_Papers_of_the_Presidents_of_the_U/v6DaAwAAQBAJ.

85   *"It was a nice speech"*: Arizona Daily Star, June 15, 1970.

86   *"When I was eighteen, Vine Deloria's book"*: "Charlie Hill—Leading the Life of an Indian Comedian," YouTube, November 4, 2016.

86   *"The Indian people are exactly opposite of the popular stereotype"*: Deloria Jr., Custer Died for Your Sins, 148–149, 164–168.

87   *"a little wooden Indian who hardly dared look right or left"*: Roberta Jean Hill, Dr. Lillie Rosa Minoka Hill (Minneapolis: University of Minnesota Press, 1998), 76.

87 *"After attending Catholic school, Minoka-Hill attended the Women's Medical College of Pennsylvania"*: Edited by Kathleen Ratteree and Norbert Hill, *The Great Vanishing Act* (Golden, CO: Fulcrum Publishing, 2017), 81.

87 *"He fought in Green Bay"*: *On and Off the Res' with Charlie Hill*, directed by Sandra Osawa, 1999.

88 *"It was an Indian meeting ground"*: Interview with Author.

88 *"They were often abandoned by the federal bureaus"*: Steiner, *The New Indians*, 186–187.

88 *"We watched Jackie Gleason"*: Interview with Author.

88 *"I didn't realize until later what kind of brainwashing"*: *On and Off the Res' with Charlie Hill*, directed by Sandra Osawa, 1999.

89 *"I was eight years old and I sent away for this dummy"*: "Charlie Hill—Back Home and Sovereign," *Indian Country Today*, November 4, 2016.

89 *"He had grown up watching his mother, a doctor"*: Interview with Author.

89 *"Norbert Sr. was the vice chairman"*: *Austin American-Statesman*, April 27, 1980; *Mansfield News-Journal*, May 5, 1980.

89 *"He would tell jokes and my mom would just stare at him"*: "Charlie Hill—Leading the Life of an Indian Comedian," YouTube, November 4, 2016.

89 *"As a kid, on Saturdays, after all the work was done"*: IndianCountryTV, "Charlie Hill—Back Home and Sovereign," YouTube, November 4, 2016; Elizabeth Blair, "Native American Comic Living The 'Indigenous Dream,'" *Morning Edition*, NPR, June 21, 2012.

90 *"Reading and writing were his main things"*: *Green Bay Press-Gazette*, September 15, 1991.

91 *"I usually go up twice a night and get onstage around twelve times a week"*: Interview with Author.

93 *"These false impressions have been delivered one year after another"*: *Orlando Evening Star*, November 18, 1966.

94 *"Television sitcoms picked up on the trend"*: *I Love Lucy*, Season Two, Episode Twenty-Four, CBS Television, May 4, 1953.

95 *"J. Carrol Naish will figure prominently"*: *Variety*, September 30, 1960.

95 *"Life with Luigi, despite high ratings"*: *Akron Beacon Journal*, December 29, 1952.

96 *"We're getting sick of the kind"*: *Detroit Free Press*, May 29, 1955.

96 *"Having taken away the Indian's lands, we persist"*: *Dayton Daily News*, March 23, 1957.

96 *"We tried to use genuine Indians in feature roles"*: *Baltimore Sun*, January 13, 1957.

96 *"Instead of showing so many Hollywood Indians"*: "The American Stranger," *Kaleidoscope*, NBC Television, November 19, 1958.

97 *"I voted for [contestant] number two"*: *To Tell the Truth*, CBS Television, August 27, 1957.

97 *"Television's portrayal of the Indian is not justified"*: *Cincinnati Enquirer*, January 17, 1960.

98 *"I have a three-year-old son"*: *Boston Globe*, January 9, 1961.

98 *"Writers and producers know nothing of Indian life"*: *Des Moines Register*, March 27, 1960.

99 *"By the late 1940s and 1950s, this Indian's ongoing appearances"*: Dustin Tahmahkera, *Tribal Television: Viewing Native People in Sitcoms* (Chapel Hill: The University of North Carolina Press, 2014), 1.

99 *"Leaders of 19 Oklahoma Indian tribes met at the state capitol"*: *Wisconsin State Journal*, February 1, 1960.

99 *"Television has painted the American Indian"*: *Cincinnati Enquirer*, January 17, 1960.

99 *"Television makes the younger generation think"*: *Denton Record-Chronicle*, January 13, 1960.

100 *"There is no excuse for TV producers to ignore the harm"*: *Allentown Morning Call*, July 2, 1960.

100 *"Indian war drums are sounding again in Oklahoma"*: *Cincinnati Enquirer*, January 17, 1960.

100 *"Politically, it is convenient to have Indians not as people"*: *On and Off the Res'* with Charlie Hill, directed by Sandra Osawa, 2009.

101 *"There are huge stereotypes that every one of us deals with"*: Interview with Author.

103 *"Those aren't Indians!"*: IndianCountryTV, "Charlie Hill—Back Home and Sovereign," YouTube, November 4, 2016.

103 *"About three months ago I worked up in Minneapolis"*: PM East, Westinghouse Broadcasting Company, Inc., August 18, 1961.

104 *"I'm going to go for it. I'm going to find a way"*: *Green Bay Press-Gazette*, October 13, 1977.

104 *"When he was sixteen, he learned that the comedian"*: *On and Off the Res'* with Charlie Hill, directed by Sandra Osawa, 1999.

104 *"For the past hundred years Indians have been held back"*: Paul R. McKenzie-Jones, *Clyde Warrior: Tradition, Community, and Red Power* (Norman, OK: University of Oklahoma Press, 2015), 80.

105 *"respect for American Indians' right to embrace"*: McKenzie-Jones, *Clyde Warrior*, 177.

105 *"Clyde Warrior joined with Paiute activist Mel Thom"*: Steiner, *The New Indians*, 69.

105 *"You could feel there was a squaring off"*: Steiner, *The New Indians*, 50.

106 *"Throughout the country, Indians are doing battle"*: Hunter S. Thompson, *The Great Shark Hunt: Strange Tales from a Strange Time* (New York: Simon & Schuster, 2003 edition), 379–383.

106 *"Whether an Indian writes a letter or brushes his teeth"*: *American Indian Culture and Research Journal* (Berkeley, CA: University of California Press, Volume 22, Number 4, 1998).

106 *"I read a book called* Indians of the Americas*"*: *The Dick Cavett Show*, ABC Television, June 12, 1973.

106 *"Charlie Hill was impressed and inspired"*: *On and Off the Res* with Charlie Hill, directed by Sandra Osawa, 1999; Joel Samuel, YouTube Channel, January 28, 2007.

107 *"About the American Indian Theatre Ensemble Company"*: La MaMa Experimental Theatre Club Archive.

108 *"Thank you for your letter"*: *On and Off the Res' with Charlie Hill*, directed by Sandra Osawa, 1999.

108 *"We started going to ceremonies"*: *A Good Day to Die*, directed by David Mueller and Lynn Salt, 2010.

109 *"Police had to arrest a certain number of Indians"*: Dennis Banks with Richard Erdoes, *Ojibwa Warrior* (Norman, OK: University of Oklahoma Press, 2011), 59.

109 *"A similar movement brewed in South Dakota"*: Dee Brown, *Bury My Heart at Wounded Knee* (New York, NY: Bantam Books, 2000 Printing, 1973), 284–287.

109 *"That mountain is part of the sacred Black Hills"*: Banks with Erdoes, *Ojibwa Warrior*, 109–110.

110 *"We never went [anywhere] to cause any trouble"*: *A Good Day to Die*, directed by David Mueller and Lynn Salt, 2010.

110 *"Did you read about that in Washington"*: *The Tonight Show starring Johnny Carson*, NBC Television, November 9, 1972.

110 *"Will Rogers Jr. considered the BIA occupations"*: *Palm Beach Post*, June 2, 1973.

110 *"He had done something really astounding"*: *Chula Vista Star-News*, September 27, 1973.

111 *"Eighty-nine percent of the top executives"*: Lehman Brightman at the University of Oregon, clip 1 (1970), Knight Library, YouTube.

111 *"The most ambitious of the occupations"*: Deliah Friedler, "Activist LaNada War Jack of the Bannock Nation Details Her Time Occupying Alcatraz," *Teen Vogue*, March 21, 2019.

111 *"We, the Native Americans, re-claim the land"*: "Indians of All Tribes," Alcatraz Manifesto by John Trudell, dated November 1969, *Trudell*, directed by Heather Rae, 2005.

112 *"turning over surplus facilities right and left to white profit-making corporations"*: *KPIX News*, KPIX Television, December 15, 1969.

112 *"Members of the Hopi Nation joined the protest"*: Holliday, Wendy, *Hopi History: The Story of the Alcatraz Prisoners*, Hopi Cultural Preservation Office, https://www.nps.gov/alca/learn/historyculture/hopi-prisoners-on-the-rock.htm.

113 *"The image of a raised red fist adorned the entranceway"*: *Les Indiens*, 1976, French Television documentary; KQED News, November 24, 1969.

113 *"Chavers answers telephone calls"*: *Los Angeles Times*, October 16, 1968.

113 *"During the past two years he has been visiting reservations"*: *Baltimore Sun*, April 27, 1969.

113 *"in recognition of his long-standing interest in the welfare"*: *Baltimore Sun*, June 22, 1968; *Los Angeles Times*, October 11, 1968.

113 *"Winters secured permission"*: *KPIX Eye on the Bay News*, KPIX Television, December 27, 1969.

114 *"The state government cut off all water and power"*: *Variety*, April 8, 1970.

114 *"I don't understand why the Indians want to squat"*: *Variety*, December 29, 1969; August 12, 1970.

NOTES

114 *"The significant thing that's been accomplished by Alcatraz"*: KPIX *Eye on the Bay News*, KPIX Television, June 11, 1971.

115 *"If Bob Hope can take"*: *Lawton Constitution*, February 22, 1970.

115 *"Flanked by a pair of dancing girls"*: *Hazleton Standard-Speaker*, September 23, 1970; *Lawton Constitution*, May 8, 1973.

115 *"Paul Littlechief was born in Lawton"*: *Lawton Constitution*, May 8, 1973.

115 *"In the 1950s, Paul Littlechief's parents were mystified"*: *Lawton Constitution*, June 20, 1974.

115 *"He was eighteen years old"*: *Lawton Constitution*, May 1, 1960; *Lawton Constitution*, May 22, 1960.

116 *"A few weeks later Littlechief"*: *Pasadena Independent*, November 13, 1964.

117 *"MAPES A GO GO WITH PAUL LITTLECHIEF"*: *Reno Gazette-Journal*, September 14, 1968.

117 *"The show is one of the fastest-paced"*: *Reno Gazette-Journal*, April 12, 1969.

117 *"The act caught the attention of Sam Boyd"*: *Santa Maria Times*, May 29, 1970.

117 *"I refused to accept any more bookings in the downtown lounges"*: Associated Press, September 23, 1970.

118 *"The Indian-flavored revue is attracting sizable"*: *Lawton Constitution*, February 22, 1970.

118 *"It was for my thirteenth birthday"*: Interview with Author.

118 *"the fine comedian"*: *Lawton Constitution*, June 20, 1974.

118 *"All of their outfits were made in Vegas by a woman"*: Interview with Author.

118 *"The Landmark Hotel lured Littlechief"*: *Lawton Constitution*, June 20, 1974.

118 *"It's a wide-open field since there are no real"*: *Lawton Constitution*, May 8, 1973.

119 *"A wealthy Las Vegas attorney"*: *Lawton Constitution*, June 20, 1974.

119 *"Brock was schizophrenic"*: Interview with Author.

119 *"Inspired by the occupation of Alcatraz"*: *Lawton Constitution*, June 11, 1971; *Reno Gazette-Journal*, November 14, 1973.

119 *"It'll all work out"*: *Lawton Constitution*, June 20, 1974.

120 *"My dad quit alcohol"*: Interview with Author.

120 *"Brock Littlechief, 22, was charged in district"*: *Lawton Constitution*, November 12, 1975.

120 *"[Brock] was sent to a federal"*: Interview with Author.

120 *"It is conceded that the land where the alleged"*: State v. Littlechief, Oklahoma Court of Criminal Appeals, 1978.

120 *"Littlechief's son was placed in permanent"*: Interview with Author.

121 *"Two new Indian musicals performed"*: American Indian Press Association News Service, April 29, 1972.

122 *"My eyes! My eyes!"*: La MaMa Experimental Theatre Club Archive.

122 *"an examination of all the false stereotypes"*: American Indian Press Association News Service, April 29, 1972.

123 *"The ensemble set out on an ambitious six-week tour"*: Joel Samuel, "Legends in Comedy: Charlie Hill- Interview & Live 1983/84," YouTube, published January 28, 2007.

123 *"Jay Leno had long hair and glasses"*: On and Off the Res' with Charlie Hill, directed by Sandra Osawa, 2009.

124 *"The country's second all-Indigenous theater troupe"*: Green Bay Press-Gazette, October 13, 1977.

125 *"A firebrand Kiowa, Amos Hopkins-Dukes"*: Desert Sun, September 11, 1967.

126 *"An honest moment crept into an episode"*: Tahmahkera, Tribal Television, 23.

126 "The Andy Griffith Show *reflected evolving interpretations"*: Tahmahkera, Tribal Television, 60.

128 *"Two Indian braves from the Fakawi tribe"*: Burlesque Humor—Redd Foxx, Dooto Records, 1959.

128 "F Troop *obviously couldn't use* fuck *on the air"*: Interview with George Schlatter.

128 *"General Custer was a madman"*: Tampa Bay Times, July 24, 1967.

129 *"The Indian [is] a creature possessing"*: Steiner, The New Indians, 79–80.

129 *"From my reading and from people we consider"*: Binghamton Press, September 2, 1967.

129 *"I don't believe Custer did those things"*: Akron Beacon Journal, July 31, 1967.

129 *"As tribes in different areas began to move"*: Deloria Jr., Custer Died for Your Sins, 31.

130 *"I was born in Huron, South Dakota"*: Interview with Author.

133 *"a master rubber-faced mugger"*: Reno Gazette-Journal, September 14, 1968.

133 *"Dennis and Cree had a drummer and a Cordovox"*: Interview with Author.

134 *"Show business pros Karen and Coffee"*: Reno Gazette-Journal, March 5, 1971.

134 *"Harrah's was the big time"*: Interview with Author.

135 *"The stage bars were all over Nevada"*: Interview with Author.

136 *"When I drifted through the Commercial Hotel"*: Reno Gazette-Journal, July 10, 1981.

137 *"Three shows a night, sometimes four"*: Interview with Author.

137 *"prejudiced human beings"*: Argus-Leader, November 28, 1986.

137 *"Chartrand was killed Tuesday morning"*: Variety, September 4, 1968.

138 *"When the Mob ran things"*: Interview with Author.

138 *"Sometimes we bomb"*: Reno Gazette-Journal, March 15, 1974.

139 *"I figured I'd just get up there and talk"*: Green Bay Press-Gazette, October 13, 1977.

140 *"Charlie worked the Palomino Club"*: Interview with Author.

140 *"Letterman used to pick me up in this pickup truck"*: Green Bay Press-Gazette, November 9, 1985.

140 *"I never knew true poverty until I became a comedian"*: On and Off the Res' with Charlie Hill, directed by Sandra Osawa, 1999.

141 *"It was a real easy decision"*: Interview with Author.

142 *"We hit it off right from there"*: "Charlie Hill—Leading the Life of an Indian Comedian," YouTube, November 4, 2016.

142 *"We were running in a posse of young comedians"*: Interview with Author.

142 *"When you do stand-up comedy in front of a Native crowd"*: Indian Country Today, January 3, 2014.

142 *"I brought Dick Gregory to Saskatchewan"*: Interview with Author.

143 *"Some Indian gathering would have him come to a reservation"*: Interview with Author.

143 *"When I would do an AIM benefit"*: "Charlie Hill—Leading the Life of an Indian Comedian," YouTube, November 4, 2016; *A Good Day to Die*, directed by David Mueller and Lynn Salt, 2010.

144 *"Things won't ever be the same again"*: Banks with Erdoes, *Ojibwa Warrior*, 58.

144 *"If you look at that AIM situation, there was a lot of the hippies"*: Coast to Coast AM with Art Bell and guest Eric Burdon, February 21, 2002.

144 *"There was nothing else they could do"*: *Chula Vista Star-News*, September 27, 1973; *Palm Beach Post*, June 2, 1973.

145 *"In 1975, AIM leader Dennis Banks"*: *Salem Capital Journal*, November 22, 1975.

145 *"He liked my goddamned act"*: "In Memorial: Listen to Charlie Hill at AIM's 40 Year Reunion," January 2, 2014, https://bsnorrell.blogspot.com/2014/01/remem bering-charlie-hill-aim-west-2009.html.

145 *"Dick Gregory did a lot of material"*: *Honolulu-Star Bulletin*, November 1, 1990.

146 *"Hill asked the audience to imagine"*: "In Memorial: Listen to Charlie Hill at AIM's 40 Year Reunion," January 2, 2014.

146 *"He'd do all these 'I get no respect' jokes, one line after another"*: Interview with Author.

146 *"When you say 'white man,' it's always singular"*: *The Roseanne Barr and Johnny Argent Show*, KCAA Radio, June 1, 2007.

147 *"He'd lay the picture down on a chair"*: Interview with Author.

147 *"He was making a big deal about it"*: *Goin' Native: The American Indian Comedy Slam*, Showtime, 2009.

147 *"I called him up"*: *Roseanne Barr and Johnny Argent Show*, KCAA Radio, June 1, 2007.

147 *"It had been an old two-hundred-thirty-five-seat room"*: Interview with Author.

148 *"Charlie killed a lot of places"*: Interview with Author.

148 *"We have to get together, motherfucker!"*: *Goin' Native: The American Indian Comedy Slam*, Showtime, 2009.

148 *"an incredible respect for Indian people"*: "Charlie Hill—Leading the Life of an Indian Comedian," YouTube, November 4, 2016.

149 *"Charlie Hill, the 26-year-old Oneida"*: *Green Bay Press-Gazette*, October 13, 1977.

150 *"There was a knock on my door one morning"*: Interview with Author.

150 *"It was a revolving dining room"*: *Argus-Leader*, May 5, 1978.

151 *"Williams & Ree follow the usual pattern of such teams"*: *Variety*, September 10, 1975.

151 *"We were getting tired of working for the drunks at the Holiday Inns"*: Interview with Author.

151 *"It looked like they had a lot of experience"*: Interview with Author.

151 *"Bruce and I have ten years together"*: *Argus-Leader*, May 5, 1978.

NOTES

152 *"In the middle of the act, Bruce would hold my hand"*: Interview with Author.

152 *"Their management pushed them on Norman Lear"*: *Variety*, May 3, 1978.

152 *"Our agents started jacking us around"*: *Argus-Leader*, August 22, 1980.

153 *"When you get the TV credits, you become a recognized"*: *Argus-Leader*, August 22, 1980.

155 *"I was twenty-six years old and I was thrilled"*: *Goin' Native*, Showtime, 2009.

155 *"They wanted me to be in a sketch"*: *On and Off the Res' with Charlie Hill*, directed by Sandra Osawa, 2009.

155 *"Okay, well, how about I give you five minutes"*: Tahmahkera, *Tribal Television*, 182–183.

155 *"They had the scenery set up like it was out in the desert"*: Neyom Friday podcast, November 19, 2009.

157 *"I was sitting right next to Mitzi"*: Interview with Author.

157 *"It was almost like talking two different languages"*: Neyom Friday podcast, November 19, 2009.

157 *"From there Charlie Hill appeared on"*: Joel Samuel, "Legends in Comedy: Charlie Hill-Interview & Live 1983/84," YouTube, January 28, 2007; Interview with Norbert Hill Jr.

158 *"Charlie Hill, the Indian comic with Merv Griffin"*: Voice of Broadway, Jack O'Brian, November 14, 1978.

159 *"When Charlie returned to the greenroom"*: Neyom Friday podcast, November 19, 2009.

159 *"After Charlie appeared on Johnny Carson"*: Interview with Author.

159 *"There he was, right there on The Tonight Show"*: *Appleton Post-Crescent*, April 8, 1983.

159 *"The Bionic Woman was a breakthrough for women on television"*: Interview with Author.

160 *"It was a kick hanging with him there"*: Interview with Author.

160 *"She had her own plane and they flew up to Boulder"*: Interview with Author.

160 *"I learned a lot and became very active in Native American issues"*: Interview with Author.

161 *"I was dating a woman who was best friends"*: Interview with Author.

162 *"Those who see him as a hero"*: David Treuer, *The Heartbeat of Wounded Knee* (New York, NY: Riverhead Books, 2019), 350.

162 *"That's how my mom and dad met"*: Interview with Author.

163 *"Max Gail who plays Detective Wojciehowicz on ABC-TV's Barney Miller"*: *Stevens Point Journal*, July 26, 1979.

163 *"I learned about the Peltier story from people I knew"*: Interview with Author.

164 *"There were psychological scars"*: "Charlie Hill—Back Home and Sovereign," *Indian Country Today*, November 4, 2016.

165 *"Floyd and Dennis were taken away from their families"*: Interview with Author.

167 *"They attended Stewart Indian School in Carson City"*: Interview with Author.

169 *"That video is about that non-Native idea of what 'Native art' is"*: Interview with Author.

171 *"This goes way beyond mocking"*: *Time*, September 20, 2014.

171 *"Native Americans accused me of things"*: Washington Post, September 19, 2014.

171 *"To commit genocide, you have to dehumanize people"*: Interview with Author.

171 *"Aren't there more important issues to worry about"*: Interview with Author.

173 *"If they switch all the mascots—even something that simple"*: The Roseanne Barr & Johnny Argent Show, KCAA Radio, June 1, 2007.

173 "The Big Show *was two hours, prime time, every week"*: Interview with Author.

174 *"the only thing he was willing to do was wrestle a woman"*: St. Louis Post-Dispatch, December 7, 1979.

174 *"I loved that Charlie Hill was part of our repertory"*: Interview with Author.

174 *"They had an army sketch and [Don] Rickles was in it"*: Interview with Author; Austin-American Statesman, April 27, 1980.

174 *"Ever see a funny Indian"*: Mansfield News Journal, May 5, 1980.

175 *"I've seen comedian Charlie Hill on 'The Big Show'"*: Indianapolis News, May 5, 1980.

175 *"Hey, Charlie—looks like you got some of your land back"*: On and Off the Res' with Charlie Hill, directed by Sandra Osawa, 2009.

175 *"Part of this whole thing was—I got to meet all the comedians"*: "Charlie Hill—Back Home and Sovereign," Indian Country Today, November 4, 2016.

176 *"There was nobody better to be around than Charlie"*: Interview with Author.

177 *"The first time I ever walked onto the Comedy Store property"*: Interview with Author.

181 *"The Jim Halsey Company started as a broker for country music acts"*: Variety, November 29, 1983.

182 *"the highest-paid unknown comedy act"*: Tennessean, March 31, 1985.

183 *"Ralph Emery would ask questions and never listen to your answer"*: Interview with Author.

185 *"I've had many, many death threats"*: Interview with Author.

188 *"My name is Charlie Hill—I'm an Oneida Indian"*: Late Night with David Letterman, December 9, 1985.

188 *"She's putting finishing touches on an ambitious and risky labor of love"*: Variety, December 12, 1986.

189 *"They used a restaurant that Mitzi leased across the street"*: Interview with Author.

189 *"The Dunes was the place that really made Mitzi wealthy"*: Interview with Author.

190 *"From 1985 to 1990 my calendar was booked up nine months"*: Interview with Author.

190 *"I lived with my dad in Los Angeles and then my mom wanted"*: Interview with Author.

191 *"He loved his family dearly"*: Interview with Author.

191 *"My dad went to work just to provide for us"*: Interview with Author.

191 *"They weren't offering him anything but crap"*: Interview with Author.

192 *"We get so much respect from community members"*: Interview with Author.

192 *"Everybody sort of brings a different humor to it"*: Interview with Author.

193 *"We were all really skeptical"*: Interview with Author.

193 *"It was perfect because we always sell out in Oklahoma"*: Interview with Author.

194 *"Almost all [of it is] about"*: Tahmahkera, *Tribal Television*, 205.

194 *"People don't know the rhythm"*: Radio KOSU, Allison Herrera, March 16, 2016.

194 *"Native communities always say that humor is a big"*: *The Cuts* podcast, October 21, 2017.

195 Interview with Author.

195 *"I'm a member"*: *The Writers Panel with Ben Blacker*, interview with Sierra Ornelas, September 25, 2018; Autryvisiondsd, "Interview with Sierra Teller Ornelas," YouTube, June 21, 2010.

196 Interview with Author.

196 *"I would get to meet these filmmakers"*: *The Creative Independent*, May 10, 2019.

197 Interview with Author.

197 *"It's all about the town of Rutherford Falls"*: *Unreserved*, CBC, February 7, 2020.

197 Interview with Author.

198 *"I just feel like my [job] as a comedian is to continue"*: *Unreserved*, CBC, February 7, 2020.

199 *"The American narrative dictates that Indians are supposed to be"*: Interview with Author.

199 *"There aren't very many news articles about how twenty-five Ojibwe people"*: Laura Howells, "Open Mic," Indigenous Land, Urban Stories, 2020, http://indigenouslandurbanstories.ca/portfolio-item/open-mic/.

199 *"The sacred clown is an element that runs deep"*: Interview with Author.

200 *"In Ojibwe communities, it's Nanabozho"*: Interview with Author.

200 *"The thing non-Natives don't understand about powwows"*: Interview with Author.

200 *"Powwow emcees, for hundreds of years"*: Interview with Author.

201 *"For some of the people who have successfully moved"*: Interview with Author.

201 *"Going to powwows when I was growing up"*: Interview with Author.

201 *"I often saw powwow emcees telling jokes"*: Interview with Author.

201 *"For anyone who's ever attended a powwow"*: Brian Daffron, "Master of ceremonies," *Indian Country Today*, June 4, 2008.

201 *"repertoire of jokes"*: *The Missourian*, July 11, 2001.

202 *"We're taking the stage persona of the powwow emcee"*: Interview with Author.

203 *"one of the most beloved public figures"*: *Navajo Times*, March 25, 2010.

204 *"after eating mutton stew from a sheep that had drunk from the Puerco"*: Wade Davies, *Healing Ways: Navajo Health Care in the Twentieth Century* (Albuquerque: University of New Mexico, 2001), 134.

204 *"Throughout the 1980s, Vincent Craig"*: *Los Angeles Times*, November 29, 1994.

204 *"I saw him at the Farmington Civic Center"*: Interview with Author.

205 *"Vincent Craig! Man, I was thinking of trying"*: *Arizona Daily Star*, September 25, 1998.

205 *"Just like everybody else on the reservation"*: Taos News, September 16, 1999.
206 *"I'd open for Vincent Craig at Native community events"*: Interview with Author.
208 *"Most comedy teams, when they're on, there's a friction"*: Neyom Friday podcast, November 19, 2009.
208 *"When I started, there were three Native comedians"*: Interview with Author.
209 *"I saw James and Ernie perform when I was just a kid"*: Interview with Author.
211 *"I do this just so I can be treated as an equal"*: Interview with Author.
214 *"You need to know what a community is going through"*: Interview with Author.
215 *"I was very small and too young to go to school"*: Interview with Author.
217 *"There's a young Cree comedian"*: Interview with Author.
217 *"Other comedians hate me"*: Interview with Author.
217 *"He stole material, and I really have a problem with that"*: Interview with Author.
217 *"Don Burnstick stole Jeff Foxworthy's material"*: Interview with Author.
217 *"It is wrong on multiple levels"*: Interview with Author.
218 *"White comics can just go onstage"*: Interview with Author.
218 *"Yeah, people said I was doing Foxworthy"*: Interview with Author.
218 *"I was sitting in the makeup chair when the producer came in"*: Interview with Author.
219 *"They wanted to fucking kill each other"*: Interview with Author.
219 *"We let Burnstick close"*: Interview with Author.
219 *"I made lifelong friends that week"*: Interview with Author.
219 *"The first Native person I ever saw on TV"*: Interview with Author.
220 *"I grew up watching SNL"*: Interview with Author.
220 *"It was the young comics who moved it forward"*: Lara Rae, Facebook, February 20, 2020.
221 *"Charlie Hill liked encouraging other people"*: Interview with Author.
221 *"Charlie and I talked for years about getting something on TV"*: Interview with Author.
221 *"I pitched the idea of a Native comedy special pretty hard"*: Interview with Author.
222 *"I was born in East Los Angeles in 1961"*: Interview with Author.
223 *"My mom is from the Bay Mills Reservation in Michigan"*: Interview with Author.
224 *"I was in the second grade, going to this white school"*: The Dark Mark Show with JR Redwater, May 4, 2019.
224 *"Early on we did a show in Albuquerque"*: Interview with Author.
224 *"It was remarkable"*: Interview with Author.
225 *"There was the issue of who was contributing the most"*: Interview with Author.
225 *"We were eating at Tony Roma's"*: Interview with Author.
225 *"opened so many doors"*: Interview with Author.
225 *"Every Native American I meet tells me"*: Interview with Author.
225 *"I saw this show with an all-Native lineup"*: Interview with Author.
226 *"I think the influence we had"*: Interview with Author.

227 *"There's a lot going on in our home with all of the foster kids"*: Interview with Author.

228 *"Rejection I can deal with"*: Jonny R. podcast, Episode 36, March 3, 2019.

228 *"I sing as loud as I can to keep my focus"*: Interview with Author.

230 *"It'll be tough with all the kids"*: NDN Way w/ Jonny R.

231 *"I had to move because of the travel"*: Interview with Author.

232 *"I'm Tonawanda Seneca"*: Interview with Author.

232 *"It was hard starting out because we didn't have the resources"*: Interview with Author.

233 *"There's very little visibility when it comes to Native people"*: Interview with Author.

233 *"I don't like being viewed as at-risk"*: Interview with Author.

235 *"I think I was the first Native woman to do it"*: Interview with Author.

238 *"It pretty much just makes us feel like"*: "Sacred Standing Rock," *Rise*, Episode #106, Viceland, August 17, 2017.

239 *"It was against the law for Native peoples to form a political organization"*: Joseph, *21 Things*, 72–74.

239 *"other than an Indian"*: Joseph, *21 Things*, 27.

239 *"The interests of corporations"*: Out in the Open, CBC Radio, April 21, 2018.

239 *"Canada and the United States both justified their jurisdiction"*: Robert F. Berkhofer Jr., *The White Man's Indian: Images of the American Indian from Columbus to the Present* (New York: Vintage Books, 1979), 123.

239 *"Canada still invokes the Doctrine of Discovery"*: Arthur Manuel, *Unsettling Canada: A National Wake-Up Call* (Toronto: Between the Lines, Sixth Printing, 2015), 3.

239 *"Canada, Australia, New Zealand, and the United States"*: Manuel, *Unsettling Canada*, 176–177.

240 *"I am helping to handle logistics"*: Vincent Schilling, "An Activist Profile: Dallas Goldtooth of the 1491s," *Indian Country Today*, May 8, 2014, https://indian countrytoday.com/archive/an-activist-profile-dallas-goldtooth-of-the-1491-s -bFzWST0u30qHWa91V3_nqw.

241 *"It was the harrowing combination of the oil giant's complete lack"*: Naomi Klein, *This Changes Everything* (New York, NY: Simon & Schuster, 2014), 330.

241 *"Ten days after the BP gusher was plugged"*: Klein, *This Changes Everything*, 332.

241 *"Canada's Imperial Oil spent $13 billion"*: Klein, *This Changes Everything*, 145.

241 *"Its massive craters could be seen from outer space"*: Klein, *This Changes Everything*, 327.

241 *"The expansion of offshore drilling"*: Klein, *This Changes Everything*, 311.

241 *"Meanwhile, the companies responsible for the accidents"*: Klein, *This Changes Everything*, 149.

241 *"Think tanks like the American Enterprise Institute"*: Klein, *This Changes Everything*, 282.

242 *"I have a baby"*: "Sacred Standing Rock," *Rise*, Episode #106, Viceland, August 17, 2017.

242 *"I couldn't just stand by. I have family members"*: Interview with Author.

NOTES

242 *"I drove the whole Tulsa donation van up there by myself"*: Interview with Author.

242 *"At its peak, we had nine to ten thousand people"*: Interview with Author.

242 *"A lot of folks saw it on social media"*: *The Extraordinary Negroes* podcast with guest Dallas Goldtooth, January 29, 2018.

243 *"I went back up to Standing Rock and made a short film"*: Interview with Author.

243 *"I was super tired—but my mind was on fire"*: *The Cuts* podcast, October 21, 2017.

244 *"So many hippies showed up"*: Interview with Author.

245 *"It was so powerful"*: Interview with Author.

245 *"I got my first phone calls to work in TV after Standing Rock"*: Interview with Author.

247 *"We had very little sleep Thursday night"*: *APTN National News*, APTN, May 9, 2018.

247 *"The families are dealing with such heartache"*: *Calgary Herald*, April 28, 2018.

247 *"We have always done the ethnic thing"*: Interview with Author.

248 *"Is the crowd laughing because the jokes"*: Sylvia McAdam Saysewahum, Facebook Page.

248 *"After seeing the outrage [and] counter-outrage"*: Twitter.com/Dalby, May 7, 2018.

248 *"They hosted a country music festival every year here"*: Interview with Author.

249 *"Hundreds [and] hundreds of hate mail"*: The APTN National News, May 9, 2018.

250 *"I wasn't prepared for the backlash"*: Interview with Author.

250 *"Fuck a bunch of"*: *Indian Country Today*, April 6, 2016.

251 *"Apparently my comedy was taken out of context"*: *Superior Telegram*, October 7, 2017.

252 *"I was really on the fence and apprehensive"*: *Grand Forks Herald*, April 7, 2016.

252 *"I just want to say to Ralphie that his nonapology"*: *Native America Calling*, Koahnic Broadcast Corporation, April 13, 2016.

252 Native America Calling, Koahnic Broadcast Corporation, April 13, 2016; *The Interrobang*, April 13, 2016.

253 *"We spoke right before I had to do a gig"*: Interview with Author.

254 *"Sometimes these life lessons are hard"*: Interview with Author; The *Jonny R.* podcast, guest Adrianne Chalepah, January 26, 2018.

255 *"All my comedy buddies think I'm making"*: *The Roseanne Barr & Johnny Argent Show*, KCAA Radio, June 1, 2007.

255 *"They hired white people because white people were the ones"*: Interview with Author.

256 *"Only ten percent of Indian tribes have"*: Jason Morgan Edwards, "Charlie Hill: 'The Indian Spirit is America,'" *Indian Country Today*, March 21, 2013, https://indiancountrytoday.com/archive/charlie-hill-the-indian-spirit-is-america-Njj-OCTbT06doBJMDJR5KA.

256 *"It would seem with all these casinos"*: Interview with Author.

295

NOTES

256 *"Charlie was the real deal"*: Interview with Author.

256 *"We got in on the ground floor"*: Interview with Author.

257 *"David Letterman was a friend of my dad's"*: Interview with Author.

257 *"He came up with funny things when he was joking around"*: Interview with Author.

257 *"At some point he lost the desire"*: Interview with Author.

257 *"He came from an era where social media wasn't the way"*: Interview with Author.

258 *"He didn't get support"*: Interview with Author.

258 *"We walked through Greenwich Village"*: Interview with Author.

259 *"I talked to him on the phone"*: Interview with Author.

259 *"By the time Charlie was on"*: Interview with Author.

259 *"He was the first genuinely"*: Interview with Author.

260 *"He never called attention"*: Interview with Author.

260 *"Right before he died"*: Interview with Author.

260 *"I want to make sure we take"*: *The Late Show with David Letterman*, CBS Television, January 10, 2014.

260 *"Throughout history there are"*: Interview with Author.

264 *"What we realized"*: Interview with Author.

265 *"Putting 'Aunty's Choice' "*: Interview with Author.

265 *"Indians—we think about these massacres all the time"*: *Pow Wow Life*, Episode 22, Powwows.com, April 1, 2019.

266 *"The scene was based"*: Interview with Author.

266 *"There was only one time"*: Interview with Author.

266 *"They have found a way"*: Patrick Thomas, review of *Between Two Knees* Oregon Shakespeare Festival, https://www.talkinbroadway.com/page/regional/other /or2.html.

267 *"Somebody came up to the usher"*: Interview with Author.

267 *"We were so happy"*: Interview with Author.

267 *"It can be really difficult"*: *Pow Wow Life*, Episode 22, Powwows.com, April 1, 2019.

268 *"This was our best attempt"*: Radio KLCC, Interview with the 1491s, April 9, 2019.

269 *"Most Native comics"*: Interview with Author.

269 *"I used to watch a TV show in the early 1990s"*: Interview with Author.

Index

INDEX

INDEX

Brown Eyes, Lucas, 101–2, 197
Brownlow, Kevin, 11
Bruce, Lenny, 55, 58
Bruce, Louis, 110–11
Buck, Gene, 45
Buck Fuffalo, 151
Burdon, Eric, 144
Bureau of Indian Affairs (BIA), 91, 204
    and education of Native Americans,
        23
    and film portrayals of Native
        Americans, 73
    medicine shows and, 11
    Native American protests and,
        110–11
    and Native Americans in Wild West
        shows, 8–10
    Termination Act and, 84
burlesque, 11, 42, 45
Burnstick, Don, 214–21
    childhood of, 215–16
    heritage of, 215–17
    in interactions with other comedians,
        217–19
    Native American issues and,
        214–16
    sense of humor of, 214–18, 220
    stand-up and, 214, 217–18
    television appearances of, 218–20
Bury My Heart at Wounded Knee
    (Brown), 161
Buttram, Pat, 114

California, 25, 72, 81–84, 118, 161,
    232, 262, 265
    and absence of Native Americans in
        media, xii–xiii
    Brown Eyes and, 101–2
    Curtiss and, 54, 56–60
    Hill and, 124, 139–42, 145–49,
        190–91, 258–59
    Miles and, 237

Native American protests and,
    111–14
Omaha and, 179–80
Peltier case and, 163–65
Rogers and, 48, 50–51
Rogers Jr. and, 50–51, 81–83
stand-up and, 29–30, 124, 139–42,
    145–48, 152, 167
and Williams and Ree, 151–54,
    256
Yaffee and, 223
Cambridge, Godfrey, 118
Campbell, Glen, 131
Canada, 9, 13, 142–43, 196
    Banzo and, 199
    Boushie shooting and, 246–47
    Burnstick and, 215, 218
    Clift and, 80
    Curtiss and, 57
    education in, xii, 6–7
    and films and videos of Native
        Americans, 17–18
    Hebert and, 70–71
    Hill and, 186
    Humboldt Broncos memorial and,
        246–48
    and legal rights of Indigenous
        peoples, xi–xii, 239–40
    McMahon and, 71, 185–86
    and marginalization of Native
        Americans, 238–39
    Miles and, 235–36
    Miller and, 211–13, 222
    mining, logging, and petroleum
        operations in, xi–xii
    oil spills and, 241
    powwows and, 200–201
    and Williams and Ree, 246–48
Caponera, John, 269
Carlin, George, 127, 150, 196,
    252
Carlisle, Kitty, 97, 192

INDEX

About the Author

KLIPH NESTEROFF is the author of the critically acclaimed book *The Comedians: Drunks, Thieves, Scoundrels and the History of American Comedy*. He has been hailed as the "human encyclopedia of comedy" by *Vice* and the "king of comedy lore" by *Los Angeles* magazine.